STUDIES IN AFRICAN AMERICAN HISTORY AND CULTURE

edited by

GRAHAM HODGES
COLGATE UNIVERSITY

A GARLAND SERIES

DEAD OR ALIVE

FUGITIVE SLAVES AND WHITE INDENTURED SERVANTS BEFORE 1830

DANIEL MEADERS

GARLAND PUBLISHING, INC.
NEW YORK & LONDON / 1993

Library of Congress Cataloging-in-Publication Data

Meaders, Daniel, 1945–
    Dead or alive : Fugitive slaves and white indentured servants before
1830 / Daniel Meaders.
       p.   cm. — (Studies in African American history and culture)
    Includes bibliographical references (p.).
    ISBN 0–8153–1007–2 (alk. paper)
    1. Fugitive slaves—Southern States—History. 2. Indentured servants—
Southern States—History. 3. Southern States—History—Colonial period,
ca. 1600–1775. 4. Afro-Americans—Southern States—History. I. Title.
II. Series.
E450.M48   1993
975'.00496—dc20   93–14202
                                       CIP

Printed on acid-free, 250-year-life paper
Manufactured in the United States of America

TABLE OF CONTENTS

ACKNOWLEDGMENTS

The investigator of fugitive slaves and white indentured servants during the colonial period must have the patience of a Job in order to make sense of the thousands of fugitive ads in the local newspapers. He also must have the support, sympathy and encouragement from his family and advisor. They should be saluted.

My first debt of acknowledgement is to my advisor John Blassingame. Without his assistance, his encouragement, his sensitive criticisms, this major piece of investigation would have never seen the light of day. Thanks are due to the staffs of the New York Public Library, The New York Historical Society and the Schomburg library and the libraries of Yale and Columbia.

My special thanks to Delia Perez and my mother Margaret Meaders. The writer is especially grateful to Dorothy Woolfolk, Flo Bergin, Gwen Williams and especially Michele Brenner for doing the major part of the typing as well as checking notes and sources. My thanks also to Charles Williams, Andy Gill, Fred Wallace, Cora Anderson, Estelle Paris, Susan Stevens, Wayne Gibbons, Victoria Ford and Zipporah Brown.

I owe a debt of gratitude to Professor Myschelle Spears of Maryland University for her spiritual support. And I am especially grateful to Loretta and Tarina Meaders for their sacrifices in the years gone by.

Much of the financial assistance for this work came from the Woodrow Wilson Foundation and the Martin Luther King Heritage House.

Dead or Alive

INTRODUCTION

This is a study about the American fugitive slave and the indentured servant in the thirteen American colonies, with an emphasis on the Southern section during the seventeenth and eighteenth centuries, and their yearning to be free; it is a study, too, about their resistance to unpaid labor, against the breakup of families, against the whip, the rope, the chain, the branding iron, and the gun.

In December 1738, two English convict servants from Virginia absconded, leading the master to publish a fugitive advertisement claiming, "They are bold, stout Fellows, and will make Resistance; and if taken, must be well guarded, or they will escape." In October 1763, "A Short well made Negro, named Ben, formerly the property of Hugh Bryan of Indian land, where he is well known" escaped from his owner, William Williamson, an absentee rice planter, owner of thirty-four slaves and a member of the Commons House in South Carolina. After offering twenty pounds for Ben's capture, Williamson noted in his advertisement that "but, as the said fellow has declar'd he will not be taken alive, whoever delivers his head, shall be intitled to a reward of Fifty pounds."[1] Whether it took the form of feigned obsequiousness, poison, arson, self-mutilation, flight, or insurrection, resistance is an activity that cannot be ignored in American history.

In an attempt to play down the theme of resistance and maltreatment, historian Ulrich B. Phillips in his *Life and Labor in the Old South* claimed blacks were "more or less contentedly slaves, with grievances from time to time but not ambition." In his *Slavery in Alabama*, James Sellers noted: "Unquestionably some slaves ran

---

[1]Pennsylvania Gazette, January 28, 1728; *South Carolina Gazette,* July 2, 1763; Walter B. Edgar and N. Louise Bailey eds., *Biographical Directory of the South Carolina House of Representatives* (4 vols., Columbia, S.C., 1977), II: 720-728.

away because the master or overseer treated them with cruelty, though cruel and harsh treatment of slaves was the exception, as we have already noted." After describing two fugitives who had been whipped, Sellers concluded that the blacks were "probably habitual rogues and truants, the most unmanageable of the lot on the plantation. The harsh punishment which scarred them may have been provoked, though not justified, by their own recalcitrancy."[2]

Both Phillips' and Sellers' examination of plantation records, slavery laws and local newspapers helped the reader to understand the planter's world; the black's and the white servant's dreams and feelings and hopes have been basically ignored and their interviews, narratives, autobiographies and poems have been passed over without due attention. After commending a noted black fugitive named Solomon Northup for his slave narrative, Phillips claimed that "ex-slave narratives in general, and those of Charles Ball, Henry Box Brown and Father Henson in particular, were issued with so much abolitionist editing that as a class their authenticity is doubtful."[3]

As valuable as the slave accounts are to historians hoping to write about the heritage of African-Americans and the distinctiveness of the black experience during the nineteenth century, it is far more difficult to draw upon such data during the colonial period in America because the fugitive slave's, as well as the indentured servant's personal records are mostly unavailable. Still the historian can paint a realistic portrait of chattel slavery and indentured servitude even if the slave's and the servant's records are few in number during the colonial period, and even if he has to rely on the planters documents. Here the fugitive notice, a planter's document, will be the primary source of evidence. In his *Slavery in Mississippi*, Charles Sydnor claimed that "Newspaper advertisements constitutes one of the chief sources of information concerning fugitive slaves." He maintains that these ads "are not

---

[2]Ulrich B. Phillips, Life and Labor in the Old South (Boston, 1939), 196; James B. Sellers, *Slavery in Alabama* (University, Ala., 1950), 268.

[3]Phillips, Life and Labor, 219.

biased. Here was no case of attacking or defending the institution of slavery."[4]

Filled with stereotypes, threats, and cries of betrayal on one

---

[4]Charles Sydnor, Slavery in Mississippi (New York, 1933), 125; Carter G. Woodson, ed., "Eighteenth Century Slaves as Advertised by their Masters," in *Journal of Negro History I* (April 1916), 163-216; Lorenzo J. Greene, "The New England Negro as seen in Advertisements for Runaway Slaves," *Journal of Negro History*, 29 (April 1944), 125-46; John W. Coleman, *Slavery Times in Kentucky* (Chapel Hill, 1940), 218-244; Sellers, *Slavery in Alabama*, 277-281; Joe Gray Taylor, *Negro Slavery in Louisiana* (Baton Rouge, 1963), 174-79; John Blassingame, *The Slave Community: Plantation Life in the Antebellum South* (Rev. and enl., ed. New York, 1972-1979), 198-206; Eugene D. Genovese, *Roll Jordan Roll: The World the Slaves Made* (New York, 1972, 1974), 648-657; Peter H. Wood, *Black Majority: Negroes in Colonial South Carolina from 1670 through the Stono Rebellion* (New York, 1974), 238-268; Gerald W. Mullin, *Flight and Rebellion: Slave Resistance in Eighteenth Century Virginia* (New York, 1972), 74-110; Betty Wood, *Slavery in Colonial Georgia, 1730-1775* (Athens, 1984), 169; Daniel C. Littlefield, *Rice and Slaves in Colonial South Carolina* (Baton Rouge, 1981), 142-164; Windley A. Lathan, *Runaway Slave Advertisements, a Documentary History from the 1730's to 1790* (4 vols., Westport, Conn., 1983), I: 1-5; Marvin L. Michael Kay and Lorin Lee Cary, "Slave Runaways in Colonial North Carolina, 1748-1775," *The North Carolina Historical Review*, 63 (January 1986), 1-39; See also Herbert Aptheker, "Resistance and Afro-American History: Some Notes on Contemporary Historiography and Suggestions on Further Research," in *In Resistance: Studies in African, Caribbean, and Afro-American History*, Gary Y. Okihiro, ed. (Amherst, 1986), 11-15; Alan D. Watson, "Impulse Toward Independence: Resistance and Rebellion Among North Carolina Slaves, 1750-1775," *Journal of Negro History*, 63 (Fall 1978), 317-328; Michael P. Johnson, "Runaway Slaves and the Slave Communities in South Carolina, 1799 to 1830," *The William & Mary Quarterly*, 3rd Ser. 38 (July 1981), 396-417; Lawrence Towner, "A Fondness for Freedom: Servant Protest in Puritan Society," *The William and Mary Quarterly*, 3rd Ser., 19 (1962), 201-219.

hand and offers of forgiveness and flattery on the other, these ads
caused the author initially to throw his hands up trying to
understand this document. Should the planter's felicitous
phraseology and self-serving logic be accepted as fact? Even if the
fugitive notices reflected how the planter felt, need it be the gospel
truth? Charles Sydnor came away from the fugitive ads with this
conclusion: "some slaves were not only intractable but even
dangerous and savage." Lorenzo Greene in his *The Negro in
Colonial New England* concluded that the "most common offense
[by blacks] was running away" and that fugitive flight was one of
the "variety of crimes perpetuated by Negroes."[5] Whereas the
planter might have thought that the blacks were little more than
savages and criminals, no black fugitives have ever painted so
harsh a picture of themselves.

Kenneth Stampp in his book *The Peculiar Institution* thought
that flight was "an important form of protest against slavery" and
after his examination of the fugitive notices, he, too, found
planters calling blacks 'unruly scoundrels' and 'incorrigibles scamps'
but he rejects this by concluding that "most of them seemed to be
'humble', 'inoffensive', and 'cheerful' slaves."[6] After examining 1,500
fugitive notices in the local Virginia colonial newspapers, Gerald
Mullin argued in his *Flight and Rebellion: Slave Resistance in
Eighteenth-Century Virginia* that the "acculturated slaves we know
best were the most successful rebels of the century" because "they
possessed skills, exhibited fluency in the English language," had a
"sensible demeanor" and an "intelligent adaptive manner in
speaking situations." Mullin, like Stampp, taking the planter at his
word without qualification, examined the ads and found a black
man named Davy described as a 'great hypocrite, of mild
expression,' another as a 'fair spoken, deceiving slippery chap' and,

---

[5]Sydnor, Slavery in Mississippi, 125; Lorenzo J. Greene, *The
Negro in Colonial New England* (New York, 1942, 1968), 145.

[6]Kenneth Stampp, *The Peculiar Institution* (New York, 1956),
110.

another called an 'artful insinuating fellow.'[7] How can the black's or servant's personality traits be understood without interviewing the fugitive himself? Were the planter's descriptions stereotypes? Were the impressions for the moment or for all time? Because the planter describes the black or the indentured servant in so many ways, this study begins with a chapter called "The Fugitive Notice as Evidence" showing how the descriptive data in the fugitive notice varies from colony to colony and from period to period, how the ads have both an impressionistic and a quantitative value and how they only unravel a small portion of the history of fugitive flight in America.

Because so much attention has been devoted to slavery's effect on the black's personality structure and because so much attention has been devoted to the loyal, docile, cheerful, grinning slave (better known as Sambo), it was necessary to include in this study the white indentured servant, to show that the blacks varied response to slavery was a natural human response. In my chapter, "Passing for Free," the servant, whether he be Irish, German, English, Dutch, or whether he was a carpenter, shoemaker or weaver, was not above bowing, grinning, scrapping his feet, stuttering and tipping his hat if that could pave the way for his escape. Feigned obsequiousness was just another tactic in the battle of wits between the fugitive and the planter.

John Blassingame, in his study *The Slave Community*, maintained that the "plantation was a battlefield where slaves fought masters for physical and psychological survival," and that "There is overwhelming evidence, in the primary sources, of the Negro's resistance to his bondage and of his undying love for freedom." Peter H. Wood in his book *Black Majority: Negroes in Colonial South Carolina from 1670 through the Stono Rebellion* states that "No single act of self-assertion was more significant among slaves or more disconcerting among whites than that of running away." And in his dissertation, "A Profile of Runaway Slaves in Virginia and South Carolina from 1730 through 1787," Lathan A. Windley questions the "Sambo thesis," by asking "Why, (1) if they [slaves] were truly docile and submissive, did they run

---

[7]Mullin, *Flight and Rebellion: Slave Resistance in Eighteenth-Century Virginia*, 89, 91.

away, and (2) why did the slaveowners and planters of eighteenth-century Virginia and South Carolina enact laws to prevent the escape of these Sambos and punish them when caught?"[8]

---

[8]Blassingame, The Slave Community: Plantation Life in the Antebellum South, 192, 284; Wood, *Black Majority*, 239; Windley, *A Profile of Runaway Slaves*, 150.

CHAPTER I
THE FUGITIVE NOTICE
AS EVIDENCE

To understand the fugitive's world, every class of source must be examined, for neither the indentured servant nor the black left many personal records behind during the colonial period. "The fundamental problem confronting anyone interested in studying black views of bondage," wrote John Blassingame, "is that the slave had few opportunities to tell what it meant to be a chattel."[9] The colonial planter, too, left few letters, diaries, memoirs or autobiographies describing his experiences during chattel slavery or indentured servitude. The document, then, that has been chiefly used to study the fugitives is the fugitive notice, an advertisement that did not originate in America; the *London Gazette*, one of England's oldest newspapers, began publishing such advertisements in 1665, long before the American colonists published their first newspaper, the *Boston News-Letter*, in 1704.[10] Advertisements were placed in the local newspapers by planters searching for their servants or slaves. Before studying the fugitive, an examination is needed of these notices in order to determine their trustworthiness.[11]

In 1667, Master Thomas Joyner placed an advertisement in the *London Gazette* asking for the return of three white servants: Richard Martin, Richard Evans, and John Kiercombe. Three

---

[9]John Blassingame, ed., Slave Testimony: Two Centuries of Letters, Speeches, Interviews and Autobiographies (Baton Rouge, 1977), xvii.

[10]Lawrence C. Wroth, *The Colonial Printer* (Portland, Me., 1938), 19.

[11]Carl L. Becker "What is Evidence?" The Relativist View - "Everyman His Own Historian," in *The Historian as Detective: Essays on Evidence*, Robin W. Winks, ed. (New York, 1968), 3-23. See E.H. Carr, *What is History?* (New York, 1962); Jacques Barzun, Henry F. Crass, *The Modern Researcher*, (New York, 1857), 49.

months later an Englishman published an advertisement describing the fugitive John Brown, about twenty two-years of age, as "a tall black man with short black hair."[12]

More creative, more passionate, more detailed, larger and more numerous than the English ones, the American fugitive advertisements came in all sizes, the standard size being three by six inches, numbering from a ten-word sentence to a three hundred word paragraph and listing both the master's and the fugitive's name as well as the fugitive's physical description, residence, religion, occupation, musical instrument played, whip marks, branding scars, complexion, personality traits, number of known children, and relatives, possible weapons carried, past offenses, and probable destination.

The *North Carolina Gazette* published this advertisement in 1778:

> RUN away from the subscriber in Bladen county, a Negro man named CEASAR, about 5 feet 5 or 6 inches high, about 20 years of age, tolerable well set, has a scar on one of his hips, and I believe has lost one of his teeth. He was seen on Cape Fear, making northwardly, is very sensible, and has some papers or letters by which he passes, pretending to be going on my business. A reward of £10 will be given to any person who shall apprehend and confine him in any gaol in this state, so as I can get him, or shall execute him according to law, he being outlawed the 14th of April 1778.
>
> THOMAS AMIS[13]

In 1786, the noted Virginia leader George Mason printed this:

> Ranaway a few days ago from the Subscribers living in Fairfax county, Virginia, two slaves, viz. Dick, a very lusty well made Mulatto fellow, about 25 years of age, has bushy hair or wool, which he generally combs back, large features

---

[12]*London Gazette*, September 20-23, December 27-30, 1667.

[13]New Bern *North Carolina Gazette*, May 1, 1778.

and eyes, a grumb down look when spoken to, is a subtle artful fellow, well acquainted both in Maryland and Virginia, beats a drum pretty well, and has been formerly a waiting Man; he took with him a light coloured country cloth coat with white metal buttons, a short green ditto, a white cloth waistcoat, a red ditto faced with black velvet, a round hat half worn, and common shoes and stockings; he ran away some time ago, when he worked on board a bay craft, by the name of Thomas Webster. WATT, a stout Negro fellow, remarkably black, about thirty five years of age, has lost some of his teeth before, which in some measure affects his voice, has had cross paths lately shaved on his head, to conceal which it is probable he will shave or cut close the rest of his head. He is an artful fellow, has a down look, and seems confused when examined; he took with him a brown cloth coat, a pair of black breeches, and a variety of cloathes not known. They will perhaps change their names and pass for free men; and it is probable they may have a forged pass. They will probably make for the eastern-Shore or for the state of Delaware or Pennsylvania. The above reward, or five pounds, for either of them will be paid for delivering them to the subscribers, or for securing them in gaol and giving us notice, so that we get them again, and if brought home all reasonable charges paid. All captains or skippers of vessels, and others, are hereby warned at their peril from taking them on board or employing them.

George Mason.
George Mason, Jun.[14]

N.B. All Captains or Skippers of vessels and others are hereby forewarned, at their peril, from taking them on board, or employing them.

Was the fugitive advertisement an objective description of the fugitive or was it a form of propaganda designed to justify the publication of the advertisement in the first place? "As I have been always tender of my slaves" claimed one planter in Virginia, "and

---

[14]Alexandria *Virginia Journal & Alexandria Advertiser*, September 30, 1786.

particularly attentive to the good usage of them, I hope wherever these fellows may be apprehended that they will receive such moderate correction as will deter them from running away for the future."[15]

The fugitive notice was not a love letter, nor was it a diary or memoir written for future publication in a scholarly journal; it was like a warning bell, a tocsin designed to instill dread and anxiety into the fugitive. "Toney is an obstreperous sawcey Fellow, and if he should be kill'd in taking, I am willing to allow any Man that will bring me his Head Ten Pounds" said one owner in 1745. This was the *South Carolina Gazette's* first dead or alive notice. Twelve years later that gazette published the first dead or alive notice describing a black woman. The slave's owner, Mary Ellis, looking for a thirty year old woman named Catherine, asserted: "Whoever takes the said wench dead or alive, and delivers her to me, shall have a reward of 10 pounds."[16]

The North Carolina advertisements also contained death threats. In 1774, one planter declared: "if the said Abraham doth not surrender himself, and return home, immediately after the Publication of these Presents, that any Person may kill and destroy the said Slave by such Means as he or they think fit, without Accusation or Impeachment of any Crime of Offense for so doing or without incurring any Penalty of Forfeiture thereby."[17]

The North Carolina dead or alive notices, often couched in legal jargon, devoid of any apparent emotion, were penned by the court justices. In 1778, planter Ann Barron of Craven County filed a complaint with two justices, James Davis and John Fonville, about the escape of Lewis who was "supposed to have gone to Virginia." The *North Carolina Gazette* published Barron's advertisement:

These are therefore to command the said slave forthwith to

---

[15]*Virginia Gazette* (Purdie, Dixon), January 14, 1767; *Maryland Gazette*, October 5, 1786.

[16]*South Carolina Gazette*, June 1, 1745, February 3, 1757.

[17]New Bern *North Carolina Gazette*, September 2, 1774.

surrender himself, and return home to his said Mistress. And we do also require the sheriff of the said County to make diligent search and pursuit after the said slave, and him having found, to apprehend and secure, so that he may be conveyed to his said mistress, or otherwise discharged as the law directs. And the said sheriff is hereby empowered to raise and take with him such power of his County as he shall think fit, for apprehending the said slave. And we do hereby, by virtue of an act of assembly of this state concerning servants and slaves, intimate and declare, if the said slave doth not surrender himself, and return home, immediately after the publication of these presents, that then any person may kill or destroy the said slave, by such means as he or they may think fit, without accusation or impeachment of any crime or offence for so doing, or without incurring any penalty or forfeiture thereby.

JAMES DAVIS.
J. FONVILLE.

N.B. Whoever apprehends the said slave, and secures him in Newbern gaol, shall have 50 dollars reward, and handsomely rewarded if secured in any other gaol in this state.

ANN BARRON.[18]

The local newspapers in South Carolina published thirty-six dead or alive fugitive notices between 1732 and 1780, representing 3% of the total number of advertisements published during that period. The gazettes in North Carolina published eleven dead or alive notices constituting 5% of the total and published between 1775 and 1799. Virginia gazettes published forty-one dead or alive notices during 1736-1780 representing 3% of the total advertisements published there. The gazettes in Georgia published six dead or alive notices between 1763 and 1776 which amounted to 8% of the total number published. Maryland published one of these notices during 1729 and 1800 which amounted to less than 1% of the overall number of advertisements. None of the northern colonies published dead or alive notices and none of the gazettes in the Northern colonies took out dead or alive notices against

---

[18]New Bern *North Carolina Gazette*, March 6, 1778.

white servants, men or women. Every colonial gazette, too, contained a fugitive advertisement where the planter offered to forgive the fugitive. "As I have reason to believe," said one planter about his black fugitive named Agrippa who had "always behaved himself extremely well, I have Reason to believe if the said Agrippa, will return to his master, of his own Accord, he shall be forgiven."[19]

Why a black or a servant escaped is a question that fugitive specialists need to address in their studies, but what the advertisements show is that some planters failed to investigate the reasons or that they honestly did not know. On August 30, 1745, master William Roberts, a clockmaker from Annapolis, fired off an advertisement describing John Powell, an English servant of the same trade. Six days later, Roberts wrote cancelling the search: "Whereas John Powell was advertised last week in this Paper as a Runaway, but being only gone into the Country a Cyder-drinking, being returned again to his Master's Service." Christopher Lowndes, thinking that his servant had fled by cart on February 19, 1750, placed a fugitive advertisement in the *Maryland Gazette* two days later. One month later he wrote that his servant named Michael Wallace, who had been advertised "about a Month ago," was found "dead near the Head of South River, after the melting away of the last great Snow, in which it is supposed he lost himself and perish'd."[20]

The planter often gave unrealistic reasons for the fugitive's escape. Master Joseph Holdstock placed a fugitive advertisement in the *Pennsylvania Gazette* in 1769, describing a thirty-four year old blacksmith named Hopkins Driver who made off twenty-three times: "Although he is used well while he stays at work, yet he is so very lazy, and fond of running away, this being the 23rd time, that the public are requested to look sharp after this fellow." Maryland planter Charles Carroll, a signer of the Declaration of Independence, felt that John Plutt, an English convict servant, "is of a lazy Disposition, which is the only Cause of his running

---

[19]*South Carolina Gazette*, November 15, 1770.

[20]*Maryland Gazette*, August 30, September 6, 1745, February 19, 21, March 21, 1750.

away."[21]

An abused fugitive might complain, but some planters scoffed at the notion of maltreatment in their advertisements. Fourteen year old Hager of Maryland absconded in 1766 and this black woman had "a scar under one of her Breasts supposed to be got by a whipping" and "an Iron Collar about her neck." She was "supposed to be harbour'd in some Negro Quarter, as her Father and Mother Encourages her in Elopements, under a Pretense that she is ill used at Home." Three months later eighteen year old Nan and her one year old daughter named Doll of the same colony made off and the planter wrote: "This Wench, with her deceitful Ways and lying tongue, passes with some sort of People by shewing her Marks and pretending to be ill used with a great deal of Barbarity; she is pretty well marked, which she never got for her good behavior."[22]

Most advertisements left no hint about what caused an escape. Scores of advertisements must be examined before a planter mentions a reason for flight, but this hardly means that the planter was a model of benevolence. Planter John Ducoins published an ad, the only one in his lifetime, in the *Gazette of the State of Georgia* on September 30, 1784:

> RUN AWAY from the subscriber, A NEGRO WENCH, named MARY, about 35 years of age, a little pitted in the face with the smallpox, and has some white spots upon her hand and arm. A reward of half a guinea will be given to any person that will deliver the said wench to the subscriber, and if harboured or concealed by any white person, on conviction therof, a reward of two guineas.
>
> JOHN DUCOINS.[23]

Ducoins does not show any signs of being violent, yet on

---

[21]*Pennsylvania Gazette*, August 31, 1769; *Maryland Gazette*, July 26, 1753.

[22]*Maryland Gazette*, October 2, 1776, January 29, 1767.

[23]*Gazette of the State of Georgia*, September 30, 1784.

October 13, 1785 a planter, Thomas Lane, wrote in this gazette that Ducoins had captured a slave called Barber and placed him in a boat and sailed down the Savannah river. "After saying he was not afraid of any man, and how valiantly he had behaved during the late war", Ducoins "threw his sword and cut the Negro in several places, in his back, legs and arms and afterwards threw him out of the boat" reported Lane. A week later, Ducoins denounced Lane's account, calling it "a pitiable detail of the ill treatment the said Negro received from his master previous to his elopement." Lane called on three justices to verify his claims. One justice examined Barber and "found four wounds in his head" and his "skull bone bare." Another justice found "live vermin" in Barber's wound.[24]

If a planter felt his fugitive was possessed by the "Devil", should that view be treated seriously or should it be shrugged off? In North Carolina in 1798, a planter who last saw a black woman fugitive heading toward "the woods." The planter maintained that "the Devil did possess her. She would no longer stay."[25] Some planters possessed a low estimation of the fugitive, making it fruitless to trust their point of view without looking behind the words. Jim, a black, had escaped twice and his master from Delaware said that he had not "ranaway without any cause from me," because of "his own vile villainous disposition."[26]

Planter Francis Le Brasseur, a Charlestown store owner, fired off an advertisement in February 10, 1733 offering to hire or sell a sixteen year old black fugitive named Parris. The black returned a week later, but on March 2, 1734 Le Brasseur published another advertisement ordering Parris's return and threatening that if he "refuse to surrender, knock him down, or shoot him with a small shot about his Breech to make him stand."[27] Later, Le Brasseur wrote:

---

[24]Ibid., October 13, 1785.

[25]Edenton *State Gazette of North Carolina*, March 10, 1798.

[26]Wilmington *Delaware Gazette*, August 12, 1795.

[27]*South Carolina Gazette*, February 10, 1733, March 2, 1734.

Against my Negro man nam'd Parris, from this day forth
denounced War is: For now the Dog is grown so wicked he's
runaway without a Ticket which he shall never have, I tell ye.
Nor maigre soup to fill his belly. If he don't halt at your
command Pray knock him down to make him stand or
pepper him well about the A-e Be gar, dis make one pretty
farce.[28]

Parris returned and Le Brasseur put, "a chaine and 3 spurrs on
each of his legs." Parris still made off again. Le Brasseur probably
wrote this unsigned piece:

Whereas a stately *Baboon* hath lately slipp'd his Collar and
run away: He is big-bond'd full in Flesh, and has learn'd to
walk very erect on his two Hind-Legs, he grins and chatters
much, but will not bite, he plays Tricks impudently well and
is mightily given to clambering, whereby he often shews his
A----.
If anyone finds him, or will send any news, of him to----
Office, in----street, shall be rewarded proportionately to the
Merit of the creature.[29]

Can the advertisements be trusted as evidence if the fugitive's
feelings are not discussed? Again, the planter brought to the
fugitive advertisement all his illusions, all his fantastic reflections
of reality, as well as his frustrations. "That this slave shou'd
ranaway and attempt getting his Liberty," said one planter in
Maryland "is very alarming, as he has been always too kindly used,
if any Thing by his Master, and one in whom his Master has put
great Confidence, and depended on him to overlook the rest of his
slaves and he has no kind of Provocation to go off." The planter's
name was Thomas Ringgold, a slavetrader and assemblyman and

---

[28]Ibid., March 30, 1734.

[29]Ibid., May 4, 1734, quoted in Peter Wood, *Black Majority*,
245-6. See also Winthrop Jordan, *White Over Black* (Chapel Hill,
1968), 238.

the black's name was Toby who "intended to pass for a Free-man."
Some notices were unwittingly realistic. One South Carolina
advertisement describing a black contained a threat: "Flog him so
as not to take his life," requested the planter, "for though he is my
property, he has the audacity to tell me he will be free, that he
will serve no man and that he will be conquered or governed by
no man." Many planters acknowledged that the fugitive wanted
freedom, not out of sympathy, but to alert the public about the
fugitive's ultimate goal. One fugitive, "A mulatto man named Jim
who is a Slave," claimed one planter, "but pretends to have a Right
to his Freedom" because his "Father was an Indian."[30]

Planters seemed dumbfounded by the fugitive's desire for
freedom. Three English convicts fled in 1766 from Cecil County,
Maryland and the planter asserted: "As they have now gone off
without the least Cause of Complaint, have lived extremely well,
and have behaved with the greatest Ingratitude, it is hoped every
Person will, as far as it lies in their Power, hinder their getting
off." Similarly, Charles, a black man escaped from Virginia, from
"no Cause of complaint, or Dread of Whipping, (for he has always
been remarkably indulged, indeed too much so) but from a
determined Resolution to get Liberty, as he conceived, by flying to
Dunmore."[31]

The fugitive notice can be used quantitatively. A fugitive
advertisement in the local newspapers implied that a black or
white servant had rebelled, that the planter did not know his
whereabouts, and that he needed assistance to track down the
fugitive. A count of fugitive advertisements during any time period
will reveal the *minimum* number of fugitive escapes during that
period. The *Pennsylvania Gazette* during 1729-1780, published
approximately 4,731 advertisements describing 4,565 white servant
men, 415 white servant women, 462 black men and 46 black
women. Had it not been for the long and uninterrupted
publication run of this gazette, it would have been impossible to

---

[30]*Maryland Gazette*, February 20, 1755; *South Carolina Gazette*,
December 1, 1770.

[31]*Virginia Gazette* (Purdie), November 18, 1775; *Maryland
Gazette*, May 8, 1766.

know that hundreds of fugitives, both black and white, had escaped in that colony. An understanding of the newspaper's contemporary role, then, as well as its use as a source for the quantification of fugitive advertisements is needed to gauge the scope of fugitive resistance in early America.

North Carolina, first settled by the English in 1663, had no newspaper in its early beginnings. Fifty-two years later it had 7,500 whites and 3,700 blacks and still no newspaper. By 1752, when the colony had 20,000 whites and 10,000 blacks it got its first newspaper. During the period between 1752 and 1800, the colony had twenty-six sets of different newspaper publications, but few survived. Between 1751 and 1783 the total number of available issues was thirty-one, most of which were mutilated. Between 1752 and 1800 these newspapers contained about 167 fugitive advertisements describing 174 black men, 23 black women, and 6 white servants. In 1790 North Carolinians had about 100,600 slaves, which means the fugitive number appears too low for that state given the population and too low to make a probable guess of how many fugitives escaped.[32]

Delaware, whose Swedish settlement took root in 1643, never had a large number of slaves. The 1790 census listed 8,887 slaves, 59,096 white inhabitants, but no white servants. Delaware's first newspaper, *The Wilmington Courant*, began publication in July of 1762 and discontinued five months later. Twenty-three years later the *Delaware Gazette* began publication followed by *The Delaware Courant* in 1785 and *The Delaware Eastern Shore Advertiser* in 1796. Together these three papers published 112 advertisements between 1762 and 1800 describing 107 black men, 17 black women, and 3 white servants. Over ninety percent of Delaware's

[32]Hugh T. Lefler and William S. Powell, *Colonial North Carolina: A History* (New York, 1973), 1-20; Evarts B. Greene and Virginia D. Harrington, *American Population Before the Federal Census of 1790* (New York, 1932), 160; Clarence S. Brigham, *History and Bibliography of American Newspapers* 1690-1820 (2 vols., Mass., 1962) II: 758-781.

newspapers are missing.[33]

Whites settled in Georgia in 1733. Planters brought blacks to Georgia during the 1740's and the latter numbered 420 in 1751, 1,066 in 1753, 3,578 in 1760, 7,800 in 1766, and 29,264 in 1790. No continuous count was kept of white servants, but considering there were eighty-six white indentured servants in Savannah in 1737. Georgia's first newspaper, the *Georgia Gazette*, ran from 1763 to 1776, when the Royalists closed it during the Revolutionary War. After the war it resumed under the title *The Gazette of the State of Georgia*, continuing from 1783 to 1788. In 1788, James Johnston, the publisher, changed the title back to *The Georgia Gazette*, which title remained unchanged until 1802. The Georgia newspapers published 641 notices describing 712 black men, 94 black women, and 11 white servants but this is in the context of publications being available for only seventeen of the thirty seven years of the existence of the Georgia press in the eighteenth century.[34]

English settlers, accompanied by blacks, first inhabited South Carolina in 1670 or 1671. The settlers in 1695 outnumbered the blacks by four to one. By 1708, the black population of 4,000 equaled that of the whites. In 1751 the blacks numbered 40,000, the whites 9,000. On the eve of the Revolutionary War (1775), the blacks numbered 100,000, the whites 60,000. Census data for Indian slaves are scarce and for white indentured servants are non-existent.[35]

---

[33]John Munroe, *Colonial Delaware: A History* (New York, 1978), 3-79; Greene, *American Population Before 1790*, 12; Brigham, *History and Bibliography of American Newspapers*, I: 77-86.

[34]Kenneth Coleman, *Colonial Georgia: A History* (New York, 1976), 1-10; Green, *American Population*, 180-182; Brigham, *American Newspapers*, I: 111-134.

[35]J.H. Easterby and Ruth S. Green, eds., *The Colonial Records of South Carolina* 1st ser.; *The Journal of the Commons House of Assembly, 1736-1750* (9 vols., Columbia, 1951-62), 1736-1739, Jan. 17, 1739, 590; 1739-1741, 595-7; *South Carolina Gazette*, Jan. 25,

Thomas Whitmarsh published South Carolina's first newspaper, the *South Carolina Gazette*, on January 8, 1732. Whitmarsh died in 1733 and in 1734 the Timothy family purchased the paper and published it until December 1775 when it was suspended by the British. This paper had fifteen months of missing publication. An examination of the *South Carolina Gazette* (1732-1775), *South Carolina Gazette and County Journal* (1765-1775), *South Carolina and American General Gazette* (1764-1784), *South Carolina Gazette and General Advertiser* (1783-1785), *South Carolina Weekly Gazette* (1758-1764), *Gazette of the State of South Carolina* (1777-1780), (1783-1785), *Royal Gazette* (1781-1782), and the *Royal South Carolina Gazette* (1780-1782), yields 2,171 fugitive notices. These notices described 2,336 black men, 436 black women, 344 white servants, and 15 Indians.[36]

During the period 1670-1732, that is the period before the founding of South Carolina first newspaper, scores of blacks and servants made off, especially after 1720. South Carolina officials, for example, complained to the London authorities about the Spanish harboring runaways in St. Augustine and the violation of the 1726 agreement between the two countries concerning the return of fugitives. Six months after Thomas Elliott and other planters near Stono complained about fourteen blacks absconding to St. Augustine, Governor Arthur Middleton in June 1728 wrote to London about the Spanish receiving and harboring "all our Runaway Negroes."[37]

The *South Carolina Gazette* gave little coverage to the black flight to St. Augustine and the planters showed scant concern in their fugitive advertisements about the flight to Florida, leaving the

---

1739; Wood, *Black Majority,* 306, 311-12.

[36]Daniel E. Meaders, "South Carolina Fugitives as Viewed Through Local Colonial Newspapers with Emphasis on Runaway Notices, 1732-1801," *Journal of Negro History,* 60 (April 1975), 288-319; Green, *American Population,* 174; Brigham, *American Newspapers* I: 1037-1038.

[37]*Parish Transcripts,* New York Historical Society, Box I Folder 2: 1, Folder 4: 19.

impression that St. Augustine posed no threat. The gazette did note on January 17, 1739, that South Carolina's governor, William Bull, had complained: "The Desertion of our Slaves is a Matter of importance to this Province" that "the most effectual Means ought to be used to discourage or prevent it for the Future." Two days later, Captain Caleb Davis told the Assembly he had "lost" nineteen slaves to the Spanish, and that twenty-five other blacks had left Port Royal. A month later, Speaker of the House Charles Pinckney reported: "Several Negroes who lately attempted to fly from this province to St. Augustine," but, he noted, they were "apprehended."[38] An examination of 404 fugitive notices during the period between 1732 and 1745 shows no mention of St Augustine as a suspected fugitive destination.

To allay white anxieties, authorities might have kept the St. Augustine escapes out of the public eye. But the citizenry in and around Charlestown had probably heard of "Simon Felix Argular, alias Brigadier, formerly the Slave of John Barton and who heretofore joined in Stealing the Barge of late Gov. Johnson and ran away with a Gang of Slaves from the Province to Augustine." Argular, age forty, born in St. Augustine, had been captured by American troops in St. Augustine, ferried to England where the Secretary of State interrogated him and sent back to South Carolina where he was again interrogated by the Council about his role concerning the "Seducing" of blacks to go to St. Augustine.[39]

South Carolina Governor John Hammerton's inquiry showed that the Creek Indians killed Felix Argular's father, a Spaniard, in St. Augustine; that the Indians took seven year old Felix to South Carolina and sold him to a John Stanyarne for two barrels of rice. A few days later Stanyarne sold the young Felix to John Barton who lived in St. Philip's parish in Charlestown. Barton kept Argular working on a plantation for twenty years before he sold

---

[38]*South Carolina Gazette*, January 17, 1739; *Par. Trans.*, Box 1, Folder 10.

[39]*Par. Trans.*, Box 1, Folder 26-28; Jane Landers, "Spanish Sanctuary: Fugitives in Florida 1687-1790," *The Florida Historical Quarterly*, 63 (January 1984), 296.

him to one Pendarves, a planter from whom Felix absconded.[40]
While at large Felix met Hercules, a black who also escaped from
Pendarves. Hercules told Felix "that there was a gang of them
goeing to runaway to St. Augustine in Governor Johnson's Boat
or Barge." Felix, Hercules, one Indian, and eight other blacks took
Johnson's boat and sailed to St. Augustine in four days. The
fugitive advertisements in the 1730's in the *South Carolina Gazette*
show no mention of Hercules, Argular or Pendarves.[41]

In 1749, thirty-five petitioners from Prince William parish
located near the southern section of South Carolina, had traveled
to the Assembly in Charlestown and testified that "of late several
attempts had been made by Negroes to Escape to St. Augustine,
and particularly one in that Parish, to wit, about Seven weeks ago
when six Negroes belonging to Joseph Butler and one belonging
to Sarah Woodward ran away met the Boat belonging to Mr.
Alexander McPherson." Again, the *South Carolina Gazette*
published no fugitive advertisements describing blacks going to
Florida. Neither McPherson nor Butler nor Woodward published
advertisements in 1749.[42]

The largest number of undocumented fugitives occurred during
the Revolutionary War. Historian David Ramsey estimated that
South Carolina lost about 25,000 slaves. About 100,000 blacks
lived in South Carolina in 1775, but after the war, in 1785 the
number had dropped to 80,000. Despite the mass flight, the
newspaper coverage was scanty. In 1775, 1776 and 1777 the *South
Carolina Gazette* published eleven fugitive notices. The publisher,
Peter Timothy, suspended the paper in 1777 and later that year he
published the *Gazette of the State of South Carolina* which also
contained eleven fugitive advertisements. A fire in the printing
shop halted publication from January 15, 1778 to June 24, 1778,
but Timothy, along with Nicholas Boden, managed the paper until
February 9, 1780. The British seized Timothy, and while being
taken to St. Augustine he drowned en route and the paper did not

---

[40]*Par. Trans.*, Box 1, Folder 26-28.

[41]*Par. Trans.*, Box I, Folder 26-28.

[42]*Par. Trans.*, Box 2, Folder 9: 16-25.

appear again until August 27, 1783. Between 1777 and 1783 planters published forty-two advertisements describing fifty-four blacks in the *Gazette of the State of South Carolina.*[43]

It is a mistake to assume that as soon as the fugitive made off that the planter reached for the fugitive ad. Some planters used the fugitive advertisements as a followup to their personal contacts. On June 17, 1762 merchant Henry Callister of Maryland wrote to Thomas Smith claiming he had sent a servant named "John King to Queen Ann's County where he was to receive a considerable sum of money" but Callister received a letter from Queen Ann's County claiming that King had fled to Virginia with the 150 pounds. Callister had hoped to catch King "unless he was aboard some vessel and outward bound." Unable to find the fugitives, Callister wrote the *Maryland Gazette* owner Jonas Green on July 3, 1762: "I must beg the favor of you to insert the enclosed advertisement in your next Gazette and to recommend to the Printer in Virginia, a Duplicate."[44] Two weeks later the *Maryland Gazette* published the merchant's advertisement:

Chester River, Maryland, 2d July, 1762.
> RAN away from the Subscriber, a few Days ago, an Indented Servant, Assistant in a Store, who calls himself John King, and may now go by his true Name, William Augustus Taubert.
> He is a Londoner, a young Man of slender make and low: But he is not so young as his Aspect seems to shew, and he is yet older in Art and Experience. He is too genteelly dressed for a servant but his Capacity intitled him to that indulgence, provided his Integrity were answerable. He had Variety of Cloathes, but chiefly affected to wear a Lead colour'd fine Sagathy Coat. He had an affected Swing in his Gait, and is very apt to intrude into Gentlemens Company,

---

[43]David Ramsey, *The History of the American Revolution* (2 vols., London, 1793), II: 293; Henning Cohen, *The South Carolina Gazette* 1732-1775 (Columbia, 1953), 1-10.

[44]*Henry Callister's Papers*, New York Public Library, 5 vols., III: 526-528.

especially of the mercantile Class. He carried off with him, or perhaps has sold or exchanged, a pretty little Bay Horse, with a Star in his Forehead.

His Aunt, the Widow of the late *John Rawlings*, lives on the Eastern Branch of *Patowmack*. There he will probably make his first Stage from *Annapolis*, on his Way to *Hampton* for *London*. There is a Man in Pursuit of him, who has his Indenture; but is apprehended he will not cross *Patowmack* after him.

Whoever secures the said Runaway in any Jail, in *Virginia* or *Maryland*, and sends Notice by the Post, shall be paid FIVE POUNDS of the Currency of the Province where taken, upon his Jail Delivery, and TEN POUNDS (if taken in *Maryland*) or FIFTEEN POUNDS (if taken in *Virginia*) and itinerant Charges, if brought to his master.

Masters of Vessels will please to take Notice.

H. CALLISTER.[45]

William Hunter, owner of the *Virginia Gazette*, did not publish Callister's advertisement and Green himself might not have published it had Callister not contacted Green's brother who happened to be at his house when King escaped. Jonas Green's brother recommended that the Naval office be notified and that the advertisement be posted in their offices. Without these key contacts Callister's efforts to capture John King would have been even more difficult and expensive. Callister fired off letters to four different friends, including Green and Hunter, contacted the Naval office, the post office and acknowledged, too, that "I have a man in pursuit of the Runaway."[46] The tracking operation was expensive, but Callister remained optimistic: "I am not without hope of overtaking the fox, tho not with[out] great expense." Was the loss of labor, the loss of a horse, the loss of 150 pounds, the cost of the ad, the postage fees, the capturer's reimbursement fees,

---

[45]*Maryland Gazette*, July 18, 1762.

[46]*Callister Papers*, III: 528.

worth the capture of one fugitive?[47]

The planter devised a number of different methods to cope with the expense of fugitive advertisements. For the mass escape of fugitives, the planter published not separate advertisements for each fugitive, but one advertisement for all. Again, according to a fugitive advertisement on August 4, 1768, in the *Pennsylvania Gazette* Hopkins Driver, a thirty-four year old white servant made his first escape. During the next twelve months he had escaped twenty-three more times. For three and a half years there was no mention of Driver, until July 16, 1772. Rather than publish twenty-three different notices for the various escapes, the planter published, in all, three different advertisements and apparently relied on other means to recapture Driver who was described as "fond of running away." An English servant from Maryland who left in irons was advertised "being 43 times he has absconded." His master did not publish any advertisements following any of the other 42 escapes.[48]

Some planters wanted little or no publicity about an escape. George Washington published two fugitive advertisements in his lifetime though twenty different blacks make off. In 1761, he placed an advertisement not in his local colonial newspaper in Virginia, but in the *Maryland Gazette* describing four black men: Perez, Jack, Neptune and Cupid. In the *Virginia Gazette* in 1775 he published an advertisement describing Thomas Spears and William Webster, two indentured servants. But when a black named Paul escaped two decades later, overseer William Pearce discussed the effectiveness of the fugitive advertisement with President Washington who said: "I had no other objection to the advertising of Paul than that of having my name appear therein, in any papers

---

[47]Ibid., III: 530.

[48]Charleston, South Carolina *City Gazette and Daily Advertiser*, November 11, 1796; *Pennsylvania Gazette*, August 4, 1768, July 16, 1772; *Maryland Gazette*, August 20, 1761.

North of Virginia."[49] In 1798, at Mount Vernon, the gray haired Commander complained to George Lewis, a steward, in Philadelphia "that the running off of my Cook has been a most inconvenient thing to this family." Instead of publishing an advertisement in the *Pennsylvania Gazette* to alert the citizenry in Philadelphia, Washington asked him to use "indirect enquiries of those who know Hercules" to flush out the cook and to contact a Clement Biddle who will "take proper measures" to have Hercules returned.[50]

Landon Carter, a wealthy planter from Virginia, left a diary that spanned the years from 1758 to 1778, detailing his daily plantation operations. His diary entries listed thirty-two fugitive escapes; the local newspapers in Virginia showed one fugitive notice describing Isham in March 1775, and another in March 1776, describing Phil, a black who had made off "twice before." Why Carter chose Phil and Isham for publication and not the thirty other fugitives is a mystery. How Carter found time to publish fifty essays for the *Virginia Gazette* and not time to publish more than two fugitive advertisements is even more mystifying. And George, a black "stayed out" ten years and no advertisement was published to alert the public.[51]

On the one hand, the colonial gazettes are filled with advertisements showing thousands of planters unhesitantly using the advertisement as a deterrent and on the other a number of planters who were either reluctant to use the advertisements or did not use them at all. Why one planter would publish an

---

[49]John C. Fitzpatrick, ed., *The Writings of George Washington from the Original Manuscript Sources 1745-1799* (39 vols., Wash., 1931-44), XXII: 289; *Maryland Gazette*, August 30, 1761; *Virginia Gazette* (Purdie), May 5, 1775.

[50]Fitzpatrick, *The Writings of George Washington*, XXXIV: 170, XXXVI: 79, 123, 148.

[51]Jack P. Greene, ed., *The Diary of Colonel London Carter of Sabine Hall 1756-1778* (2 vols., Charlottesville, 1965), II: 990, I: 218; *Virginia Gazette* (Dixon and Hunter), March 4, 1725; *Virginia Gazette* (Purdie), March 29, 1776.

advertisement and another would not might have been a question
of money or of trying to lull the fugitive into believing that the
escape was successful. Whatever the case, the fugitive notice, like
other classes of evidence, should not be treated uncritically, or
presumptively, though the account seems, at first glance, to be
believable, and logical. A planter's account might be greeted with
less skepticism if he claims a fugitive desires to be free, but should
it be embraced with confidence, if the planter calls the fugitive a
grinning monkey, a thief, a liar, and hypocrite? One must
challenge, contest and raise questions about every ad, and use
caution to guard against being misled.

Even if the data is accepted provisionally, this would be better
than to pass over it entirely. Allan Gallay in his article "Jonathan
Bryan's Plantation Empire: Land Politics, and the Formation of a
Ruling Class in Colonial Georgia" tells how this planter
accumulated 10,000 acres of land and 300 slaves on the eve of the
Revolution through the use of his councillor's office and his
planter connections. Gallay claims that "there are few records of
how Bryan operated his plantations." Using John Martin Bolzius
as a source for 1742, he concludes that the slaves were "well
treated and as a result, were contented and worked efficiently."
Since Bryan's slaves left no narratives behind, one can only guess
how they felt, but Bryan himself did publish a fugitive
advertisement in 1764 describing three black fugitives and another
in 1768 in the *Georgia Gazette* offering a reward for the capture of
"Ten Negro men" who made off in a canoe.[52]

Unlike the fugitive notice, the slave narrative or autobiography
provides evidence about the experience of chattel slavery. It tells
of the blacks' dreams and their hopes, their fears and their
superstition, their weaknesses, and their strengths. It is true that
few fugitive blacks left written testimonies during the eighteenth
century whereas the planter left behind thousands of fugitive

---

[52]Allan Gallay, "Jonathan Bryan's Plantation Empire: Land
Politics, and the Formation of a Ruling Class in Colonial Georgia,"
William and Mary Quarterly, 3rd Ser., 45 (April 1988), 276; See
Gallay, *The Formation of a Planter Elite* (London, 1989), 16-18, 23-
24, 164-165; *Georgia Gazette*, October 25, 1764, August 31, 1768.

notices. It is true, too, that it is difficult to corroborate these testimonies. As John Blassingame pointed out, the reader must be on guard for the shortcomings of these records. Did they constitute the whole truth and nothing but the truth? Were they representative of the black experience? Were they propaganda tracts? Were they written by abolitionists?[53]

Despite any shortcomings the narratives might have, they are superior to the fugitive advertisements as evidence because they offer more details about blacks, and their families as well as the planters and their families. In the fugitive notices it is difficult to know who is tormenting the slave. The planter might describe a fugitive as having been "corrected," but the corrector may not have been him, but rather his wife. Silvia Dubois maintained that her master Minical Dubois "did not treat me cruelly." She "tried to please him and he tried to please me and we got along together pretty well--except sometimes I would be a little refractory, and then he would give me a severe flogging." Dubois had "plenty to eat, plenty of clothes, and plenty of fun--only my mistress was terribly passionate and terribly cross to me. I did not like her and she did not like me, so she used to beat me badly."[54]

The white woman's harsh hand is evident in the narratives. James D. Mars, a fugitive from Connecticut, remembered that his parents' master, Reverend Thompson, married a woman slaveholder from Virginia who moved to Connecticut just after the Revolutionary War. Mars' father was a "man of considerable muscular strength, and was not easily frightened into obedience." Thompson's wife told his father "if she only had him South, where she could have at her call a half dozen men, she would have him stripped and flogged until he was cut in strings, and see if he would do as she bid him."[55]

The slave narratives captured the slaves' love for their family

---

[53]Blassingame, *Slave Testimony*, xviii.

[54]Silvia Dubois, *Silvia Dubois, (Now 116 Years Old): A Biography of the Slave who Whipt her Mistress and Gained her Freedom* (Ringos, N.J., 1883), 55.

[55]James Mars, *Life of James Mars* (Hartford, 1867), 5.

members and how their separation caused them grief. Julius Melbourn's mother was "entirely black," while his father, whom he never saw, was "a whiteman." Melbourn wrote: "The day my mother was separated from me is among my earliest and most painful recollections." He was three years old and he remembered the "scalding tears as they fell upon my face." He remembered the "shrieking and madness of her grief" and the "clink of the hammer used in riveting the rings which enclosed her wrists and fastened them to a bar of iron. My poor mother was soon marched off with a gang of slaves, and I have never seen or heard of her since."[56]

The fugitive notices showed slave families absconding, but they never reveal how a planter could singlehandedly terrorize them. Minister David George, a fugitive, was born in Essex County, Virginia. His parents John and Judith were Africans. He had four brothers and four sisters. His master's name was Chapel "a very bad man to the Negroes. My oldest sister was called Patty; I have seen her several times so whipped that her back has been all corruption, as though it would rot." George had a brother named Dick, who "ranaway" twice and was captured with the help of horses and dogs. Chapel and his sons held Dick down and gave him "500 lashes, or more," and "washed his back with saltwater and whipped it in as well as rubbed it in with a rag" and sent him to "work pulling off the suckers of tobacco."[57]

"I also have been whipped," recalled George; "many a time on my naked skin, and sometimes till the blood has run down over my waistband but the greatest grief I then had was to see them whip my mother, and to hear her, on her knees, begging for mercy." He concluded: "Master's rough and cruel usage was the

---

[56]Julius Melbourn, *Life and Opinions of Julius Melbourn; with Sketches of the Lives and Characters of Thomas Jefferson, John Quincy Adams, Julia Randolph, and several other Eminent American Statesmen. Edited by a late Member of Congress* (Syracuse, 1847), 8-10.

[57]Account of the Life of Mr. David George, from Sierra Leone in Africa; Given by Himself in a Conversation with Brother Rippon of London, and Brother Pearce of Birmingham," *Baptist Annual Register for 1790-93*, 473-474.

reason of my running - away."[58]

The slave narrative depicts what the fugitive slave felt about his condition, or what was his attitude toward his master and planters in general. This does not mean that the planter's records, including the fugitive notices, should be ignored. But the records must be made to complement each other in order to depict in all its complexity the relationship between the slave and the master. Gerald Mullin's study, draws not on the slave narrative, but on hundreds of fugitive advertisements and uses a number of planter letters and diaries to suggest that some planters were "benevolent", "indulgent" and even "gentle." He believed that these "patriarchs" had "sharply equivocal feelings, about beating" their 'people.'[59] Can Mullin's view be verified, or qualified without consulting the slave? Silvia Dubois said her master's wife "whipped me until she marked me so badly I will never lose the scars here upon my head today, and I will never lose them if I live another hundred years."[60]

Moses Grandy claimed that a Mr. Kemp "used me pretty well; he gave me plenty to eat, and sufficient clothing." But Jemmy Coates was a "severe man." Grandy said: "Because I could not learn his way of hilling corn, he flogged me naked with a severe whip, made of a very tough sapling, this lapped around me at each stroke; the point of it at last entered my belly and broke off, leaving an inch and a half outside."[61] Narrative after narrative tells about the maltreatment of blacks under the planter and if this is shrugged off or played down, then our understanding of the fugitive's world will suffer for it. This in no way suggests that other source materials or categories of evidence such as letters, diaries, public correspondence, court records, or vestry minutes should be played down. Indeed, in order to understand the white servant's flesh and blood experience during the late seventeenth century and

---

[58]Ibid.

[59]Mullin, *Flight and Rebellion*, 24.

[60]*Silvia Dubois*, 55.

[61]Moses Grandy, *Narrative of the Life of Moses Grandy* (Boston, 1844), 7.

in order to understand why they choose to escape, one must draw
on the Maryland court records. Yet, if the servants had left behind
a large body of narratives telling about their experiences under
indentured servitude, then this source of evidence would carry
more considerable weight than police records regarding many
aspects of their lives.

CHAPTER II
FUGITIVES: A PROFILE

The overwhelming majority of fugitives, servants and slaves, were men.[62] Of the 1,946 indentured servants advertised in the *Pennsylvania Gazette* during the period between 1729 and 1780, only 196, or 12%, were women. Between 1732 and 1775, the 1,668 blacks advertised in the South Carolina local newspapers included 271, or 16%, women. And between 1736 and 1780, of the 961 black fugitives advertised in the local Virginia gazettes, 84 of them or 8% were women. During the same period, of the 356 Virginia white servants advertised, 33, or 9%, were women. Because men outnumber women does not necessarily mean that women fugitives desired freedom less than men. In his diary, William Byrd of Westover had his hands full trying to deter a black woman whose determination equaled that on any man's. He wrote:

June 24, 1710 - Negro woman & seven cattle were gone away
June 28, 1710 - Negro woman was found again they thought had drowned herself
Aug. 10, 1710 - My cousin's John brought home my Negro G-1 that ranaway three weeks ago.
Nov. 6, 1710 - The Negro woman ran away again
Nov. 11, 1710 - I had a letter from home which told me all was well except a Negro woman who ran away and was found dead[63]

---

[62]Blassingame, *Slave Community*, 202; Mullin, *Flight and Rebellion*, 55-56, 77-78.

[63]William Byrd, *The Secret Diary of William Byrd of Westover*, 1709-1712; Louis B. Wright and Marion Tinling, eds. (Richmond, 1941), 195, 197, 215, 216, 254, 257.

Demographically the men had the edge: they outnumbered
women in the general population, causing an imbalance in the
sexual ratio. In South Carolina, the slave ratio - 180 men to 100
women in the 1730's, was probably shaped by the slave trade
imbalance, for the merchants preferred men rather to women. On
June 27, 1755, Henry Laurens, South Carolina's leading merchant,
wrote Thomas Mears, a Liverpool merchant and claimed that "Men
slaves from 18 to 25 Years of age turn to best Account, tall able
People of any Country but Callabers." Two months later, Laurens
told Wells, Wharton and Doran, a merchant group from St.
Christopher's that the "best Cargoes for our Market are those that
have most full grown Men. The Men generally bring us from £3 to
£6 Sterling more than the Women & £4 or £5 more than what you
call Men boys of 14 to 16 years of age. The last Cargo we sold was
from Angola about six Weeks ago. It consisted of 116 Men, 45
Women, 49 Boys, & 33 Girls."[64] The planter preferred male to
female servants: Of 20,657 English servant registrations during the
years 1654 to 1775 only 18% were of women.[65]

The uneven sex ratio among fugitives sprang, too, from the
added tasks placed on fugitive women's shoulders, especially those
who took their children with them while en route to their
destinations. An unsuccessful escape could endanger the child. On
September 18, 1755, the *Maryland Gazette's* editor reported that
Master John Hill from Kent county was "conveying home a Servant

---

[64]Wood, *Black Majority: Negroes in Colonial South Carolina
from 1670 through the Stono Rebellion*, 160; Philip M. Hamer,
George C. Rogers, eds., *The Henry Laurens Papers* (9 vols.,
Columbia, S.C., 1968-1980), I: 253, 315.

[65]For some interesting hypotheses about the sexual ratios of
indentured servants in the seventeenth-century see Wesley Frank
Craven, *White Red and Black: The Seventeenth-Century Virginian*
(Charlottesville, 1971), 5-8; Wood, *Slavery in Colonial Georgia
1730-1775*, 169; David W. Galenson, *White Servitude in Colonial
America: An Economic Analysis* (Cambridge, London, New York
1981), 24-26; Mildred Campbell "Social Origins of Some Early
Americans," in *Seventeenth-Century America*, James Morton Smith,
ed. (Chapel Hill, N.C., 1959), 63-89.

Woman who had a Child in her Arms about six Weeks old, he struck the Woman with a Switch sundry Times, and the End of the Switch reaching the Child's Head, kill'd it in her Arms."[66]

Despite these hardships, women with children, including those in various stages of pregnancy, managed to slip away. The Pennsylvania fugitive advertisements during the period between 1729 and 1780 described six pregnant white servants and seven servant women with children which amounted to 2% of the total number of female servants who escaped during that period. These same advertisements did not describe any black women in that category. In South Carolina the advertisements described seven pregnant women and fifty-four other women who carried away a total of seventy-six children between 1732 and 1775, amounting to 23% of the total number of female fugitives. No pregnant fugitive women were reported as carrying their other children off.

How far could these women travel before tiring? One planter in 1773, in Pennsylvania wrote that a seventeen year old Irish servant named Jane McDole was "pretty far advanced in her pregnancy." Molly, a black of South Carolina, was pregnant and carried two children with her when she escaped in 1796, but the owner predicted that she "would not be able to travel far."[67] A notice in one Virginia paper in 1793 described a black woman, Beck of North Carolina, who formerly belonged to a master named Morris, who had emancipated both her and her two children in North Carolina. She had, nevertheless, been "apprehended and sold agreeable to an act of Assembly of North Carolina." Her new owner from when she had been away apparently knew she would be back. "I have got the two children from Mr. Morris since the wench went away."[68]

Leaving the children behind, a tactic fraught with danger, was one method the fugitive woman used to increase her chances of remaining at large. Margaret Brown, a servant, had "four or five

---

[66]*Maryland Gazette*, September 18, 1755.

[67]*Pennsylvania Gazette*, October 20, 1773; Charleston, *South Carolina Daily Advertiser and City Gazette*, July 1, 1796.

[68]Richmond *Virginia Independent Chronicle*, May 5, 1793.

Children, and has left two behind her" claimed her master. One twenty-three year old Irish woman of Pennsylvania had a young child about 6 weeks old, and was reported by a one planter as having, "come in the night into an out Kitchen of Mine, and left the child, which was almost perish with cold, before it was perceived." In Maryland in 1786, one planter said that Dinah "appears to be with a child," and Peggy, a "tall black woman," was said to have "left a young child behind."[69]

That these women escaped at all was remarkable, especially from Landon Carter who examined his slaves to determine whether they were sick or malingering. In 1770, he wrote in his diary about two black women: "2 Sarahs came up yesterday pretending to be violent ill with pains in their sides. They look very well, had no fever, and I ordered them down to their work upon pain of a whipping." One Sarah, Manuel's Sarah, "swore that she would not work any longer and run away and is still out." According to Carter's diary, the pregnant women engaged in work stoppages rather than attempts to leave the plantation, a tactic used only as a last resort. Carter wrote that "Wilmot of the fork whenever she was with Child always pretended to be too heavy to work and it cost me twelve months before I broke her." Criss of Mangorike had escaped, but Carter captured her. She received a "severe whipping" and according to Carter has been a "good slave ever since only a cursed thief in making her Children milk my Cows in the night."[70]

With assistance, the pregnant fugitive or the women with children faced fewer difficulties. Jack, a black, according to the *Virginia Gazette*, "had carried off a wench his wife and child about one years old." White servant Andrew Bartell had "taken his wife (who is likewise servant to subscriber), his child age three months with him." Traveling as a unit did not always work out. James Murphy, age thirty-four, took "a woman with him he calls his Wife, whose name is Phoebe but as she is big with child, he may leave

[69]*Pennsylvania Gazette*, January 21, 1746, May 4, 1755; Baltimore *Maryland Journal* and *Baltimore Advertiser*, June 8, 1786.

[70]Greene, *Carter's Diary*, I: 372.

her by the way."[71]

The men rarely took children, but a black named Bow age forty took his twelve year old son named Bow, according to a South Carolina fugitive advertisement. Servant Henry Carpenter, by trade a carpenter, had "a son with him of 13 years old." Sampson, age fifty-eight, a "very lusty Negro Man has taken with him a Boy twelve or fourteen years of Age named Sam."[72]

How old was the typical fugitive? In the most active stage of his life, the typical fugitive servant was between seventeen and thirty years old. During the period between 1729 and 1750, the *Pennsylvania Gazette* published 1,099 advertisements describing 1,090 fugitive servants of whom 251, or 66%, had their ages listed; 174, or 69%, of these servants were between sixteen and twenty-five years old; 240, or 86%, between sixteen and thirty. Between 1770 and 1775, of the 270 male servants who had their ages listed, 250, or 92%, were between sixteen and thirty. For the twenty-four women whose ages were listed, 96% of them were between the ages of sixteen and thirty. During the period between 1773 and 1790, the *Maryland Gazette* and *Baltimore Advertiser* published advertisements describing 192 blacks of whom 111 had their ages listed. Of these fugitives, 59% were between the ages of thirteen and twenty-five; 79% were between the ages of thirteen and thirty and 18% between thirty and fifty. Of the 247 servants advertised, 94 had their ages advertised and 67% of these servants were between the ages of fifteen and twenty-five; 83% between fifteen and thirty and 11% between thirty and fifty.

Although more blacks than servants fell between the ages of thirty and fifty, the average ages of the two groups did not differ markedly. In the *South Carolina Country Journal* during the years 1772-1774, the jailer published advertisements describing 229 recaptured blacks of whom 114 or 50% had their ages listed. Twenty-six percent of these fugitives were between the ages of

---

[71]*Virginia Gazette* (Purdie), June 11, 1767; *Pennsylvania Gazette*, June 11, 1772; *Maryland Gazette*, July 17, 1756.

[72]*South Carolina Gazette*, February 29, 1748, January 7, 1761; *Maryland Gazette*, July 8, 1745; *Pennsylvania Gazette*, October 1, 1749.

fifteen and twenty-five, 59% between fifteen and thirty. Forty percent of the fugitives were between the ages of thirty-one and fifty-five meaning that the older fugitive captives outnumbered the younger ones. Perhaps the older fugitives had gained such notoriety that it was easy to find them and drive them out of their haunts or perhaps as the fugitives grew older their ability to remain at large diminished.

Caution should be used in employing the advertisements as a source to measure ages mainly because some planters seem to be guessing at the fugitive's age. Thomas Burke was "36 or 38 years of age" according to a Pennsylvania advertisement. William Brown of the same colony was "about 30 or 40 years old" and Harry, a black, was described as "age upwards of 40 years."[73]

Fugitives need not always be in their prime. A Maryland servant, reported one planter, was "about 70 years old," and his Hair and Beard was almost white tho it is suppose he cut them off." Another servant of Pennsylvania, "a fresh colour old man, grey hair'd about 60," made his escape.[74] How does one account for the elderly fugitive? Some fugitives were forced into servitude because of prior offenses. The thirty year old William Kean of Virginia had been teaching school in November 1764 but because of his "Ill conduct was obliged in May 1765 to come under indenture." Another planter's servant, Edward Carlton of Maryland, "has five years to serve, besides runaway time and charge which is considerable."[75]

Some fugitives were children. "A Negro boy named Jack, he is about 12 years of age" ran away in 1760 in South Carolina and was "supposed to be harboured by his father Cupid." Catherine Ochlier of Pennsylvania was between thirteen and fourteen years old when she escaped and "it is supposed she has gone to New York." Thirteen year old Thomas Moughan of the same colony was

---

[73]*Pennsylvania Gazette*, February 4, April 25, 1754; *New York Gazette*, November 9, 1747.

[74]*Pennsylvania Gazette*, May 14, 1741, July 13, 1759.

[75]*Maryland Gazette*, May 3, 1748, May 13, 1765.

supposedly "enticed away by his father."[76] The indenturing of young servants came about largely because the servants' parents placed them into servitude at an early age. In Maryland in 1668, the court noted that John Dobb had "hand over" his "Daughter Sarah unto Morgan Williams and his wife for and during the term of four years." And Edward Ryall and his wife Ishell in the same court "doe bind their child Judith with Christopher Percy until she was over Twenty Years of Age."[77]

The typical white fugitive was European born. Although the English, Dutch and Irish constituted over 90% of the fugitives described in the fugitive ads, nationalities such as the Germans, Scots, Welshmen, Swiss, and French also had rewards on their heads. The Pennsylvania notices show during 1729-1750 that of the 246 fugitive servants whose ethnicity was described, 169, or 69% were Irish, 42, or 17% English, 17, or 7%, Dutch, and 8, or 3%, were Welshmen. But in Maryland, of the 178 advertisements that described the servant's ethnicity between 1745 and 1764, 86, or 48%, were English, 69, or 36%, Irish, 11, or 6%, were Scotch, 7, or 4%, Welshmen and 1%, Prussians. Like Maryland, Virginia's English servants outnumbered the other ethnic groups. Virginia gazettes published 107 servant advertisements with ethnic characterizations between 1736 and 1768: 52, or 49%, were English, 40, or 37%, Irish, and the Scots and Welshmen each accounted for 7%.

Save for South Carolina and Georgia, the fugitive advertisements rarely listed the African's nationality, ethnicity, or geographical origin. The Mandingoes, the Guineas, the Iboes, the Coromantees and other African national groups were mentioned in the South Carolina notices. Constituting the largest group of Africans in South Carolina, 104 Angolans were listed in the fugitive

---

[76]*Pennsylvania Gazette*, November 20, 1755, May 29, 1759; *South Carolina Gazette*, August 16, 1760.

[77]*Archives of Maryland*, LIV: 247, 597.

advertisements during the period between 1732 and 1780,[78] making them proportionately the largest noted African fugitive group in South Carolina.

By describing one fugitive as Angolan, or a Mandingo, or by calling one an Irishman and another a Scot, the planter was making a stab at ethnic differentiation, as a tactic simply to speed capture. This was futile because the planter himself could not make the fine distinctions between the various African nations. In 1777, one planter wrote that an African had "been in the country about 7 years, was imported with a cargo of Eboes. I could not make out what country he was or neither can he tell his master's name, he answers to two names, Boston or Monday."[79]

When questioned about his identity, the fugitive himself could not always identify his country of origin or his ethnic group. Whether this was feigned or real ignorance is difficult to tell. The jailer in South Carolina wrote that Tom, a black captive, said, "his master is dead and cannot tell, the name of his country." Another African in that jail "cannot tell his own or his master's name, nor his country."[80] Some fugitives denied their country of birth in order to go undetected. Betty Dawson, a white servant, was "born in Ireland but denies her country" claimed her owner in Pennsylvania. Servant Charles South of Maryland "is an Irishman but will not own it." Convict servant, Mortimour Sales "pretends he is an Englishman, but the Brogue on his Tongue discovers him to be an Irishman."[81]

One fugitive sought to make his ethnicity known to the colonist in order to win his freedom. Job, the Son of Solomon, the Grandson of Abraham and a Fulani priest in the eastern part of

---

[78]Hamer, *The Laurens Papers*, I: 295; Littlefield, *Rice and Slaves*, 8-11.

[79]*South Carolina American and General Gazette*, April 10, 1777.

[80]*South Carolina Country Journal*, April 27, 1767, September 5, 1769.

[81]*Pennsylvania Gazette*, July 15, 1756; *Maryland Gazette*, June 24, 1746, August 25, 1763.

Senegal known as Bundi. Captured by a party of Mandingoes while en route to the Gambia River where he hoped to sell two slaves to the English slavetraders, later Job himself was captured and sent to Annapolis, Maryland in 1730 and sold for 45 pounds to Alexander Tolsey, a tobacco planter who lived on Kent Island, in Queen Anne's County. Job escaped to Dover, Delaware, hoping to find a sympathetic planter who might help him return to Africa, but the authorities captured him in 1731 and placed him in a jail. Thomas Bluett, an attorney and a missionary, and his friends had heard about Job's imprisonment and asked to see the Muslim fugitive. Bluett, who would later pen Job's narrative, found that the fugitive, "could not speak one Word of *English*. Upon our talking and making signs to him, he wrote a Line or two before us, and when we read it, pronounced the words *Allah* and *Mohammed;* by which, and his refusing a Glass of Wine we offered him, we perceived he was a *Mahometan;* but could not imagine of what Country he was, or how he got thither; for by his affable Carriage, and the easy Composure of his Countenance, we could perceive he was no common Slave."[82] Bluett and his group found an "old Negroe man, who lived in that Neighborhood, and could speak the Jallof," a language related to Pulsar and finally they found Job's master and the reason why he had escaped. Job was eventually sent back to Bunda.[83]

Most planters probably used black interpreters, for how else could they communicate with the African, especially since no documents show planters trying to learn the African languages. The South Carolina jailer in 1760 reported the capture of "Four New Negroes who can speak no English, but what I can learn from my fellow who understands their country language and can speak

---

[82]Phillip D. Curtin., ed., *Africa Remembered: Narratives of West Africans from the Era of the Slave Trade* (Madison, Milwaukee, London, 1968), 17, 18, 40-41; Allan D. Austin, *African Muslims in Antebellum America: A Sourcebook* (New York, 1984), 75-93; Douglas Grant, *The Fortunate Slave: An Illustration of African Slavery in the Early Eighteenth Century* (London, 1968), 68-77.

[83]Grant, *The Fortunate Slave*, 42-44.

to them, their names are Ned, Tom, Dick and Harry."[84]

The planters have left little evidence of what they knew about African nationalities. Laurens was one who left evidence about his views toward African nations. He did have slave preferences: "There must not be a Callabrar amongst them. Gold Coast or Gambia are best, next to them the Windward Coast are prefer'd to Angolas." He preferred the Gambians and the "Gold Coast" blacks because they were tall and black; disliked the Iboes and the Callabrars because they were suicidal and praised the Angolans because they were docile.[85]

Laurens never indicated that he asked these captives about how they felt about themselves. In fact whether the Africans were from the Gold Coast or Central Africa, Laurens complained about the captives in America being "full of infirmities." He could not sell the Gambia cargo in 1755 "Oweing to one fourth part them being Invalids with many disorders."[86]

Just as the listing of nationalities in the fugitive advertisements was used as an aid to capturing a fugitive, so was the listing of names. Two Africans escaped in 1761, in South Carolina, and the owner said: "They were brought from Charlestown a day or two before they went away, are not named, and can speak no English."[87] To remedy this problem, a few planters mentioned both the African and the European name of the fugitive, "his name is John" wrote Henry Laurens in his fugitive advertisement about a Mandingo who could "speak no English" but "he will more readily answer to the name of Footabea which he went by in his country." One planter said in his advertisement that "the Wench's country name is Cumba, but her proper name is Tyra."[88]

The planter named the blacks after the days of the week:

---

[84]*South Carolina Gazette*, September 20, 1760.

[85]*Laurens* I: 295.

[86]Ibid., I: 128, 172, 327.

[87]*South Carolina Gazette*, December 5, 1761.

[88]Ibid., August 27, 1753, August 12, 1765.

Monday, Tuesday and Friday, after months: January, February, March, April, May, June, July and December; after large cities: London, Bristol, Durham, Dublin, Boston, Charlestown, Richmond; and after Colonies: Carolina, Virginia, and Georgia. Fugitive advertisements show that both black and white servants were given names that encapsulated a certain personality or physical trait. Dick, a black, was "known by the name of Preaching Dick." Another advertisement read: "A very big Negroe man named Sampson." One planter wrote: "A servant woman named Margaret Barnes but commonly goes by the name of hopping Pegg. She is remarkably short and limps." And lastly, one black fugitive's "tongue is so glib that he is nicknamed lawyer."

The fugitive advertisements show that a number of blacks and servants had trades or handicraft skills that might have given them a certain amount of autonomy, status, and individual control of their work; this might have freed them from the routine of plantation labor. These occupations included bakers and blacksmiths, carpenters and tailors, coopers and brickmakers, weavers and millers, wheelwrights and tanners, masons and hatters, shoemakers and butchers, sawyers and joiners, clock makers and sadlers; there were other non-plantation workers who included schoolmasters, doctors, ferrymen, waiters, houseservants, sailors, bartenders, jockeys, dancemasters and newspaper carriers.

Because the planter was determined to track down the fugitive, it would seem logical that he would mention the fugitive's occupation in order that his description would be even more accurate. But strangely enough most of the fugitive notices do not list the fugitive's occupation. The *Pennsylvania Gazette* published advertisements during 1729-1775 describing 210 skilled servant fugitives which amounts to only 13% of the total number that escaped during that period. What were the occupations of the other 87%? In 1776, that paper published fugitive advertisements describing twenty-four servant women but not one advertisement listed their occupations.

The South Carolina fugitive advertisements had the same shortcomings. South Carolina gazettes described 242 fugitives performing non-plantation duties but that was equal to only 15% of the total number of fugitive blacks. What of the other 85%? Was the fugitive who did not have his occupation listed a plantation laborer? Or does the researcher have to resort to mere conjecture? One planter claimed that his servant was a blacksmith, but the servant has "always deny'd it."[89] William Eddis, the English traveler, visited America during 1769-1777 and met many colonists, one of whom was a planter. The planter had "purchased a servant as an assistant to his garden having been previously informed that he had originally acted in the capacity and was qualified for the undertaking." Dissatisfied with his job, the servant absconded and was later captured. The servant said the Captain who sold him said he should "avow some particular calling in order to secure a more comfortable job."[90]

Some fugitives, who did not have a trade, pretended to have one. One servant in Pennsylvania "pretends to know something of several trades but knows nothing of any" said one planter. Servants who had trades would feign the mastery of another trade. One English servant was "By Trade a Shipcarpenter, but will pretend to be a sailor."[91]

Some planters engaged in boasting and scaling the heights of hyperbole rather than giving an accurate description of the fugitive. Peter Deerfoot, a black, was "an indifferent shoemaker, a good butcher, ploughman, and carter, an excellent sawyer and waterman, understands breaking oxen well, and is one of the best scythemen, either with or without a cradle, in America." John Winter was a "very compleat House Painter; he can imitate Marble or Mahogany very exactly, and can paint Floor Cloths as neat as any imported from Britain."[92]

A number of planters thought the reader would know the fugitive's occupation because some fugitives were so well known.

---

[89]*Virginia Gazette* (Parks), April 6, 1739.

[90]William Eddis, *Letters from America Historical and Descriptive Comprising Occurrences from 1769 to 1777 Inclusive* (London, 1792), 29.

[91]*Pennsylvania Gazette*, August 15, 1745; *Maryland Gazette*, 1750.

[92]*South Carolina Gazette*, September 10, 1763; *Maryland Gazette*, July 3, 1760.

Jack, a black, of South Carolina was "so well known in those parts as to require no further description," claimed one planter. And one black named Sancho was so "well known in Charlestown, as to want no further description having for many years used to go in pilot boats."[93]

On the other hand, if a planter wished to sell a fugitive "on the run" it made sense to note the fugitive's craft. The fugitives Jack and Sophie of the Guinea country made off in 1763 according to a South Carolina advertisement. The planter made no mention of the fugitives' occupations in the body of the advertisement but in his postscript he claimed, "the said Negro is a very sensible fellow, and good marketman, good butcher, good plougher, and mower, the wench is also fit for use in a plantation, they are both young. If any person is inclinable to purchase the above Negroes may apply to the above subscriber who is willing to dispose of them."[94]

What did it mean to be an artisan in America? To Benjamin Franklin, "The Husbandman is in honor here, and even the Mechanic, because their Employments are useful. The People have a saying that God Almighty is himself a mechanic, the greatest in the Universe; and he is respected and admired more for the Variety, Ingenuity, and Utility of his Handyworks, than for the Antiquity of his Family."[95]

Unlike Franklin's idyllic description of the free artisan, Landon Carter's description of his craftsmen was less romantic: "I do believe my old Carpenters intend to be my greatest rascals." One carpenter, Guy, could not do anything right, for he "does not go about any job be it ever so trifling that he does not make three weeks or a month of it at least." When Guy should have taken three days to put new ceilings in Carter's Mudhouse he was taking over four days. On the fifth day "Guy actually runaway," reported Carter only to "return a week later and here had his correction for

---

[93]*South Carolina Gazette*, February 17, 1757, September 5, 1761.

[94]*South Carolina Gazette*, September 10, 1763.

[95]*The Writings of Benjamin Franklin*, Albert H. Smyth, ed. (10 vols., New York, 1906-7), IX: 606.

running away in sight of the people."[96]

In 1784, George Washington had a number of skilled slaves; they included wagoners, carters, cooks, gardeners, carpenters, smiths, millers and knitters. Two years later, Washington described four carpenters Isaac, James, Sambo and Tom Nokes. He claimed that Carpenter James was "a very worthless fellow, and cuts himself on purpose to lay up." Years later the President was telling his plantation manager that "Thomas Green (overlooker of the Carpenters) requires you pay close attention, which I believe it will be impossible to get any work done by my Negro Carpenters, in the first place because it has not been in my power when I am away from home."[97] In short, the fact a fugitive was a craftsman did not necessarily mean he was to be treated differently.

When separated from their wives skilled slaves expressed discontentment and even ran away. Robert Carter's two carpenters, Negro Talbot and Negro Sam, made off in 1779. Sam had left the Cancer plantation in Prince William County because he had a wife in Charles City County. Carter told planter John Pound that "Sam thinks it is a hard case to be separated from his wife," and "is not to return to Cancer." Neptune, a brickmaker, found that he was to be to sold to George Washington in 1787, but the Commander noted that this black "seems a good deal disconcerted on account of a wife which he says he has at a Mrs. Garrard from whom he is unwilling to be so far removed."[98]

Whatever their status and no matter how they were treated, some fugitive craftsmen received a sense of fulfillment from their occupations and did not see themselves as purely instruments of labor. In Maryland, one planter wrote that his fugitive servant had a "Pair of large carv'd Brass Buckles, of his own Make, which he bragg of very much." In another advertisement one Irish servant "talks much about the Bricklayer's and Carpenter's Business" and

---

[96]*Landon Carter's* Diary, I: 369-70.

[97]Fitzpatrick, *The Writings of George Washington*, XXXIV: 502

[98]Robert Councillor, "Carter Papers, Duke University Manuscript Division" (Durham, North Carolina), Letter book 3-2-110; Fitzpatrick, *Washington's Writings*, XXIX: 19.

another servant barber was "fond of expressing his Calling."[99] The planter's notices unwittingly show that the fugitives loved to sing, dance, and play musical instruments. One black fugitive can "whistle like a fish, in particular a tune called the Black Joke." Abraham, a black fugitive from Delaware, "takes a delight in singing." John Murphy, a white servant, "sings extraordinary well being followed out in the playhouse in London." Margaret Philips, a servant of New Jersey, "can sing and dance the ropes with many other tricks." John, a black, "may be found playing on his fiddle which he took with him." And an English servant who was "in the army is a good drummer, can play several instruments."[100]

Some drank heartily. One fugitive servant was described as "a fellow of few words, until he is in liquor, and then very talkative." Some were expected to act foolishly. Servant Thomas Lane "can play on the fiddle, and dance, and loves liquor. And "when in liquor he is subject to fits" and Lane's "barks like a dog and crowing like a cock caused him to be captured by his former master." A twenty-one year old black named Bacchus "when drunk cuts a foolish awkward, stupid figure, and can scarce articulate a word so as to be understood."[101]

Cockfighting, playing magical tricks, card playing and fortune telling were part of the fugitive's pastimes. Johnny, a black fugitive of Virginia, was "remarkable for cockfighting, card playing and many other games." Jacob Parrot, a twenty-one year old servant from Maryland was "a lover of dancing, singing, carding, racing, cockfighting." An English servant in Pennsylvania "plays a great many antic tricks such as making a piece of silver dance in a glass full of water, and filling a tin cup full of wheat with one grain." Servant John Robinson plays "cards, dance and tells fortunes by

---

[99]*Maryland Gazette*, December 6, 1749, October 11, 1764,

[100]*Pennsylvania Gazette*, August 16, 1750, October 7, 1750, December 13, 1759.

[101]Ibid., May 22, 1755, September 4, 1766; Baltimore *Maryland Journal* and *Baltimore Advertiser*, May 26, 1788, December 11, 1789.

the cards, and pretends to know something of the sleight of the hand."[102]

Some liked to read. A planter characterized an English servant fugitive as having "good learning and number of books with him." Another servant was "very apt to inquire about the News and is a good writer and yet denies he can write." Convict servant Edmund Roper was "well instructed in learning and law." William King, a servant, "understands Latin and is fond of talking about it." Adam, a black, "can read and write which he is apt to brag of."[103]

The religious fugitive might read the Bible or preach about God or debate religious subjects. Servant Barney Kean was "a native Irishman and a great arguer about religion." Master Thomas Love said of a black fugitive: "I expect the chief of this conversation to be on Religion."[104] Peggy a "likely Negro woman" can "spell a little, which she is very fond of shewing."

The advertisements show, too, that the fugitive took pride in his appearance. One black fugitive was described as having "bushy hair of nether wools which he combs and dresses neat by frizzing." One slave called Jack had "a very black complexion, a dimple in each cheek, his hair trimmed to a roll and by frequent combing his hair grown to a prodigious length." Advertisements also show planters complaining about the fugitives' appearance. Andrew of North Carolina was "dirty, slovenly in general appearance, His hair thick and short and matted" and the planter "question if it was ever

---

[102]*Virginia Gazette* (Rind), October 6, 1773; *Pennsylvania Gazette*, May 21, 1752, June 11, 1772.

[103]Baltimore *Maryland Journal*, July 27, 1777, February 25, 1785; *Virginia Gazette*, September 3, 1768; *Pennsylvania Gazette*, June 13, 1771; Alexandria *Columbia Mirror* and *Alexandria Gazette*, January 31, 1798.

[104]*Pennsylvania Gazette*, January 7, 1773; Baltimore *Maryland Journal*, February 25, 1777, February 13, 1787.

combed."[105]

Some fugitives liked to brag about their physical prowess. Jack, a black, who stood six feet five inches, "values himself much on his strength and activity." One servant "values himself for fighting, wrestling and driving a team." Tom Salter, a fifty year old black shoemaker of Maryland, "when in liquor values much of his manhood."[106]

White servants tried to make themselves look good by decorating themselves with tattoos. The "Figure of a Woman and a Cherry tree" was tattooed on Richard Kibble's chest. John Flack has "under his right breast" a picture of "Adam and Eve sitting under a tree." And John Peters "is marked in the middle of his Breast with the Picture of a Woman and several Children before her, on one Arm a Crucifix, on the other, the Jerusalem Arms."[107]

Fighting, too, was part of the daily lives of fugitives. A servant tailor's "Face was much bruised and had black Eyes, occasioned by Fighting" before he made off. Frank, a black, sustained an injury "occasioned by the Bite of a Person who was engaged with in a fight."[108]

Soldiers, though they later became servants, spun long tales about their past exploits. One planter felt that Daniel Rawson might give himself away because he "brags of having seen a brand of Man of War." William Cook had been in the "East Indies on board a Man of War and boast much of it."[109] Thomas Conner, an Irishman "has been a soldier in *Flanders* and talks much about it."

The fugitive women enjoyed the company of their men. Kitty

---

[105]Baltimore *Maryland Journal*, February 27, 1787; *Virginia Gazette*, March 19, 1797; *Wilmington Gazette*, April 6, 1797.

[106]*Virginia Gazette* (Dixon), December 18, 1777, *Pennsylvania Gazette*, June 6, 1751.

[107]*Virginia Gazette*, March 12, 1738, October 28, 1737.

[108]*Maryland Gazette*, March 10, 1763, December 10, 1767.

[109]*Maryland Gazette*, January 27, 1763, August 25, 1763, November 16, 1772.

Owens, a twenty year old servant, who had "fair hair, fresh complexion, light blue eyes, thin lips" was a "great singer and talker, and is fond of men." Another servant woman was "fond of drink and like Sailor Company much." They enjoyed children. One servant was "very fond of children often called them love and lovely." They were capable of infatuation. Maria, a thirty-five year old black woman, "hardly discernable from a white woman, hath left behind her three young children, a good master and mistress and is going towards New York after a married white man who is a soldier in the Continental Service." A jailer in Charles County, Maryland notified the local gazette that he had custody of a black named Frank who had a "woman's osnabrig petticoat, which he says he took from his sweetheart by way of a love memorandum."[110]

Whatever the nationality or the racial group, some fugitives remembered well their homeland and their cultural roots. One Irish servant "sings a good deal in Irish" and "expressly talked about it, bragged about it, sang about it." Robert Ryan was described as being "talkative and is apt to mention the part of country he come from." Ceasar, an African, "boasts much of his family in his own country and it being a common saying with him that he is no common Negro." Donna, another fugitive, "says he come from a Place of the Name in the IBO country in Africa; who served in the Capacity of the Canoe man."[111]

The fleeting impressions gleaned from the phraseology of fugitive advertisements show that the fugitive was both a complex and a dynamic individual who exhibited all the timeless and universal traits of any bound laborer, but despite all the singing and dancing, praying and drinking, despite all the bragging, game playing and primping, the fugitive had to expect the worst. Tom was a "great Dancer and Card player and at times played all the Clothes away from his back" but he had an iron collar strapped around his neck before he escaped. Charles Harding, a thirty year old black from

---

[110]*Pennsylvania Gazette*, February 17, 1773, August 7, 1776; *Maryland Gazette*, August 5, 1772.

[111]*Pennsylvania Gazette*, February 14, 1760, November 27, 1766; *Maryland Gazette*, November 20, 1780; *Virginia Gazette*, December 31, 1772.

Maryland, was a "carpenter and joiner by trade," who could "read and write" and "play on the violin." He had escaped in 1765 and remained at large until 1772 when he was recaptured and sold to Samuel Owings who wrote in his fugitive advertisement that Harding had "upwards of Forty Scars in his Head of different sizes," and that his back had been "unmercifully whipped from his Neck to his Knees, which he said was by his former Master."[112] Harding probably typified the transient status of the fugitive. One day Harding might be nailing boards together or playing the violin, still another day on the run trying to pass for a freeman and another day he might be captured and find himself being "unmercifully" whipped. In short, the fugitive's day to day life should not be viewed as something immutable or fixed in a permanent state, but as something that was constantly in a state of flux.

---

[112]*Maryland Gazette*, July 6, 1772.

CHAPTER III
FUGITIVE LAWS

Five days before Christmas of 1606, three ships – the *Discovery*, the *Susan Constant*, and the *Godspeed* – left London for Virginia. On April 26, 1607, the ships entered with one hundred Englishmen and five boys aboard Chesapeake Bay's southern opening. After two weeks of reconnoitering and an encounter with the Chesapeake Indians from the Cape Henry area, the English disembarked on May 14, and started America's first permanent settlement. They named it Jamestown in honor of King James I, who had allowed the Virginia Company of London to organize and finance the expedition. Through his Privy Council in England, the King controlled the stock company, the seven-man Virginia Council and its powerless presidency.[113]

The Virginia Council elected Edward Wingfield as their first president in the Spring of 1607, but later accused him of pilfering supplies and alienating the Indians. He was ousted and John Radcliff was appointed on September 10, 1607. John Smith, a twenty-eight year old councillor who criticized the gold hungry colonists who wished "to live idly among the Indians," was appointed in 1608. He organized labor gangs and goaded the Indians to trade with the settlers, all of which kept the colony from floundering; but, because of Smith's overbearing manner, the

---

[113]Alexander Brown, *The Genesis of the United States* (2 vols., Boston, 1890), I: 85, 156; Edmund Morgan, *American Slavery, American Freedom: The Ordeal of Colonial Virginia* (New York, 1975), 71; Charles Andrews, *The Colonial Period of American History* (4 vols., New Haven, 1934-1938), I: 99-102; Wesley Frank Craven, *The Southern Colonies in the Seventeenth Century, 1607-1689* (Baton Rouge, 1949), 84-90; *The Jamestown Voyages Under the First Charter, 1606-1609: Works Issued by the Hakluyt Society*, 2nd Series, Philip Barbour, ed. (2 vols., Cambridge, 1969), I: 168-70.

Company recalled him in September of 1609.[114]

Tired of complaints about incompetent presidents, bickering councillors, and discontented settlers, the London Company took control of the colony on May 23, 1609; the King relinquished his authority over the Virginia Council. The Company appointed Lord De La Warre (Thomas West) as the colony's first governor who answered to the Company itself, not to the councillors. With Smith gone, the councillors chose councillor George Percy as president of the Council until De La Warre's arrival in June, 1610. Hoping to keep the colony alive, Percy tried to develop Indian ties, find a cash crop, and organize the laborers, who consisted of servants and free men, unskilled laborers and craftsmen, soldiers and yeomen. They cleared the land, planted the crops, built the forts, stood guard, walked patrol, as well as joined together to seize the Indians' land, destroy their corn, mock their religious idols and kill them if necessary.[115]

In 1609, Percy, Captain Martin and a contingent of settlers, camped forty miles southeast of Jamestown, had spotted an island named Nansemunde and had hoped to barter it from the king of Mancemonde. Percy dispatched two messengers to the king's home, but they vanished and as a result Percy "Beate the Salvages outt of the Island burned their howses Ransaked their Temples Took

---

[114]Wesley Frank Craven, "The Virginia Company of London" in *The Jamestown 350th Anniversary Historical Booklets*, Nos: 1-6 (Williamsburg, Virginia 1957), 2; Brown, *The Genesis of the United States*, I: 139, 141; Barbour, *Jamestown Voyages*, I: 144, 145, 166; Virginia Bernhard, "Poverty and the Social Order in Seventeenth Century Virginia," *Virginia Magazine of History and Biography*, 85 (April 1977), 141-155; Edmund Morgan, "The Labor Problem at Jamestown, 1607-1618," *American Historical Review*, 76 (June 1971), 595-611; Edward M. Wingfield; *A Discourse of Virginia* (Boston, 1860), 16. See Alden T. Vaughn, *American Genesis: Captain John Smith and the Founding of Virginia* (Boston, 1975); Philip L. Barbour, "The Honorable George Percy, Premier Chronicler of the First Virginia Voyage," *Early American Literature*, 6 (1971), 7-17.

[115]Morgan, *American Slavery, American Freedom*, 79-80; Barbour, *Jamestown Voyages*, II: 410.

downe the Corpes of their deade kings from their Toambes and caryed away their pearles Cop and braceletts, wherewith they doe decore their Kings funeralles."[116]

Percy left Martin in charge of Nansemunde and returned to Jamestown; Martin followed Percy shortly after, leaving a Lieutenant Sicklemore in charge and in danger. Seventeen of Sicklemore's men "did take Away A Boate from him by force and wente therein to *Kekowhaton* pretendinge they wolde trade there victwells," wrote Percy, "Butt they were served acordinge to their desertts for nott any of them weare heard of after And in all lykelyhood weare Cutt of and slayne by the Salvages and within fewe dayes after Liestenantt *Sicklemore* and dyvrs others weare fownd also slayne with their mowthes stopped full of Breade beinge donn as it seamethe in Contempte and skorne thatt others mighte expecte the Lyke when they shold come to seeke for breade and reliefe amongste them."[117] So long as the settlers thought the road to survival led to the Indian community, the council presidency could expect more escapes.

To survive, the settlers ate dogs, cats and mice as well as boots, shoes and other leather goods. Corpses of captured Indians were dug up and eaten. One settler ""murdered his wyfe, Ripped the childe outt of her woombe and threw itt into the River and after chopped the Mother in pieces and salted her for his foode." Percy executed him. And again, "To eate," said Percy; "many our men this starveinge Tyme did Runn Away unto the Salvages whom we never heard of after." When De La Warre's deputy, Sir Thomas Gates, and Sir George Sommers arrived from Bermuda on May 23, 1610, they found a settlement of sixty men reduced from five hundred. They saw two settlers, one who cried "there was noe god"

---

[116]George Percy, "Trewe Relacyon of the Proceedings and occurrentes of Memente which has happened in Virginia from the Tyme Sir Thomas Gates was shippwracket upon the Bermudes on 1609 until my departure out of the County which was Anno Domini 1612," *Tyler's Quarterly Historical and Genealogical Magazine*, 3 (1922), 262-5.

[117]Percy, "Trewe Relacyon," 265; Morgan, *American Slavery, American Freedom*, 73.

go off to the Indians only to be slain. Percy and Gates had prepared to evacuate when Lord De La Warre and ships packed with three hundred men arrived on June 10, 1610 with supplies.[118]

Determined to crush the rebellious settler, particularly the fugitive, Governor De La Warre drafted the *Lawes Divine, Morall and Martiall*, demanding the death penalty for "speaking maliciously" against God, for blasphemy, for murder, for sodomy, for adultery, for rape, for theft and for trading with the Indians. One law read: "No man or woman, (upon pain of death) shall runne away from the Colonie, to Powhatan or any savage Werowance else whatsoever."[119] In 1610 George Percy recalled a "Conspiracy plotteinge amonst" some of the iron miners "to Runn away" in a boat. The Governor caught the miners, called for "the marshalle law to be executed," and hanged one fugitive.[120]

De La Warre, seriously ill, left Virginia on March 28, 1611, leaving Percy in charge of about two hundred men. Sir Thomas Dale arrived two months later and "brought with him three hundred men besides great store of Armour, Municyon victualls and vissyon" wrote Percy. He "ordered new laws sett downe good Articles which were well observed all our men being setto work some to plants some to sowe corne and others to build boates and houses most employed in one thing or another." Dale, like his predecessors, "wente against the Mancemondies with a hundrethe men in Armour" and Percy recalled "where he had encounters and skirmishes with the salvages bothe by lande and water, many of his company being wounded." Dale, too, witnessed the spectacle of settlers engaging in work stoppages and absconding to the Indians. In 1618, Dale supervised the construction of Fort Henrico in honor of Prince Henry. The fort was "almost finished" when many of Dale's men "bienge Idile and not willeinge to take paynes did Runne Away unto the Indyans." Dale had those who were captured

---

[118]Percy, "Trewe Relacyon" 267, 269, 276; Morgan, *American Slavery, American Freedom*, 73.

[119]William Strachey, *For the Colony in Virginia Brittannia: Lawes, Divine, Morall and Martial* (London, 1612), 14.

[120]Percy, "Trewe Relaycon," 272-273;

"hanged," "burned," "broken upon the wheles," "staked" and "shott to death;" robbers were "bownd faste unto Trees and so sterved [...] to deathe."[121] By such stern measures, Dale slowed settler flight. But what about a profitable commodity for the stockholders? The settlers found little gold and silver in Virginia and sassafras, wine, silk, iron and tar brought little or nothing in revenues. In 1612, John Rolfe tried tobacco. It worked. By 1617, the colonists had exported 20,000 pounds to England.[122] In 1619 Sir Edwin Sandys, a House of Commons member, a critic of "divine right" government, and the Virginia treasurer, saw the need for more settlers who would live in Virginia permanently. He offered fifty acres "headright" to anyone who paid the passage of a man to Virginia and if one lacked the money to buy a few headrights, he could join with others and share the profits. The Company itself sent servants to work its land for seven years.[123]

Sandys rescinded the *Lawes Divine Morall and Martiall*, and granted settlers the rights of Englishmen. For the indentured servant who agreed to work from four to seven years in return for ship passage, this meant court privileges and the right to freedom dues: food, clothing, shelter and fifty acres of land.[124] Planters elected representatives to the Assembly who shaped policy and enacted laws. Sir George Yeardley, the first governor under Sandys' new program called the Assembly together annually. The Virginia Company's new program depended on tobacco as the major source of revenue, as well as exports of bricks, iron, and glass, the recruitment of tradesmen from abroad.[125]

On March 22, 1622, the Powhatans tried to destroy the infant colony. They killed 347 settlers. Because of the poor living conditions and food shortages, thousands more died. By 1624 the

---

[121]Ibid., 275-280.

[122]Morgan, *American Slavery, American Freedom*, 90, 130, 134.

[123]Ibid., 92-97.

[124]Ibid.

[125]Ibid., 95-97.

number of colonists shipped to Virginia totaled over 5,000, yet the total number that remained alive was 1,275. King James took over; Sandys retired.[126] Between 1624 and 1640, though the number of colonists in Virginia jumped to 8,100, the planters were short of laborers to work their tobacco fields. It cost six pounds to start a laborer out with food and clothes, and this laborer could expect to produce about 2,500 pounds of tobacco a year. With a few laborers, a plot of land, and tobacco seeds the planter could make good money in a year's time.[127]

To protect his profits, the planter needed laborers who would not escape, who would not hire themselves out to another planter, and who would not seek protection in an Indian community. In March 1642, the Virginia Assembly criticized harborers who ""entertain and enter into covenants with runaway servants and freemen," and levied a fine of twenty pounds of tobacco for each night the harborer hid a servant. Counterfeit certificates found on the fugitive would result in punishment. Servants who stayed out would have to serve "double the tyme of service soe neglected." A second offender could be "branded in the cheek with the letter R and passe under the statute of incorrigible rogues." And fugitive servants who left their "peice, powder and shott" with their Indian harborers could be executed. Nineteen years later the Assembly called for the cutting of the fugitives' hair "close above their ears." Fugitives who resisted their owners with "violent hand" served two extra years of indentured time.[128]

---

[126]Ibid., 98-99, 100-101; Alden T. Vaughn, "Expulsion of the Salvages: English Policy and the Virginia Massacre of 1622," *William and Mary Quarterly*, 3rd Series, 35 (January 1978), 34-57.

[127]Morgan, *American Slavery, American Freedom*, 404, 106-107, 175-176; Philip A. Bruce, *Economic History of Virginia in the Seventeenth Century* (2 vols., New York, 1907), I: 595, 597.

[128]*The Statutes at Large, Being a Collection of All the Laws of Virginia*, William W. Hening, ed. (13 vols., Richmond, 1809-23), I: 118, 253-255; Winthrop D. Jordan, *White Over Black: American Attitudes Toward the Negro 1550-1812* (Chapel Hill, 1968), 71-82; Bradley Chapin, *Criminal Justice in Colonial America*, 1606-1660

What of the blacks? In 1624 Virginia had 1,300 settlers of whom twenty-two were black, but the court or statutory records told nothing about whether the blacks were legally slaves. Sixteen years later the court ordered two captured white servant fugitives, Victor and James Gregory, to receive thirty lashes each and a year of additional time. A black, John Punch, on the other hand, had to "serve his said master or assigns for the time of his natural life here or elsewhere." This was enslavement. A month later six servants and a black named Emanuel escaped from Captain William Pierce of Virginia; they took the captain's skiff, corn, powder, and guns, only to be recaptured on the Elizabeth River. Christopher Miller, the ringleader, received thirty "stripes," was "burnt in the cheek with the letter R to work with a shackle on his legg for one minimum whole" year and to serve seven extra years. The others received whippings and extra time. The court mentioned nothing about the black's time because he might well have already been a slave.[129]

By 1661, Virginia had roughly 6,000 white servants and 2,000 blacks out of a total population of 25,600. It had, too, its first law concerning the black, but which aimed at the servant who had indenture time to lose and not specifically the black (probably enslaved) who had no indentured time to lose, and which provided that the servant "serve for the time of the said Negroes absence as they are to do for their owne by a former act."[130]

(Athens, Ga., 1983), 136-137; A. Leon Higginbotham, *In the Matter of Color: Race and the American Legal Process* (New York, 1978), 32-40.

[129]Evarts Greene and Virginia Harrington, *American Population Before The Federal Census of 1790* (New York, 1932), 136; *Minutes of the Council and General Court of Colonial Virginia 1622-1632, 1670-1676*, Henry R. McIlwaine, ed. (Richmond, 1924), 241, 466, 467.

[130]Morgan, *American Slavery, American Freedom*, 311, 404; Hening, *Virg. Statutes*, II: 26; Adele Hast, "The Legal Status of the Negro in Virginia, 1705," *Journal of Negro History*, 54 (1969), 217-239.

In the Act of 1669, the Assembly said that the "punishment of
refractory servants resisting their master, mistris or overseer cannot
be inflicted upon Negroes, nor the obstinacy of many of them by
other than violent means supprest." If the black died, the court
promised the planter that the act would be "an accompted ffelony"
and that he would be "aquitt from molestation, since it cannot be
presumed that prepensed malice (which alone makes murther
ffelony) should induce any man to destroy his own estate."[131]
Execution has a sense of finality to it. Once buried, memories of
the fugitive, the reason for his death and how he was killed may
have faded away. But if the planter chose to dismember the
fugitive as stated in the 1705 act by cutting off an ear, hand, foot
or testicle, he placed a lasting picture in the black's memory,
"reclaiming this incorrigible slave and terrifying the others from
like practices."[132]

In 1707, "King" Robert Carter of Corotoman complained to the
court about two blacks, Henry and Dinah. "To deter these Negroes
and others from ill practices," the court permitted Carter to cut off
the fugitives' toes. On October 10, 1727, Carter described
Ballozore as an incorrigible rogue and claimed that "dismembering
will reclaim him." He ordered his overseer to take out a court
order to cut off the fugitive's toes. "I have cured many a Negro of
running away by this means," claimed Carter. In 1723 the Assembly
absolved owners and surgeons of manslaughter if the mutilation
killed the black.[133]

The planter stopped at nothing: whippings, branding, mutilation,
as well as racial incitement and divide and conquer tactics and
terror. But could he stop the determined fugitive who had little to
lose and everything to gain? The "incorrigible" fugitive brought no

---

[131]Hening, *Virg. Statutes* II: 270.

[132]Hening, *Virg. Statutes* III: 460-461.

[133]Quoted in Morgan, *American Slavery, American Freedom*,
313; *Robert Carter's Letters*, University of Virginia, 72, 3807;
Hening, *Virg. Statutes* IV: 132-33; Philip J. Schwarz, *Twice
Condemned: Slaves and the Criminal Laws of Virginia, 1705-1865*
(Baton Rouge, 1988), 80-81.

revenue to his owner; a lifetime of enslavement brought no cheer to the black. English law protected the white servant because the planter feared that widespread servant maltreatment might slow migration. In 1661, the lawmakers complained that the "barbarous usuage of some servants by cruell masters bring soe much scandall and infamy to the country in generall, that people who would willingly adventure themselves hither, are through feare thereof diverted, and by that meanes the supplies of particuler men and the well seating of his majesties country very much obstructed." The lawmakers ordered the planters to "provide for his servants competent dyett, clothing and lodging and that he shall not exceed the bounds of moderation in correcting them beyond the meritt of their offenses."[134] In either case the Virginia colony led the way in America for the treatment of fugitives.

Seven years after Maryland's first permanent settlement took place in 1634, that colony's Assembly decreed that any servant who attempted to leave the province could "suffer pains of death." Servants who made off within the colony served ten extra days for each day missing. In 1672, a planter accused John Richardson of having gone off for forty-eight days; the court ordered Richardson to serve 480 days. Maryland legislators excluded branding or shaved heads to deter flight and declined to specify in their statutes whether a servant could be lashed. Local courts, however, called for servant whipping. On February 16, 1659, the Kent County Court in Maryland contended that a servant named "Mouse" was "a Constant Runaway From his Maisters Service" and ordered him punished with "25 good Sound Lashes and if hereafter the said servant shall runn away againe, The Court doth order that any of the inhabitants shall finde him shall whipp him home againe."[135]

By 1707, blacks outnumbered white servants in the colony — 4,656 to 3,003 and the question of how to control the blacks arose.

---

[134]Hening, *Virg. Statutes* II: 117.

[135]Craven, *The Southern Colonies in the Seventeenth Century*, 191-194; *Archives of Maryland*, J. Hall Pleasants and Elizabeth L. Merritt, eds., et al. (71 vols., Baltimore, 1883-1970), I: 107-9. II: 146, LIV: 184, 452; *Laws of Maryland*, William Kilty, comp. (2 vols., Annapolis, 1800), Act of 1715, Chap. XLIV.

In 1663, the lawmakers ordered the servant who absconded with
a black "to serve for the time of the Negro's absence." The
Assembly, in 1695 and 1723, criticized black holiday gatherings,
claiming these meetings encouraged embezzling, bartering, and
insurrection. The legislators ordered authorities to whip blacks
without passes. They feared, too, that "many Negroes absent
themselves from their master's service and run out into the woods
and there remaining killing and destroying hogs and cattle."
Maryland treated the black's refusal to surrender as a felony.[136]

Maryland enacted no dismemberment laws. But on June 4, 1692
the St. Mary's Court heard that "Thomas Courtney of St. Maries
County hath lately most barbarously dismembered and cutt off
both the ears of a certain mulatto girl." Courtney contended the
woman's thefts and frequent escapes "forces him to use such
severity" and that as she was his slave he could treat her "as he
pleased." Because the slave was "born of an English woman and a
Christian," the court set the girl free. The court made a
"distinction between mulattoes and Negroes, not equalizing them
in point of servitude," and referring to the "scandal of Christianity"
as a concern. Fearing this abuse might touch the white servant, the
courts warned planters that the denial of rest and sleep, meat,
drink and lodging after the third offense was grounds for setting
servants free.[137]

Unlike Maryland or Virginia, fugitive laws in South Carolina
wavered little over the status of fugitive blacks. In 1690, twenty
years after the first contingent of blacks arrived in South Carolina,
lawmakers had begun to write statutes forcing servants, blacks, and
Indian slaves to have passes or face imprisonment. Military patrols
were ordered to capture the fugitive and to kill black resisters.[138]

---

[136]Greene, *American Population* 24; *Arch. of Md.* I: 489, 533,
VII: 204-205, XIII: 546-49.

[137]*Arch. Md.*, XIII: 292, 293, 302, 307, 457-459.

[138]Wood, *Black Majority*, 271-284; *Statutes at Large at South
Carolina*, Thomas Cooper and David J. McCord, eds. (10 vols.,
Columbia, 1836-41), VII: 355; M. Eugene Sirmans, "The Legal
Status of the Slave in South Carolina, 1670-1740," *Journal of*

In 1712, fugitive blacks, men or women, who left their masters, could expect to be "publicly and severely whipped, not exceeding forty lashes" if they remained at large over twenty days. A second escape could result in being "branded with the letter R." A third meant that the black could be whipped and have "one of his ears cut off." The fourth could cause the male fugitive to be "castrated" and the woman to lose another ear and to be branded on the other cheek. And for the sixth attempt the black could expect his achilles heel to be severed.[139]

Leaving the planter was one thing; escaping with the "intent" to leave South Carolina was another. The punishment was forty lashes and branding "in the forehead with a hot iron." The ringleader or the instigator of this escape could be executed. White men, characterized as "evil and ill-disposed persons" who persuaded a black to abscond, could be fined twenty-five pounds according to a 1722 Act. The white man who successfully sent a black out of the colony could be executed.[140] During the eighteenth century the South Carolina lawmakers made few revisions in their slave statutes. In 1751, however, they felt that the death penalty for blacks who enticed other blacks to leave the colony was a "punishment too great for the nature of the offence."[141] To accuse the black of enticement meant little if the black did not have arms, ammunition or boats to make good the escape.

These laws were put into practice, according to Dr. Francis Le Jau, an English missionary of the Society for the Propagation of the Gospel in Foreign Parts, who arrived in Charlestown in 1706, and later moved to St. James' parish in Goose Creek. Though Le Jau declined to baptize a slave without the master's consent and though this baptism, this spiritual cleansing of the soul, had nothing to do with emancipation, he was a man made proud each

---

Southern History, 28 (1962), 462-473.

[139]Cooper and McCord, eds., *South Carolina Statutes*, VII: 357-60.

[140]Ibid., 357-358.

[141]Ibid.

time he baptized a black or white. From January 1, 1711 to June 30, 1712, he "Christened 11 infants Marryed 2 couples Buried 2 Men New Communicants 3. Actuall Communitcants on Easter Sunday 37 among whom 5 Negroes." Because he worked hard to save souls, it angered him to see needless deaths take place. Two hundred whites and as many more blacks had died in 1711. The physicians said that the "Aire has been infected," but the Reverend Le Jau believed that it was "the Irreligion and Lewdness of too many Persons, but chiefly the Barberous usage of the poor Slaves."[142]

Le Jau complained about a fugitive law which stated that a "Negroe must be mutilated by amputation of Testicles if it be a man, and of Ears if a Woman. I openly declared against such punishment grounded upon the Law of God which setts a slave at liberty if he should loose an Eye or tooth when he is Corrected." He complained, too, about a "hellish Machine" called a "Coffin" where they are "crushed almost to death, and he keeps them in that hellish Machine for 24 hours commonly with their feet Chained out, and a Lid pressing upon their stomack, this is a matter of fact universally known when I look upon the ordinary cause that makes those poor Souls run away, and almost dispaire I find it is imoderate labour and want of Victualls and rest."[143] The castrated black could expect permanent infertility, irritability, mental depression, passive behavior, decreased libido and a likely death within three years.[144]

In October 1710, William Fry and William Sadler, Baptist Church elders in Charlestown, South Carolina, asked the Baptists of South Moulton, Devon, England "Whether a master may and

---

[142]"The Carolina Chronicle of Dr. Francis Le Jau 1706-1717," in *University of California Publications in History*, Frank J. Klingberg, ed., 53 (1956), 86, 108; Charles S. Bolton, *Southern Anglicanism: The Church of England in Colonial South Carolina* (Westport, Connecticut, 1982), 109.

[143]Klingberg, *The Carolina Chronicle*, 108, 120-121

[144]*Textbook of Endocrinology*, 5th ed., Robert A. Williams, ed. (Philadelphia, 1974), 46.

not Sinned against God, by making a Eunuch of his slave for being absent (without his master's leave) from his business for the space of 30 daies?" Fry thought planters had no right to castrate a black without the magistrate's permission or out of revenge with the aim of bringing about a slave's death. But he did not completely rule out castration since such laws "preserved order" among a "Sort of rude, unpolished people, whose Nature requireth a Stricter hand over 'em." On October 28, 1711 a majority of the Devon church members concluded that "the Master Acting according to the Law of your Province, in gelding his Slave, hath not Committed any crime" because the master had bought the slaves and thereby had a right "to keep them in order and under government; and for self preservation, punish them to prevent farther Mischief that may ensue by their running away and [?] rebelling against their Masters." Thus, masters guilty of such acts could receive communion in the church.[145]

North Carolina enacted no castration laws, but its records show that between 1762 and 1767 fourteen blacks who were not listed as fugitives were castrated, two of whom died. Fugitives who had crossed the border and were recaptured were killed, and blacks carrying guns were subjected to the lash. White servants merely served two days for every day absent. The courts prohibited planters from whipping a servant when naked without court permission.[146]

---

[145] "Baptists Face the Barbarities of Slavery in 1710," in *Journal of Southern History*, 29, William G. McLoughlin and Winthrop D. Jordan, eds., 29 (1963), 495-501. See also: Orlando Patterson, *Slavery and Social Death: A Comparative Study* (Cambridge, Mass., 1982).

[146]*The State Records of North Carolina*, Walter Clark, ed. (26 vols., Goldsboro, 1886-1907), VI: 740; XXII: 819, 825, 830, 834, 837, 843, 850; Ernest James Clark Jr., "Aspects of the North Carolina Slave Code, 1715-1860," *North Carolina Historical Review*, 39 (April, 1962), 148-153; R.H. Taylor, "Humanizing the Slave Code of North Carolina," *North Carolina Historical Review*, 2 (July, 1925), 323-325; Alan D. Watson, "North Carolina Courts, 1715-1785," *North Carolina Historical Review*, 60 (January 1983), 24-36.

Because many of the original settlers migrated from Virginia to North Carolina in the 1660's, the North Carolina fugitive laws, first published in 1741, resembled Virginia's. These settlers, mostly small tobacco farmers, shipped a million pounds of tobacco during the seventeenth century. North Carolina never had a large number of blacks until after the Revolutionary War. Nor did the colony appear to have a large number of indentured servants. The blacks numbered 6,000 in 1730, 141,000 in 1767 and by 1790 they were 100,570.[147]

Of the original thirteen colonies, Georgia was the only colony founded after 1688. Lying between the Savannah and Altamaha Rivers, it became a colony in 1732 at the urging of General James Oglethorpe, a Parliament member and Georgia's first governor. Oglethorpe and the trustees who governed the colony for twenty-one years had prohibited slavery in Georgia because the king wished to provide an opportunity for poor debtors and criminals from England to work out their salvation in the New World.[148]

Because Georgia's frontier fanned southward toward the Spanish settlement of Florida, the authorities feared that the blacks would run southward. In 1742, author Benjamin Martyn felt that the *"Spaniards* at St. Augustine would be continually inticing away the Negroes or encouraging them to Insurrections; and a single Negro could run away thither without Companions, and would only have a River or two to swim over." Martyn said the authorities forbade slave importation into Georgia because they feared black insurrections, which would cause whites to quit work and leave Georgia for South Carolina and they feared that Georgia would

---

[147]Marvin L. Michael Kay and Lorin Lee Cary, "A Demographic Analysis of Colonial North Carolina with Special Emphasis upon the Slave and Black Populations," in *Black Americans in North Carolina and The South*, Jeffrey J. Crow and Flora J. Hatley, eds. (Chapel Hill, 1988), 73; Greene, *American Population*, 162-164;

[148]Kenneth Coleman, *Colonial Georgia: A History* (New York, 1976), 1-20.

come under planter control.[149]

By 1750, Georgia admitted slaves; by 1751 this colony had 400 slaves; thirty years later Georgia had 29,264 blacks. In 1758, black fugitives received twenty lashes if caught without a pass, twenty lashes for traveling seven or more miles together, death for maiming or wounding a white person, and death for leaving the province. A white colonist or free Indian received two to four pounds for capturing a black man, woman or child crossing the southside of the Altamaha River. And if a captor brought back not the body but the male slave's ears and scalp, he received one pound. If they captured a male fugitive on the Southside of the St. John River, they could receive fifteen pounds sterling, a woman or child, five to ten pounds sterling. Again the "Scalps with two ears" of a male fugitive could earn the captor thirty shillings sterling.[150]

In 1758, the Georgia lawmakers enacted slave laws because of the numerical increase of blacks, as well as to restrain violent planters. The lawmakers wrote: "And whereas Cruelty is not only highly unbecoming those who profess themselves Christians but is odious in the eyes of all men who have any sense of virtue or humanity therefore to restrain and prevent barbarity being exercise towards slaves."[151] The Assembly declared that a white who "willfully killed" a black had to compensate the owner and could not hold an office place or employment, civil or military, within the province. The second offense could result in execution. If the first offender could not compensate the owner, he had to serve seven years in jail. Planters who killed a black in a "sudden heat or passion" had to pay a 150 pound fine; those who "willfully cut

---

[149]Benjamin Martyn, *Account Showing the Progress of the Colony of Georgia in America from its First Establishment* (London, 1741), 8-9.

[150]*The Colonial Records of the State of Georgia*, Allen D. Candler, ed. (26 vols., Atlanta, Ga., 1904-1916), XVIII: 137-138; Ralph Gray and Betty Wood, "The Transition From Indentured to Involuntary Servitude in Colonial Georgia," *Explorations in Economic History*, 13 (1976), 353-370.

[151]Candler, *Georgia Colonial Records*, XIX: 244.

out the tongue, put out the eye, castrate or cruelly scald, burn, or
deprive any slave of any limb or member or shall inflict any other
cruel punishments other than by whipping or beating with a horse
whip, cow skin switch or small stick or by putting irons on or
confining or imprisoning such slave every such person shall for
every such offense forfeit a sum not exceeding fifty pounds
sterling."[152]

What of New York, Pennsylvania, New Jersey, Connecticut, and
Massachusetts? The northern slave laws were less harsh than the
South's, especially the fugitive laws, which might have reflected the
North's relative lack of concern about the day-to-day security of
towns and cities. Indeed, a militia, patrol, sheriff, and constable
were neither threatened with fines nor jail if they failed to perform
their duties. In fact, the Northern fugitive laws did not spell out
the patroller's duties, rarely advocated terror to halt flight – no
whippings, brandings, chains, ear slicing, castration, or other forms
of dismemberment. Except for those who left Albany, New York
for Canada, blacks did not have to fear for their lives.[153]

New Jersey had a 10:00 p.m. curfew for blacks and Indians; New
Hampshire and Connecticut, a 9:00 p.m. curfew. Fugitive blacks or
Indians could be whipped and jailed in all the colonies. Perhaps

---

[152]Ibid., XIX: 245; Betty Wood, "Until He Shall be Dead,
Dead, Dead: The Judicial Treatment of Slaves in Eighteenth
Century Georgia," *Georgia Historical Quarterly*, 71 (Fall, 1987), 377-
398.

[153]*The Statutes at Large of Pennsylvania from 1682-1801*, James
T. Mitchell and Henry Flanders, comp. (18 vols., Harrisburg, 1896-
1915), II: 79, 235-6, IV: 62-63; *The Colonial Laws of New York
from the Year 1664 to the Revolution...*(5 vols., Albany, 1894-96), I:
147, 148, 158, 582, 763; E.B. O'Callaghan, ed., *Laws and
Ordinances of New Netherlands 1638-1674* (Albany, 1868), 10; *The
Acts and Resolves, Public and Private of the Province of the
Massachusetts Bay, 1692-1780* (21 vols., Boston, 1869-1922), I:
747-8; *Laws of New Hampshire*, Albert S. Batchellor and Henry H.
Metcalf, eds. (10 vols., Manchester, 1904-1922), II: 138-9, 292; *The
Public Records of the Colony of Connecticut*, Charles J. Hoadly, ed.
(15 vols., Hartford, 1872), VI: 390-91.

the most stringent from of punishment might have been slavery itself. Indeed, one might say the same thing about the white servant in relation to indentured servitude. If captured, the following colonies made the servant serve extra time for every day missed: New York, 2 days; New Jersey, 2 days; Pennsylvania, 5 days; and Connecticut, 3 days.[154]

Drawing comparisons between the southern and northern colonies' fugitive statutes helps little because the two regions had different social systems: plantations, and gang labor, consisting mostly of blacks, marked the southern landscape; small farms, fisheries, and shipyards worked mostly by freemen that were of the north. Better to examine the statutes of Barbados, Antigua and Jamaica, since their economies resembled the southern colonies. The English planters who constructed their first permanent settlement in Barbados in 1627 used white indentured servants to work their tobacco and cotton plantations until the middle of the seventeenth century. The Barbadian authorities complained in 1661 about the "unruliness, obstinacy and refractoriness of the servants," especially those who "frequently run from and desert their Master's service." To halt the flight, the Assembly ordered servants to serve an extra day for every two hours at large, which was not to go beyond three years of extra service. Any servant who tried to leave the island by ship could expect a shaved head and three additional years of indentured time.[155]

By the 1660's, the Barbadians had switched to sugar and relied mostly on the black to work that cash crop. Blacks numbered 20,000 in 1655 and 46,602 in 1684. The servants numbered 2,317 in 1684. At least a thousand whites left Barbados for South Carolina between 1680 and 1712, many of whom were powerful planters such as Sir John Colleton and Arthur Middleton who

---

[154]William M. Wiecek, "The Statutory Law of Slavery and Race in the Thirteen Mainland Colonies of British America," *William and Mary Quarterly*, 3rd Series, 3 (April 1977), 258-280.

[155]Richard S. Dunn, *Sugar and Slaves the Rise of the Planter Class in the English West Indies, 1624-1713* (Chapel Hill, 1972), 49, 55, 87; *Acts Passed in the Island of Barbados, From 1643-1762 Inclusive*, Richard Hall, comp. (London, 1764), 35, 38, 41.

brought along their slaves and political expertise. Between 1670 and 1730 six Barbadian planter emigrants served as governors and more became leading members of the South Carolina Commons House of Assembly. It was no accident, then, that the lawmakers printed the following preamble almost verbatim in both the Barbadian and the South Carolina codes. [156]

> WHEREAS the Plantations and Estates of this Island, cannot be well fully managed and brought into use, without labour and service of great numbers of Negroes and other Slaves: and forasmuch as the said Negroes and other Slave brought unto the People of this Island for that purpose, are of barbarous, wild and savage nature, and such as renders them wholly unqualified to be governed by the Laws, Customs and Practices of our Nation: It therefore becoming absolutely necessary, that such other Constitutions, Laws and Orders, should be in this Island framed and enacted for the good regulating or ordering of them, as may both restrain the disorders, rapines and inhumanities to which they are naturally prone and inclined, with such encouragements and allowances as are fit and needful to their support: that from both, this Island through the blessing of God thereon, may be preserved, His Majesty's Subjects in their lives and fortunes secured, and the Negroes and other Slaves be well provided for, and guarded from the cruelties and insolences of themselves, or other ill-tempered People or Owners.[157]

Shortly after 1696, the lawmakers in Barbados drew up enactments to halt flight. A black could not leave a plantation on "Saturday nights, Sundays and other Holidays" without a pass which specified both the departure and arrival time. Owners who chose not to punish a black with a "moderate whipping" could be fined 10 shillings. The Assembly called on the overseer to check "Negro-houses" every fourteen days for fugitives and weapons or be

---

[156]Dunn, *Sugar and Slaves*, 112-113.

[157]Hall, *Barbados Acts*, 112-113; Cooper, McCord, *South Carolina Statutes*, VII: 352, 371, 385.

fined 20 shillings. The black who struck a white person could expect to be severely whipped; the second offense called for the "Nose slit" and face burned with "hot iron;" and the third offense, "by order of the Governor and Council, such greater punishment as they shall think needs to inflict."[158]

For the slave hiding in the woods, lawmakers could raise up to twenty men to affect his capture dead or alive. Alive, fugitives were worth fifty shillings after six months; five pounds after twelve months; dead, the fugitive was worth fifty shillings. Killing these fugitives had little effect for by 1692 the Assembly had repealed the 1688 act. The lawmakers blamed the repeal on the "brutish and barbarous nature" of blacks. Convinced that the blacks could not be "reclaimed by any fair means" and that their "long absence" posed a threat to the island, the authorities tried to kill the blacks at a faster rate. Instead of killing the black who stayed out six months, now it would be thirty days, for those blacks who had lived on the island over a year. In 1731 a fugitive or a slave harborer could be whipped as follows: first offense, twenty-one lashes, second offense, thirty-nine lashes and a branded right cheek with the letter R; in case of other offenses punishment was discretionary except for the execution of the fugitive. Barbados did not enact laws calling for the castration or mutilation of blacks.[159]

Antigua, St. Christopher, Nevis, and Monserrat, a group of islands known as the Leeward Islands, sit close to each other and only a few days' sail from Barbados. Documents concerning the day-to-day attitudes of the Leeward planters are scarce but laws concerning fugitives in Antigua are available for the period 1690 and 1730. There were 2,172 blacks, of which 805 were men, 868 women and 499 children, living on an island of 108 square miles. There were 2,308 whites who lived there during that period. By 1708, blacks numbered 12,960 and whites 2,892. No figures on white servants are available.[160]

In February 1691 Antigua called for the execution of a slave

---

[158]Hall, *Barbados Acts*, 113-114.

[159]Ibid., 130-131.

[160]Dunn, *Sugar and Slaves*, 141.

who stayed out past three months, only to revoke the law twelve years later because of its severity toward "new ignorant slaves," and gave the justices two more options besides death: public whipping or loss of limb or member. To mute any planter outcry, the Assembly promised to pay him eighteen pounds restitution for slaves killed. A fugitive or any black who struck a white person could be whipped. If the black "hurt, wounded or disfigured" a white, he could have his "Nose slit or have any Member cut off or be punished with Death."[161]

The lawmakers in Antigua complained in 1723 that the "Laws Now in Force for the better Government of Negroes and Slaves, and for punishing such as do withdraw from the Service of their Masters, have proved too mild and gentle to curb and refrain them, and that they have so abused the Lenity of the Laws, that great numbers of them have deserted the service of their Masters and fled to the Mountains and Rocky Parts of this Island, and have armed and assembled themselves in Bands to oppose their Masters." The courts ordered the fugitive maroon ringleaders – Sharper, Africa, Papa Will and Frank – to return within a month or be killed and ordered that fugitives who lived on the island for more than one year and stayed at large for more than three months could expect death. This order included those fugitives who stayed out for a period of three months, not consecutively but "several different times within the space of two years, amounting in all to six months." Death sentences awaited groups consisting of ten or more fugitives; fines held vacillating justices in check; and bounty hunters received three pounds for a dead fugitive and six for a live captive. The planter would be reimbursed for slaves killed. Slaves harboring fugitives had to pay a ten pound fine or serve two months in jail. Whites could break down the black's door to search for fugitives, and justices could call up twenty white men to capture fugitives dead or alive. In 1716, white servants at large served double the time if they ran away. Servant harborers were whipped and forced to work three extra months. Freemen

---

[161]John Baskett, *Acts of Assembly Passed in Charibbee Leeward Islands from 1690-1730* (London, 1734), 137-139.

harboring fugitives had to pay a fine of twenty pounds.[162]

Before the English invaded Jamaica in 1655, some 1,500 Spaniards, Portuguese, Jews, Negroes, and Arawaks kept the English at bay for five years using hit-and-run tactics. In 1662, blacks numbered 514; after Jamaica's first governor Sir Thomas Madyford, a former resident of Barbados, offered thirty acres to each planter and every member of his family emigrating to the island, the black population jumped to 9,504 in 1673. About 8,000 whites lived on the island during that period.[163]

Jamaica's white servants needed a ticket to be at large or would face seven days extra time for each day they were missing. Servants with forged certificates could expect to lose their ears and to stand in pillories in 1681. Lawmakers prescribed fines for harboring a servant. A black in 1696 needed a ticket or a white escort before leaving a plantation or faced a whipping. "Rebellious blacks who stayed out over a year faced transportation or removal from the island. Had the black returned, he could be executed. Capturing a rebellious black alive was worth forty shillings; dead, twenty shillings. If the black struck the white while being recaptured, he could expect death. In Jamaica the fugitive laws were less harsh than Georgia's, Virginia's or South Carolina's statutes. Fugitives could not be castrated in Jamaica, nor could they be dismembered."[164]

One particular characteristic that stands out in Jamaica's slave code was the reconciliation between the Jamaican lawmakers and

---

[162]Baskett, *Charibbee Leeward Islands Acts, 1690-1730*, 160-163, 206-209.

[163]Dunn, *Sugar and Slaves*, 151; Orlando Patterson, *The Sociology of Slavery: An Analysis of the Origins, Development and Structure of Negro Slave Society in Jamaica* (London, 1967), 262-264.

[164]*Acts of Assembly Passed in the Island of Jamaica From 1681-1769 Inclusive* (London, 1756), 1-3, 57, 114; Robert C. Dallas, *The History of the Maroons, from their Origin to the Establishment of their Chief Tribe at Sierra Leone* (2 vols., London, 1803, 1968), I: 58-65.

the black maroon leaders. The Jamaican planters signed an agreement with the maroon community in 1738, entitled the "Treaty of Peace and Friendship" which stated that all "Hostilities shall cease." The lawmakers honored the fugitives' right to 15,000 acres within Trelawney Town; maroon-leader Captain Cudjoe, promised to hand over the fugitives who had been out up to two years, to assist the authorities in capturing the fugitives in return for a ten pound reward. In 1741, a dead fugitive brought in ten pounds for Cudjoe's troops, later reduced to three pounds.[165] Jamaica, in 1781, meted out thirty-nine lashes to fugitives without a ticket and "transportation" to another island for those blacks who lived in Jamaica for two years and stayed out two months. Authorities could hang those who returned as well as those who left the country without authorization.[166]

Statutory law was one thing; whether the planter struck a bargain, or turned his head, was another. In 1768, a planter from Georgia warned a black in his fugitive advertisement that if he "return to his duty in ten days he shall not be whipped but if not any person may bring in his head, hand or foot." George Washington told Joseph Whipple, United States Collector of Customs, Portsmouth, New Hampshire, that he would forgive Oney Judge, a black woman who left Mount Vernon in the summer of 1796: "If she will return to her former service without obliging me to use compulsory means to effect it her late conduct will be forgiven by her Mistress" and "she will meet with the same treatment from me that all the rest of the family (which is a very

---

[165]*Jamaica Acts*, 229, 230; Eugene D. Genovese, *From Rebellion to Revolution: Afro-American Slave Revolts in the Making of the Modern World* (Baton Rouge, 1979), 66-69; Robin Winks, *The Blacks in Canada* (New Haven, Connecticut, 1971); Barbara Klamon Kopytoff, "Jamaican Maroon Political Organization: The Effects of the Treaties," *Social and Economic Studies*, 25 (June 1976), 87-105 and "The Early Political Development of Jamaican Maroon Societies," *William and Mary Quarterly*, 35 (April 1978), 287-307; *Maroon Societies: Rebel Slave Communities in the Americas*, Richard Price, ed. (Garden City, N.Y., 1973).

[166]*Jamaica Acts*, 261.

numerous one) shall receive. If she will not, would oblige me, by resorting to such measures as are proper to put her onboard a Vessel bound either to Alexandria or the Federal City."[167]

The legislature offered the best of two worlds: it enacted statutes telling the planter what must be done to deter flight, but if he chose to ignore the laws, he knew at least what the legislature thought he *ought* to do, though some did as they pleased. On April 19, 1734, Lutheran pastor Johann Bolzius recalled the capture of three blacks in Georgia who "After they have received their regular punishment (they are tied to a tree half-naked and are badly beaten with long switches while having to suffer from hunger and thirst most of the day) they must continue to help our Saltzburgers build their houses."[168]

In 1773, Philip Fithian heard Robert Carter's overseer complain that "whipping of any kind does them [blacks] no good, for they will laugh at your greatest Severity." For "Sulliness, Obstinacy, or Idleness" the overseer took a curry-comb, a comb with sharp edged teeth ordinarily used on horses, and scraped the black, rubbed him down with hay, salted him, and turned him loose. He also placed a thick plank of wood on the stable floor, nailed a sharp peg, some eighteen inches long, to the plank, tied a rope to the ceiling and around the naked black, suspending him so "that his foot may just rest on the sharpened Peg, and turn him briskly round and you would laugh (said our informer) at the Dexterity of the Negro while he was relieving his feet on the sharpen'd Peg!"[169]

The planter sold fugitive blacks. Robert Carter in June of 1780 sent Will back "to his place of Residence once again free from any shackles perceiving that neither Irons nor Whipping will Subdue that stubborn disposition that governs him, in his present evil

---

[167]*Georgia Gazette*, March 2, 1768; Fitzpatrick, *Writings of Washington*, XXXV: 298.

[168]*Detailed Reports on the Salzburger Emigrants Who Settled in America*, Samuel Urlsperger, ed. (5 vols., Athens, 1968), I: 77.

[169]Philip V. Fithian, *Journal & Letters of Philip Vickers Fithian, 1773-1774: A Plantation Tutor of the Old Dominion*, Hunter Dickinson Farish, ed. (Williamsburg, 1900, 1943), 51.

doings." For Will, no more irons or flogging, but if he escaped again, Carter proposed to "Sell him, on the character of a notorious Runaway."[170]

Killing never failed to halt escapes. In 1732, planter Charles Jones of South Carolina slam the "lock of his musket" against a fugitive's head and killed him. The "justices ordered Jones to chop the black man's head off and fix it on the Pole and set it up on the Crossroad." The offense: attempted robbery. Quash, who stayed away too long, was decapitated in 1734. Caesar, a black man, unsuccessfully tried to reach St. Augustine in 1739. On his recapture, the authorities hung Caesar in chains.[171] How often a planter tortured, sold, or killed a fugitive is impossible to know; the local gazette, especially in South Carolina, reported only spectacular cases. In other colonies the newspapers rarely mention these cases.

James Carter, a slave from Alexandria, Virginia, had a brother named Henry whom the Armistead family "sold to one George Buckner of that County, without knowing of it and Buckner bearing a very cruel name my Brother would not go with him and Runaway a few days after I sawd him and persuade him to go and try Mr. Buckner but Buckner had advertise him for 20 dollars reward and thretting to send him to Millers Iron works in North Carolina." Somehow Carter persuaded his brother to go to Buckner and en route Henry met a planter who knew him "and want to take him up." Henry, frightened, ran away and Woodford sent an overseer to track down Henry who first hid under a "shelving Rock" and then jumped into the "Rappohannock River" where the overseer "begin to Stone him and Struck him on his head which put an end to his Life, these is the Last words of my Brother lord have mercy on me you have kil'd me help for god

---

[170]Robert "Councillor" Carter to Richard Sutton, June 5, 1780, *Robert "Councillor" Carter Letter Book*, IV: 2.

[171]*South Carolina Gazette*, January 29, 1732, March 16, 1734; Wood, *Black Majority*, 282-284.

sake. I am all most gone and sunk to the bottom."[172]

The planter administered whatever form of punishment he wished, even if it resulted in the serious injury or the death of a black. In the long run, the planter determined what constituted a crime or what constituted justice, and the slave could rarely voice his grievance or seek relief or sue for damages done to him. And if there happened to be an inquiry about the willful and wanton abuse of a black, nothing could be expected to be done. French traveler J. Hector St. John de Crévecoeur who emigrated to America and became a naturalized citizen in 1764 was appointed the French Consul in 1783. He had found time to visit Charlestown and walk through the woods where he spotted a cage hanging from a tree "covered with large birds of prey, fluttering about and anxiously endeavouring to perch in the cage." He discovered a black man in the cage, blind, his eyes "picked out" by the birds and his body lacerated and bloody from the bird bites. To end his misery, Crévecoeur wanted to shoot the slave; the slave himself desired that the traveler poison him. The slave had killed his overseer.[173] In 1659, the Maryland Provincial court met to hear testimony about whether Symon Ouerzee did "felloniously by chance Kill, Contrary to the peace of his Lordship, his rule & gouvermt." After beating Tony or Antonio with a "Peare-Tree Twigg" and "powring melted Lard uppon him," and hanging him by the wrists in the September cold, Ouerzee had succeeded in killing this fugitive slave, therefore what could the court do to compensate for the damage done. The court heard the testimony of Job Chandler, Ouerzee's brother, who called Tony an "ugly yelling Brute beast like." According to Chandler, the overseer had complained to him about Antonio a black who refused to eat, who refused to do any work, and who escaped and remained at large for three months. Hungry, Antonio returned to his master's house and swallowed some hominy grits only to be recaptured and killed.

---

[172]Linda Stanley, "Notes and Documents: James Carter's Account of His Sufferings in Slavery," *Pennsylvania Magazine of History and Biography*, 105 (June 1981), 336-339.

[173]J. Hector John de Crévecceur, *Letters From an American Farmer* (New York, 1957), 167-168.

The jury brought back a verdict:"Ignoramus."[174]

Had Antonio been a white servant in Maryland he might have had a better chance at survival, for the legislators permitted servants to air their grievances and seek redress in the Provincial courts. On December 20, 1664, Sarah Hall, a twenty-six year old white servant, accused her master, Thomas Wynne, of "beating and abuseing her." Witnesses were summoned, testimony was heard and accusations were made because Hall could not expect to receive a favorable judgement without backing up her grievance with facts. Two witnesses either saw Wynne box Hall's ears or kick her or threaten to hit her with a chair. The court ruled that Hall's remaining indentured time should be sold to another planter.[175]

Because a servant, even fugitive servants, had the statutory right to file a complaint in court and to give his version of what occurred between him and the planter, did not mean that the planter himself would not go to court to press charges against a maltreated servant. During the Charles County Court Proceedings, 1662-1666, a planter accused three servants of having run away, but one servant, Mathew Broune, the court claimed he made off because his "Master did not allow them Victualls Anough which appeared to bee very Malicious and of set purpos to disgrace his sayd Master by the Condition hee then Appeared in." Broune received twenty-seven lashes at the "whiping post in the publicke vew of the Peopell." Master Humphrey Warren complained in this same court that his servant, Richard Lamb "hath Severall times absented himselfe out of his Service and hath Sold his Cloathes for which abuses he humbly requesteth the boarde to Judge him according to his Demeritts and aleadgeth that he once ptended hhimselfe lame and that vey time Ranne away and that he ptended that he Could not endure to Live with his former Master Before he the said Warren bought him because his Servants did sweare soe extreamely (which was the cause he the said Warren bought him as the Warren Averreth) And now the said Warren affirmeth that there Can hardlier be A greiueosour swearer in the County." The court ruled that the sheriff should mete out twenty lashes to

---

[174]*Arch. Md.*, XLI: 204-206.

[175]Ibid., XLIX: 318.

Lamb.[176]

One of the difficult cases that the court had to grapple with was the suspicious death of a fugitive servant. Again, if a servant absconded and the authorities or the planter captured him then the court could order the escapee to serve extra time, or send him to the whipping post or have his hair cut low. The servant owner could "correct" a servant but could not intentionally kill him without being made criminally liable. Because a planter's life or limb or property was at stake, the court took special precautions to see that a thorough inquiry took place. As soon as the "Bones of a dead man wear found upon the sands on the East sid of Patomak Riuer nie the Landing of Mr. Thomas Baker by Richard Row and George Thompson" the Charles county judge on September 16, 1661, ordered Baker himself who was the Commissioner of this county court, the Port Tobacco constable, the county surgeon, and thirteen of Baker's neighbors to view the body of the servant, whose name was Evans. The major concern of the judge was the relationship between Baker and Evans. Evans was "used as well by his sayd Master as if hee had bine his owne Child," recalled one witness under oath. The surgeon who lived in Baker's house for two months before Evans died, said that "Evans did always extol his master for a good man and hee this deponant neuer did see nor heare of any abuse offered unto the sayd Evans by the sayd Baker."[177]

Seventeen people saw Evans' bones but the court could not "find any Cause why the sayd Evans shoold absent himself from his masters saruice nor how that hee shoold Come by his death Certainly any otherways then through his owne wilfulnes by running away without any cause given him." The court did consider that the servant might have died of a sleeping disease or that he might have drowned himself but it was the "Opinion of all that hee Came by his Death through his owne Idelnes and Rogish absentment."[178]

---

[176]Ibid., LIII: 538, 560.

[177]Ibid., LIII: 140-141.

[178]Ibid., LIII: 140-141.

It was rare that the planter was held responsible for killing a fugitive servant. Thomas Ward and his wife whipped a fugitive woman servant with a peach tree rod and put salt water on the wounds, despite the fact the fugitive had asked Ward to "use her like a Christian." The court fined Ward 300 pounds of tobacco for "unreasonable and unchristian-like punishment," but refused to blame the couple for the servant's death "considering her weak estate of body."[179]

The courts in Maryland probably kept a planter off guard because where one judge would allow a planter to find shelter behind some contradictory rationale, another might fine or jail or execute him. In 1664, the St. Mary's County jurors concluded that Joseph Finnchen with "malice forethought did kill and murder" Jeffery Haggman. He was hanged. In the same year, John Grammen ordered a servant to whip Thomas Simmons with a rope. Simmons died but Grammen was turned loose for insufficient evidence.[180] "Master James Lewis beat one Joseph Robinson his servant with a stick two severall times, and that the said Joseph Robinson within three hours after such beating dyed" according to Mary Baines' testimony, servant to Lewis in 1680. The Justice at St. Mary's Court did not punish Lewis but Baines was given a new master. Yet in the same court, in 1680, the justice jailed and fined Thomas King 11,350 pounds for killing his servant.[181]

Drawn up by white men who were planters themselves, the fugitive laws which showed what ought to be done, how to do it, and why it was done appear to be more of a guide than a rigid formula for law enforcement. How many planters were guided by laws, or how many lacked the stomach to carry them out is another story.

---

[179]Ibid., LIV: 9; Chapin, *Criminal Justice in Colonial America, 1606-1660*, 87, 176-77.

[180]*Arch. Md.*, LXIX: 413-414.

[181]Ibid., LXIX: 415.

CHAPTER IV
LAW ENFORCEMENT

The American legislators enacted scores of statutes that helped to inform the colonists, unify disparate opinions, and offer direction. But many of the fugitive statutes seemed ineffective, inapplicable and ambiguous. An examination of Virginia's and South Carolina's fugitive codes will reveal these difficulties, bearing in mind that Virginia, the first colony to enact fugitive statutes, lacked precedents upon which to draw. Maryland drew mostly upon Virginia's code; North Carolina's code resembles Virginia's; South Carolina adopted Barbados' preamble, and influenced Georgia's code.[182]

The planters, at every "quarter court," pressed the Virginia Assembly to enact its first statute in 1642. The preamble pointed to the "divers loytering runaways in the collony who very often absent themselves from their masters service, and sometime in two or three monthes cannot be found, whereby their said masters are at a great charge in finding them, And many times even to the losse of a year's labor before they had be found."[183] Fifteen years later the Assembly had still not solved the problem, for, in 1657, they complained that the "Huy and cries after runaway servants hath been much neglected to the greate damage and loss of the inhabitants of this collony." The hue and cry was a proclamation that called on colonists to help track down the fugitive. But would the planters ignore their plantation duties to join in hot pursuit when the fugitive belonged to someone else? To induce the planters to help themselves, the Assembly ordered the county commissioner to bring the hue and cry proclamation to the planters' attention. If the planter "made default in the speedy conveyance of any such huies and cries" he had to pay one hundred pounds. When the captor caught the fugitive, he had to send him to his owner or from "constable to constable" until the owner was found. If the constable neglected to return the fugitive,

---

[182]Wiecek, "The Statutory Laws of Slavery," 209-226.

[183]Henings, *Virginia Statutes*, I: 253-254.

the Assembly fined him 350 pounds of tobacco.[184]

Three years later the Assembly accused the constables of ignoring the fugitive: "Whereas the pursuit and takeing of runawaies is hindred chiefly by the neglect of constables in making search according to their warrants." The lawmakers felt that either the "constable shall make diligent search and inquiry through all his precincts" or face a 350 pound tobacco fine.[185]

In 1663, the Assembly promised to shoulder even more expenses because "the ordinary way of makeing pursuites after runawaye servants by hues and cryes is by experience found ineffectual for the recovery of them, and the pursuite at the perticular charge of the master oftentimes impossible for the remedy whereof." For the planter whose servant or slave had escaped to another colony or was beyond his reach, the Assembly permitted him to file a complaint with the local justice who was "authorised and impowered to issue his warrant for pressing boate and hands or other dispatches to make persuite" and the court paid the bill. This fugitive act called, too, on the Dutch planters and the northern planters "to make seizure of all such fugitive servants, and to retourne them by the next convenient passage to any of the collectors of the rivers." The Collector handed the planter a receipt; the Assembly reimbursed him. The Collector escorted the servant to his owner; the owner reimbursed the officer or faced the loss of his servant.[186]

The Assembly dispatched them all: the commissioner, the justice, the Collector, the sheriff, the constable, and the jailer. Even the Indians in 1672 were "required and enjoyned to seize and apprehend all runaways whatsoever that shall happen to come amongst them, and to bring them before some justice of the peace." The Indians received "twenty armes length of Roanoake or the value thereof in goods as the Indians shall like of" for their

---

[184]Ibid., I: 483.

[185]Ibid., II: 21.

[186]Ibid., II: 187-188.

service.[187]

Did the planter and the Assembly do all that they could? The 1669 Assembly thought that "diverse good lawes have been made to prevent runaway servants which have hitherto in greate parte proved ineffectuall cheifly through the wickednesse of servants who at and before their arrivall plott to contrive how they may ffree themselves from their master by running away to neighboring plantations." And the planters "who so faire from apprehending these knowne runawayes that some have given them assistance and directions how to escape, to the ruyne of masters of ffamilies, who have not servants enough left (whome he can trust) to follow and pursue those runawayes and others unconcerned for want of a certain reward will not endeavour to apprehend and retourne them to their masters."[188]

Another plan was to offer a one thousand pound tobacco reward to the captor after he brought the fugitive to the judge for certification, who in turn handed him or her over to the constable. If the fugitive escaped, the constable paid a one thousand pound tobacco fine to the Assembly. A one thousand pound tobacco reward, equivalent to the earnings from about eight months' labor, encouraged speculation. Why sweat on a plantation for twenty to thirty pounds of tobacco a day in wages when a laborer could wait outside the plantation and make almost a year's pay capturing a fugitive. Even the Assembly admitted the reward was "too burthensome to the publique by the greatness of the summe there granted to the taker of them up" and by 1670 the reward dropped to 200 pounds of tobacco. The constable's fine also dropped to 400 pounds of tobacco, "halfe to the publique, halfe to the informer and the fine in the former act of one thousand pounds of tobacco to be reversed."[189]

Offering unreasonably high rewards invited fraud. When the Assembly in 1670 promised to reimburse the "apprehender" who presented a "bona fide certificate," the speculator sought to palm

---

[187]Ibid., II: 300.

[188]Ibid., I: 273.

[189]Ibid., II: 277-278.

off certificates "lyable to greate errors and ffraud;" when the
Assembly rewarded the captor for each captive, the speculator tried
to take a reward "for one and the same servant taken up at sundry
tymes by sundry persons." Reward seekers jailed the freeman as
well as the fugitive; they increased the mileage to obtain a higher
reimbursement and they posed as captors, though they were the
fugitives' owners. To deter the speculator, the Assembly forced the
captor to take an oath and threatened him with a one thousand
pound tobacco fine, or the lash for fraudulent claims.[190]

An act in 1686 called for checking the captive's certificate to see
if the captor had filled it out properly: it had to include the
planter's name, residence, when and where the servant was
captured, and the servant's name. Could this work for the African
or white servant that "doth not speak English, and cannot, or
through obstinacy will not, declare the name of his or her master?"
As the lawmakers had noted in the 1705 Act, the Assembly
ordered these fugitives to be brought to the public jail in
Williamsburg and "there to be continued prisoner until the master
or owner shall be known." If the master could not be found, the
sheriff escorted the fugitive from constable to constable and at
each stop he received thirty-nine more lashes.[191]

For the speculator who stood to be compensated for travel
expenses, why bring the fugitive to his owner's home "or where the
place the said runaways have been picked up" when he could bring
him to the public jail in Williamsburg? In 1726, the Assembly
directed the captor and the escorting officer to bring the captive
to the local jail where the sheriff would post the fugitive's
description "upon the courthouse door" and the clerk would place
one on the chapel or church door. If the owner could not be
found, then the sheriff escorted the fugitive to the next local jail.
The sheriff who failed to comply could be fined 500 pounds of
tobacco. If the county clerk "neglected" to post the advertisement
in the court and the chapel, he could be fined two hundred pounds

---

[190]Ibid., III: 283.

[191]Ibid., III: 29, 456.

of tobacco.[192]

How much pressure could the jailer or the constable or the sheriff take before they complained? In 1726, the lawmakers admitted that "great trouble is given to the constable in conducting runaways and severe penaltys imposed on them for runaway escapes." Now the law officers were "exempted from paying levies," allowed "free passage on ferries," and permitted to hire out the fugitives to pay for their upkeep. The jailer could collect captor fees from the fugitive's owner and escape liability if the fugitive escaped.[193]

No colony went through a long process of searching for effective fugitive slave laws save for Virginia. Maryland's captive procedure for both servants and blacks as well as North Carolina's were probably copied from the Virginia statutes; Georgia, and the northern colonies, failed to address the problem in their codes. For South Carolinia alone, there is extensive evidence of how the colonists systematically tried to break the captive's will and the part that incarceratoin procedures, the landowners' role and public funding played in this process.

From early on South Carolina put its treasury and law enforcement staff at the planter's command. The first fugitive statute in 1690 showed the Governor, and the House of Commons, directing the captor who failed to locate the fugitive's owner to bring the captive to the "sheriff or gaoler" or face a twenty pound fine. The lawmakers, then, ordered the sheriff or jailer to place a notice describing the fugitive "upon a public place in the goal, on the penalty of fifty pounds," to pay the captor and to place the fugitive in jail or face a thirty pound fine if the fugitive escaped.[194]

South Carolina legislators showed no qualms about employing troops to track down the fugitive. Militia captains could "raise a convenient party of men, not exceeding twenty, and with them ... pursue, apprehend and take the said runaway slaves, either alive or dead." If the captain "neglected his or their duty," he could be

---

[192]Ibid., IV: 169.

[193]Ibid., IV: 170-172.

[194]Cooper and McCord, ed., *South Carolina Statutes*, VII: 344.

fined thirty pounds. Nor did the legislators have any misgivings about offering twenty shillings to blacks and Indians who captured fugitive slaves. Moreover, the Assembly, in 1712, indemnified the planters whose fugitives were executed for leaving South Carolina or enticing another black to leave because "the loss of the Negroes and other slaves that shall suffer death, or be killed by this Act, would prove too heavy for the owners of them to bear and that the owners of Negroes and slaves, may not be encouraged to detect and discover the offences of their Negroes and that the loss may be borne by the public, whose safety, by such punishments is hereby provided for and intended."[195]

Generous with the colony's monies, the House of Commons in 1714 complained that the "public treasury hath been very much exhausted by the extraordinary sums that have been allowed for criminal slaves of all sorts, without distinction." Two years later the Assembly complained that the "executing of several Negroes for felonies of smaller nature by which they have been condemned to die, have been of great charge and expense to the public, and will continue (if some remedy be not found) to be very chargeable and burthensome to this Province." All blacks guilty of felonies should be "transported" out of the colony. A maximum value of fifty pounds compensation was set for each transported black.[196] In 1717, the Assembly stopped transporting blacks because "this has encouraged Negroes and other slaves to commit great numbers of robberies, burglaries and other felonies." The planter assumed the execution costs again. By 1740 the Assembly, in response to the Stono revolt, had reassumed the costs. It doled out reimbursements "not exceeding two hundred pounds current money" for each black executed.[197]

The House of Commons lacked a record of the yearly number of fugitives who left South Carolina or had been executed; but someone seems to have counted, for the Assembly implied that the 1712 statute increased the number of felons; the 1715 Act

---

[195]Ibid., VII: 358, 362.

[196]Ibid., VII: 366.

[197]Ibid., VII: 370, 400-403.

decreased the number. During the colonial period the South Carolina authorities executed anywhere between four and twenty blacks a year or an average of eight a year, according to one historian. If that figure is accurate, then some four hundred blacks were executed between 1690 and 1740, not including the sixty blacks who were hanged and shot during the Stono Rebellion and the fifty executed in another revolt in St. John's parish, a year later.[198]

Statutes ordering the killing of fugitives probably stemmed more from racial attitudes as well as fear, blind hatred and helplessness, than from numerical threat, which was made more manifest when the blacks ignored the statutes and headed towards the Spanish areas. On October 30, 1671, the Grand Council of South Carolina found white servant Dennis Mahoon "guilty of running away from his master's service and departing out of this Colony to attain the protection of the Crowne of Spain." Mahoon was supposed to be put to death, but "made penitence and the court forgave him." Ten days later, Mahoon tried to entice two servants, John Rivers and John Cooke, to leave the Colony and the Council ordered "that he be stripped naked to the waist and receive 39 lashes." On October 15, 1672, Richard Nicrin and John Rivers were sentenced to death for trying to get to the Spanish settlement but were pardoned; the Grand Council thought the "death of the said prisoners may not only lessen the strength of this Province but perhaps not all together be a matter so well approved." Yet on November 11, 1697 the authorities in South Carolina castrated three blacks for their attempt to escape to St. Augustine.[199]

The lawmakers seemed loath to allow any attempted or actual excape by a black to St. Augustine to go unanswered, especially if the planter asked the Assembly to take action. On November 28, 1722 two planters, George Haddrel and Robert Johnson, reported

---

[198]Wood, *Black Majority*, 279-281, 318-321.

[199]*Journals of the Common House of Assembly of South Carolina for the Two Sessions of 1697*, A.S. Salley, ed. (Columbia, 1913), 20; John J. Tepaske, "The Fugitive Slave: Intercolonial Rivalry and Spanish Slave Policy, 1687-1764," in *Eighteenth Century Florida and Its Borderlands*, Samuel Proctor, ed. (Gainesville, 1975), 1-12.

"several of theirs and more people Slaves were run and they had Great reason to believe they were gon to St. Augustine." A week later the House Speaker, James Moore, said he "looked upon the same to be a matter of very great importance and ill Consequence to the Welfare of this Province" and suggested that "the Public ought to be at the Expense of sending to St. Augustine to demand the Slaves lately runn from this Government to that."[200] Nothing came of the debate other than a plan to hire a shipmaster and his sloop for 350 pounds and an Assembly spokesman for another 150 pounds. Yet by rewarding Andrew White on December 15, 1722 with twenty-five pounds for "taking severall Runaway Slaves Endeavoring to make their Escape to St. Augustine," and by giving five pounds to Harry, a black, for his "faithfullness in returning from St. Augustine to this government"[201] in 1727, the Assembly could at least claim some success in deterring escapes, though the statutes remained ineffective.

Perhaps England could help. On June 13, 1728, the forty-seven year old Council President Arthur Middleton wrote to England complaining about "the Diffcultys we Labour under from the neare situation of St. Augustine to this place who without any regard to Peace or Warr, Doe continually Fitting Annoy our Southern Frontiers" and that the Spaniards were primarily interested in "Murders and Plunder." Middleton said the Spaniards were "Harbouring all our Runaway Negroes, but since that They have found a new way of sending our own slaves to Rob and Plunder us; They are continually fitting out Partys of Indians from St. Augustine to Murder our White People, Rob our Plantations and carry off our slaves, so that we are not only at a vast expense in Guarding our Southern Frontiers, but the inhabitants are continually Alarmed, and should keep Noe Leizure looks after their crops." And "The Indians," he reported, "they send against us Are sent out in small Partys headed by two three or more Spaniards and sometimes joined with Negroes and all the

---

[200]*Parish Transcripts* (New York Historical Society), Box 1, Folder 3, 26-28.

[201]Ibid., Box 1, Folder 3, 2; Box 1, Folder 3, 2, 13.

Mischiefe they doe is on a sudden and by surprise."[202]

The Council President was probably referring to the Spaniards, arming of a group of Yamassee Indians who killed a John Edwards near Port Royal and made off with four of his slaves; this group also killed Henry Mushoe and Hazekiah Wood and carried off ten slaves in 1726. Fifteen white colonists gave chase and "they took all the said Negroes and Plunder and killed six Indians and one Spaniard."[203] Middleton in June 1728 accused the St. Augustine governor of having "fitted out a schooner manned with Spaniards and our own Runaway Slaves to steal other Slaves and rob our Plantations along the Coast who Entering North Edisto River surprised the Plantation of the David Ferguson, plundered it and Carried away seven Slaves."[204]

The Spaniards who possessed slaves in St. Augustine disregarded the Spanish King's cedula of 1733 granting freedom to blacks entering St. Augustine from the American colonies. Instead, they forced a fugitive group to ask Governor Seignior Don Manuel de Montiano in 1738 for their freedom and some land. The St. Augustine governor granted both. The blacks who settled two and a half miles from St. Augustine in a settlement named "Moosa" now had an opportunity to rebuild their lives without constraints.[205] Moosa's existence confirmed the fears of the forty-three year old James Oglethorpe, a soldier, philanthropist, and founder of Georgia, who wrote to England on February 23, 1739 "that the People of Carolina had complained to me that the Governor of St. Augustine published a Proclamation that all Negroes who could retire thither should be free. Pursuant to this Proclamation Several

---

[202]Ibid., Box 1, Folder 2, 1; *Dictionary of American Biography*, Dumas Matone, ed. (22 vols., New York, 1933-1958), VI: 599.

[203]*Par. Trans.*, Box 1, Folder 2, 1a.

[204]Ibid., Box 1, Folder 2, 2.

[205]I.A. Wright, "Dispatches of Spanish Officials Bearing on the Free Negro Settlements of Gracia Real de Santa de Mose, Florida," *Journal of Negro History*, 9 (1924), 144-195; Wood, *Black Majority*, 306.

Negroes had escaped thither by Sea, and have been received and freed."[206]

Oglethorpe did not provide evidence of who actually escaped "thither," but again on January 19, 1739 Captain Caleb Davis' letter had been received by the Assembly. Davis wrote that "some Time in the month of November last, 19 slaves belonging to the said Davis and fifty others belonging to other Persons about Port Royal ran away to the Castle of St. Augustine. Davis went to St. Augustine in "Pursuit of them where your Committee are informed he found the said slaves to be and that he applied to the Governor of that Place for a delivery of them." The Spanish governor "refused to deliver the said Slaves" because the Spanish King "declare all Slaves to be free that should desert thither from this Province."[207]

The Assembly believed the remedy for preventing flights required the setting up of committees to discuss the problem with the hope that a statute would be passed to resolve the problem. From January to April 1739 "The Committee of Conference in the case of the Negroes' desertion to St. Augustine" deliberated. In April they asked that a petition be drawn up calling on the King of England to approve the procurement of two scout boats, manned by ten men each, to "guard the Water Passages to the Southward," and to permit a forty pound reward be given for capturing blacks beyond the Savannah River. The captor received forty pounds for a black male, twenty-five pounds for a female, and ten pounds for children under twelve. The captain also received twenty pounds for "bringing in the scalps of such Men or Women Negro Slaves that are already deserted or shall hereafter desert

---

[206]*Par. Trans.* Box 1, Folder 11, 7. See "Letters from General Oglethorpe to the Trustees of the Colony and Others, From October 1735 to August 1744," *Collections of the Georgia Historical Society* (15 vols., to date, Savannah, 1840 to date), III: 1-157; *Dictionary of American Biography*, VII: 1,2.

[207]*The Colonial Records of South Carolina: The Journal of the Common House of Assembly*, November 10, 1736 - June 7, 1739, J.H. Easterby, ed. (Columbia, S.C., 1951-1953), 596; *Par. Trans.* Box 1, Folder 10, 19-20.

who shall be found beyond Savannah River and cannot be taken and brought home alive."[208]

Did these measures work? Caesar and Alleboy, two captured blacks, had not waited for an answer. On April 12, 1739 the Attorney General accused them of "deserting from their master's service and attempting with several slaves to runaway off the Province either to St. Augustine or some other place." The lawmakers ordered Alleboy whipped and Caesar hanged. Caesar asked the black spectators "to take warning by his unhappy example after which he begged the Lord's Prayers and several others in fervent and devout Manner."[209] The four or five Angolan slaves who were "cattle hunters and knew the Woods some whom belonged to Captain MackPherson" did not wait either. After wounding his son and killing another the slaves made it to Florida, one step ahead of the South Carolina troops and the Indians where the Spaniards rewarded them with "great honours, one of them had a Commission given to him and a Coat faced with Velvet."[210]

During the Stono Revolt on September 9, 1739, sixty to a hundred blacks, mostly Angolans, led by one called Jemmy, and caling for liberty, headed toward St. Augustine, slew twenty white colonists, burned down scores of houses, and just missed killing Lt. Governor William Bull. The insurrection failed and forty blacks went to their graves, while the others fled to the swamps. But the glittering haven of St. Augustine remained ever present and in November an exasperated Governor Bull thought that the "Demolition of that Place, would free us from the like Danger for the Future." Seven months later General Oglethorpe with one thousand regular troops and one thousand Indians and eight hundred Negro volunteers, overran Fort San Diego and Fort Moosa and laid siege to St. Augustine Fort which had a contingent of one thousand soldiers and fifty cannons. The siege lasted about

---

[208]Easterby, *Col. Rec. of South Carolina*, 680-682; *Par. Trans.*, Box 1, Folder 10, 25-25a.

[209]*South Carolina Gazette*, April 12, 1739.

[210]*Par. Trans.*, Box 1, Folder 11, 3-6.

a month before the Americans, who lost fifty men, began to tire
and eventually headed home where the Assembly ordered
Oglethorpe to explain why the expedition failed.[211]

The Assembly's response was to modify existing statutes and
enact some new ones. For the fugitive black who stayed out longer
than six months and was found within thirty miles of the Savannah
River, it offered fifty pounds. One hundred pounds was offered for
a black captured on the south side of St. John's River. The black's
scalp and his two ears alone brought in fifty pounds. The public
treasurer paid the captor; the owner reimbursed the government
or faced the seizure of his other slaves. If a black was executed for
"going out of the province," then the public treasurer paid the
owner the full value of the slave. Another statute gave any white
settler the right to kill a "notorious" fugitive who was at large
beyond twelve months. And "no slaves seven in number could
travel together" without a "white person in their company."[212]

The Assemblymen admitted their fears about the fugitive's
aspiration; General Oglethorpe admitted in February 1739 that the
Spanish freedom proclamation made the "Planters fear that the
greatest part of their Negroes will leave them" and that if "the
Spaniards continue to protect the Runaway Slaves Carolina will be
entirely ruined, their wealth consisting in Slaves; amongst whom
them there is a General indignation to Liberty, and a Revoltt
amongst them where they are protected by a Spanish Garrison
lying on the same Continent, will be much more difficult to quell,
than the rebellion of the Jamaican Negroes."[213]

Michael Jeanes of Charlestown published a fugitive
advertisement in the *South Carolina Gazette* on November 17,
1739, describing a "Negro man named Sampson well known in

---

[211]Wood, *Black Majority*, 309-312; Easterby, *Commons Journal*
1, September 12, 1739 -March 26, 1741; David D. Wax, "The Great
Risque We Run: The Aftermath of Slave Rebellion at Stono,
South Carolina, 1739-1745," *Journal of Negro History*, 67 (1982),
364-367; *Par. Trans.*, Box 1, Folder 11, 3-6, 29.

[212]Cooper and McCord, *South Carolina Statutes*, VII: 414-415.

[213]*Par. Trans.* Box 1, Folder 1, 7-8.

town for his painting and glazing." Sampson was likely to be "hid on Board of Vessels," but unbeknownst to Jeanes, Sampson had been organizing blacks hoping to make it to St. Augustine. Three years later Jeanes, himself a painter and glazier, asked Governor Bull and the Council not to hang Sampson for Jeanes had "Rhumatism and other Infirmities" and was "Enfeebled in his Limbs as to render him almost incapable of working his Trade" and he depended for the maintenance of his family on the "Labour of his Negro named Sampson." They hanged him anyway. Jeanes contended that Sampson's flight was not "attended with any aggravated Circumstances of Intended Mischief other than to runaway and leave the Province, and to persuade Some other Slaves to go with him with the sole design of obtaining Liberty a desire so naturally implanted in the minds of all Men and That Seldom any other consideration has been found difficult to root out." He felt that "the desire of Liberty is founded on the General Law of Nature," and believed that Sampson's flight should not be viewed as an "Evil prohibited and never ranked amongst those termed Evils in themselves by the best Civilians as well as common Lawyers."[214]

Each generation of lawmakers knew that the blacks wanted their freedom. On December 13, 1754, the Council discussed the construction of a letter to Governor Dinwiddle of Virginia about the expense of "building a Fort in the Cherokee Nation," and they discussed the militia, the Spaniards, and the blacks. They noted "we have 50,000 Negro Slaves, to whom (no doubt) an Invader would proclaim Liberty upon them Joining them..."[215] No matter what the Assembly felt about black aspirations and no matter how irrational and ineffective the laws might appear, they were determined to enforce them.

Some blacks helped the Assembly enforce the fugitive laws. Dr. William Bull informed the Commons House on March 2, 1743, that a "Negro woman belonging to Mr. Francis Ladson named Sabina had discovered the Design of several Negroes to desert to

---

[214]Ibid., Box 1, Folder 12, 32, 33, 35; *South Carolina Gazette*, November 17, 1739.

[215]*Par. Trans.*, Box 3, Folder 6, 12.

St. Augustine whereupon one of them was tried and executed and moved that the said Negro woman might be rewarded for the same." A day later the Assembly reported that two Men Slaves belonging to McFrederick Erinker, named "Jupiter and Mingo, lately apprehended one of the Negroes that was concerned in the late Insurrection and rebellion at Stono who has been since tried and executed" and "is of the opinion that the said slaves should be rewarded for that service."[216]

When Oglethorpe needed men to invade Florida and to wipe out black sanctuaries, 800 blacks volunteered — but when seventy-three black veterans returned from the war asking for restitution, the Assembly balked, claiming it "was very burthensome to the people of this province" to pay the black soldiers. William Bull overrode the Assembly and ordered that each man be paid three pounds, aware that blacks might be needed in "future Expeditions."[217]

Blacks were not allowed to have guns, or to travel in large groups, but apparently black captors did travel in gangs led by white colonists. The Assembly President Thomas Broughton on March 29, 1734 wrote of "James, a White Servant, and Prince and Cashia, Negroes of his Excellency's and Penbo belonging to Mrs. Hume having discovered and informed his Excellency where Quash, a Notorious Offender belonging to Roger Moore was concealed." A Captain Danielson and these blacks "surprised" Quash who "jumped out the Window" but "Prince and Cashia shot and took him." They were rewarded; Quash was executed.[218]

Had Quash killed his black captors, the captors' owner would have been compensated, but not their families. One planter in 1743 asked the Assembly to compensate him because a "runaway Negro man named Hannibal came to the Petitioner's Plantations, when two of the the Petitioner's Slaves attempted to apprehend

---

[216]Easterby, *Commons Journal*, 1742-1744; Wax, "The Great Risque We Run," 136-147; *Par. Trans.*, Box 1, Folder 3, 17, 18.

[217]*Par. Trans.*, Box 1, Folder 8, 32, 39, 41.

[218]*Par. Trans.*, Box 1, Folder 7, 12; *South Carolina Gazette*, March 16, 1734.

him, but he being armed with a Knife stabbed one of your Petitioner's said slaves (named Harry) in the Heart of which he instantly died, and maiming the other very much made his Escape."[219]

Because the Indians knew the escape routes, and the hideaways, the Commons House of Assembly encouraged the Indian nations to capture the blacks. On September 7, 1730, the Lords Commissioners and the "Deputies of the Cherokee Nation" in South Carolina hammered out a friendship treaty called Articles of Friendship and Commerce that included this provision: "That if any Negro slaves shall runaway into the Woods from their English Masters, the Cherokee Indians shall endeavor to apprehend them, and either bring them back to the Plantation from which they run away, or to the Governour, and for every Negro so apprehended and brought back the Indian shall receive a Gun and a Match Coat whereupon we give a Box of Vermilion, Ten Thousand Gun Flints and Six Dozen of Hatchets."[220]

The Creeks agreed to "apprehend and secure any Negro or other Slave which shall runaway from any of the English Settlements to our Nation and carry them either to the Savannah or Pallachucola Garrison" in return for "Four Blankets or Two Guns or the value thereof." If the Creeks killed any such slave "for their Resistance, or running away," they received one blanket after they produced the slave's head. The treaty stated that if any Creek Indians "kill any such Slaves for their Resistance or running away from us in apprehending them" the Assembly paid one blanket for the fugitive's head.[221]

Some Cherokees ignored the treaty and assisted the black fugitive. On May 15, 1751 a planter reported to the Assembly that a "half-breed fellow who also came down from the Cherokee Nation in company with James Maxwell did ceduce six of my Negroes to run away from me unto the Cherokees from whence he promised to conduct them some place where they might depend on

---

[219]Easterby, *Commons Journal*, 1742-1744, 387.

[220]Easterby, *Commons Journal*, 1736-1739, 106, 107.

[221]Ibid., 109-110.

their freedom."[222]

The *South Carolina Gazette* reported on May 5, 1752, that "Two likely young slaves got to that place [St. Augustine] from Georgia who were immediately made young Christians and proclaimed free by which it appears that the Spaniard continued the unjustified practice of encouraging the slaves to desert them. The Spanish employ some of the Creeks and Cherokees to seduce them away."[223]

The Tuscarora Indians stymied the lawmakers' efforts to catch the blacks heading to North Carolina. On June 6, 1735, the Assembly announced that several "Slaves have made their Escape from this Province and very probably are sheltered and Protected by the Tuscarora Indians in North Carolina Government, which has a very evil tendency." The lawmakers asked that "all proper Methods to apprehend Such Slaves, and cause them to be conveyed back to this Government" be utilized and asked the colonists to "Expell these Tuscaroras out of the Government."[224] Instead of trying to induce the Tuscaroras to help enforce the fugitive statutes, the Assembly enacted statutes in June, 1735 calling for any "Freeman or Slave, who shall kill any Tuscarora Indians to receive fifty pounds and sixty pound like current Money for every Tuscarora Indian who shall be taken alive."[225]

The Chickasaw Indians captured and returned black fugitives to the planters. On June 3, 1745, Captain Pepper told the Assembly that seven fugitive blacks had been "taken up by our Chickasaw Indians." Pepper, who "went to their town and found them in their Custody then paid them their demands and took them in my possession," and said "The Indians tell me the Negroes were looking for Canoes to cross the River in order to make their way

---

[222]*Par. Trans.*, Box 3, Folder 2, 3.

[223]*South Carolina Gazette*, May 5, 1752.

[224]*Par. Trans.*, Box 1, Folder 7, 31.

[225]*South Carolina Gazette*, June 14, 1735.

to Aloma Fort."[226]

Without the cooperation of the Indian and the black, not to mention the military patrols and the planter himself, the Assembly would have had a far more difficult time enforcing the laws against those blacks heading out of the colony. And despite the uproar in the Assembly and the declamations of William Bull and Oglethorpe, escaping out of South Carolina was a difficult task, for even the most determined black. Again, between 1732 and 1745, the *South Carolina Gazette* published hundreds of fugitive notices, but not a single advertisement mentioned Florida as a suspected destination. If most fugitives remained within the borders of South Carolina, then the Assembly's attention should have been focused on the local flights instead of the spectacular escapes into St. Augustine.

An important local official, who helped enforce the fugitive laws in South Carolina, was the Charlestown jailer. For the captive, the jail was the last stop before he again saw his owner; for many captors, this was the last stop before they headed home. Although the captor might have traveled day and night to collect his reward, the jailer first made him "swear on oath," that his name, residence, and the time and place of capture, were in fact true; that he did not own the black, and that the black did not have a legitimate pass. Once satisfied, the jailer paid the captor, admitted the fugitive, who would also be questioned about his name, residence, age, nationality and his owner's name. The jailer posted this information on the jail, court and even chapel walls. By 1732, the Assembly ordered the jailer to publish the captive notices weekly in the South Carolina Gazette, hoping the planter would step forward and claim his slave or servant.[227]

On May 27, 1734, the Provost Marshall published the first fugitive notice describing a black woman named Lucretia, and her son. It appears that either the jailer or the printer felt that the publishing of the captive notices deserved little attention or that the fugitive prisoners were few in number, for only four captive

---

[226]*Par. Trans.*, Box 2, Folder 9, 1.

[227]Cooper and McCord, eds., *South Carolina Statutes*, VII: 344, 361, 378-379, 380.

notices were published in 1734, twelve in 1735, seven in 1736 and eight in 1737. Since the keeper laid out money to the captor and expected to be reimbursed by the fugitive's owner, it seems logical that he should have published more advertisements. Besides, if the jailer did not return the fugitives to their owners on a timely basis, overcrowdedness could result.[228]

In 1772, the Grand Jurors in Beaufort County maintained that the sheriff had "no place of Confinement for Fugitive Slaves when brought to him, and that for want of such a goal many Slaves are suffered to keep out and do much mischief to the Great injury of their Owners and others as the Distance to the Charlestown Work House is so great, that when the slave is taken, People rather let them go away than take the Trouble of delivering them at so great a distance."[229] While never accusing the gaoler in their city of barring fugitives because of shortage of space the jurors complained that the "Keepers of every gaol do not publish the Names and a full description of every Fugitive Slave confined in their respective goals, together with the Names of the People to whom they belong, at least once every month in all the Gazettes of the Province."[230]

If any officer received attention, the watchmen in Charlestown did. The Assembly in 1721 passed "An Act for the keeping and maintaining a Watch and keeping Good Order in Charlestown." These watchmen went "around the Town in the Evening" and kept an eye on the blacks, particularly those blacks who "Can't give such good Accounts of themselves." The watchmen jailed the suspicious black found in the streets after curfew, shot the "obstinate" black if he "refused to stand." By 1737, twenty-one watchmen, headed by an officer, combed the streets of Charlestown, jailing and whipping blacks found after 8:00 or 9:00 at night without a "lantern with a candle lighted" or a pass.[231]

---

[228]*South Carolina Gazette*, May 27, 1734.

[229]*South Carolina Gazette Country Journal*, December 5, 1772.

[230]Ibid., June 1, October 26, 1773.

[231]*Par. Trans.*, Box 1, Folder 1, 29.

These laws did not allay the colonist's fears. In 1772, an anonymous writer named the "Stranger" wrote in the *South Carolina Gazette* that he had observed "a Country Dance, Rout, or Cabal of Negroes, within five miles distance of this Town [Charlestown] which consisted of about 60 people" who brought "bottle liquors of all sorts, Rum, Tongues, Hams, Beef, Geese, Turkies, and Fowls, both dried and raw, with many luxuries of the table, as sweetmeats, pickles." The blacks "danced, betted game, swore, quarrelled, fought and did everything that the most modern accomplished gentlemen were not ashamed of; except breaking of lamps, abusing the watch, and what is commonly called beating up the quarters, which would have endangered their safety."[232]

If this was thrue, then where were the twenty-one watchmen? Why had they not broken up the illegal assembly and jailed the curfew violators? In 1741, the Council had assailed "the town watch of Charlestown for their Neglect of Duty by which means frequent Robberies are committed and one of their officers keeping a Punch House many of the said watch repair late to their Duty sodden in liquor."[233] The Charlestown grand jurors in 1773 criticized "the Officers of the Charlestown Watch, for Neglect of Duty in not taking up every Negro found in the Streets not agreeable to Law after Tattoe, or keeping them confined until morning and acquainting their master therewith." The Grand Jurors accused the watch of "not patroling the streets on Sundays, especially during divine Service, and for not apprehending, confining them and punishing impudent noisy and troublesome Negroes, Mulattoes and Masters' Slaves especially when they found about five of them together." The Jurors said that "it is well known that one half the number of men required by law do attend their Duty on Sunday at night."[234]

Two years later the Charlestown Grand Jurors, again, blamed "the Watch Company of Charlestown for their Great neglect of Duty in not patroling the streets at night and their too frequent

---

[232]*South Carolina Gazette*, Sept. 17, 1772.

[233]*Par. Trans.*, Box 2, Folder 2, 22.

[234]*South Carolina Gazette*, June 20, 1776.

permitting Negroes, when taken up, to pass upon paying a small sum." The Grand Jurors blamed the "Inactivity of Magistrates and others, whose duty is to carry the Negro Acts into execution; and we do recommend a Revised and Amendment of the said Acts; in particular as to prevent Slaves being suffer to cook, bake, sell fruits, Dry Goods and otherwise to traffic and barter in the public market and streets of Charlestown and by those means prevent many industrious Families from obtaining an honest livelihood."[235]

No watchman, no matter how zealous, could detain every black he laid eyes on, for some blacks were free with a legal right to be at large. But the jurors complained that "All Free Negroes are not distinguished from those in Bondage or in Slavery. And Recommend that a law be made to oblige the Free Negroes to be distinguished by Badges on their Jackets or outside Garments."[236]

If the watchmen were the sole group empowered to apprehend the fugitives, the jurors might have had cause for concern, but the Assembly had enacted legislation in 1690 empowering military patrols under 'Captains' to track down fugitive blacks, long before the watchmen began walking their beat. The Captains could be fined twenty pounds for dereliction of duty.[237] In 1712, the Assembly increased the fine to thirty pounds, and added incentives. For captured blacks who had "runaway above six months" the company received forty shillings, above twelve months, four pounds from the owner and "if killed they shall receive forty shillings from the public." The 1722 Act gave the militia the "full power and authority for entering into any plantation" and searching "Negro houses" for weapons, and the power to search, seize, and carry away any black and the power to discipline those blacks found without passes by giving them "moderate whippings."[238]

These patrol laws did not "answer the intentions thereof" and in 1734 the lawmakers in "An Act for Regulating Patrols in this

---

[235]*South Carolina Gazette*, June 20, 1776.

[236]*South Carolina Country Journal*, March 8, 1774.

[237]Cooper and McCord, *South Carolina Statutes*, 346.

[238]Ibid., VII: 362-372.

Province" felt that patrols consisting of three enlisted men and one Captain, each armed with a "gun cutlass, [and] a cartridge box with at least two cartridges in it" should be stationed in each district. The patrol could apprehend and discipline blacks without passes and give them up to twenty lashes, search "Negro houses" for weapons and "beat maim and even kill such slave or slaves."[239]

This Act ordered the patrol to inspect the plantations at least once a month and, by 1737, once a week. In that year the number of men in the patrol jumped from four to fifteen. They were exempted from general militia duties, "serving in parrish offices," working on roads and jury attendance. By 1740 as a result of the Stono Revolt, the lawmakers had charted out the district — not exceeding fifteen miles — that each patrol was responsible for in that colony. The planter and overseers, women or men, between the ages of sixteen and sixty-five were ordered to perform patrol duty. Dereliction of duty, misbehavior or drunkenness could result in a forty shilling fine.[240] The Grand Jurors in 1775 in Beaufort, however, claimed that the "Patrol Act" was not being enforced "whereby many Villainies and Robberies are committed."[241]

If the watchmen's and the patrolmen's services were less than satisfactory, then any white colonist could enforce the law in South Carolina. The Assembly enacted legislation allowing any white man or woman to arrest and flog if necessary any black thought to be at large illegally — if "the free man or slave shall happen to be wounded, maimed or disabled" in capturing the black they were eligible for "relief." The 1740 Act declared that if the black fugitive attacked the white captor, the captor could kill the slave and if the white happened to be killed, his heirs would be reimbursed.[242]

What role did the white captor play in capturing the fugitive? The jail advertisements during the period between 1734 and 1744 described 152 captured black men, 18 black women, and four

---

[239]Ibid., III: 395-396.

[240]Ibid., III: 457, 573.

[241]*South Carolina Gazette*, December 15, 1772.

[242]Cooper and McCord, *South Carolina Statutes*, 392, 399.

children as well as the capture of one white servant man and one white woman servant. The jailers did not publish the captors' names during 1734-1737 but between 1738 and 1744, they published the names of 37 white men, 35 blacks, six watchmen and two wardens. These men had captured fugitives who had been hiding on plantations, on boats, in barns, or who had been roaming through Charlestown. Two blacks, Jacob and Will, were "taken up in a canoe at Wappoo Creek." Tony, a black, was captured "in Ms. Belinger's Barn" by an overseer. Jack, another black, was "taken up by watch." And "three of Captain Windham's men" captured Cuffie, a black. Forty percent of the blacks were captured on plantations.[243] The jailer listed no woman colonist among the captors.

Slaves capturing slaves and handing them over to the white authorities were reported by the planters and jailer. "London" was "taken up at Captain Beale's Plantation by one of his Negroes" and "Dick and Jack were taken up at Ms. Hume's plantation by one of her Negroes." Free blacks and Indians also captured fugitive blacks. "Cicero" had been "taken some 15 miles from Charlestown by a Mulatto freeman." "Caesar and Guinea was in the Posession of an Indian in the Cherokee Nation" after being at large for two years.[244]

Would-be apprehenders were conscientious. This was particularly true of the planter who took the time to put a captive's advertisement in the newspaper or to bring a fugitive to the jailhouse so that the rightful owner could reclaim the captive, especially the non-English speaking fugitive. A planter wrote in June 1734, "In Combabee River, two lusty Negro men. They can't speak English (or will not) but I understand by one of Negroes who is of their Country they have been out four Months."[245]

Alerting the captive's owner relieved the captor from escorting the fugitive to the Charlestown jail. One planter described in Issac and Abraham who had "been runaway five months from their

---

[243]*South Carolina Gazette*, May 17, 1735, July 23, 1741.

[244]Ibid., June 16, 1739, May 5, 1746.

[245]Ibid., June 15, 1734.

master whose name is Atkins and lives near Combabee." He noted that the owner may have "them in paying for this advertisement, and giving a small gratuity to the Negro who took them up" and "if the above slaves are not immediately owned they will be sent to the Work House in Charlestown which will be an additional expense, as they are 130 miles from town."[246]

Publishing a captive's name and his whereabouts showed the captor's willingness to obey the law, a law calling for the captive to be brought to the owner or the local constable within five days, on pain of a fine of twenty shillings. It showed, too, that the planter declined to put the fugitive to work or sell him. Indeed, one planter in his fugitive advertisement complained about the "vile practice of encouraging Negroes to runaway so they may buy cheap."[247]

If the captor could not understand the captive's language and if he could not find a translator, then he escorted the captive to the jailer who relied on the black prisoners to translate for him. In December of 1751 the jailer wrote: "A yellowish New Negro man, speaks bad English and cannot tell his Master's name, but tells other Negroes that the man who brought him, bought nine New Negro men, and one woman, most which runaway."[248] The jailer claimed that the black belonged to Benjamin Seabrook, but this planter published no fugitive advertisements in 1751 or 1752. One jailer had a black translator. "Four new Negroes" said the jailer, "who can speak no English, but what I can learn from my fellow who understands their country language and can speak to them their names are Tom, Dick and Harry."[249]

What was the difficulty in recalling a name? The planter expected the black to use his European name, while the African name was suppressed; this could cause resentment. Olaudah Equiano, the noted Ibo who was born in Benin, recalled in his

---

[246]Ibid., May 20, June 12, 1762.

[247]Ibid., September 10, 1762.

[248]Ibid., December 6, 1751.

[249]Ibid., September 19, 1760.

narrative that "while I was on board this ship, my captain and master named me Gustavus Vassa. I at that time began to understand him a little, and refused to be called so, and told him as well as I could that I could be called Jacob, but he said I should not and still called me Gustavus, and when I refused to answer to my new name, which at first I did, it gained me many a cuff, so at length I submitted, and was obligated to have the present name by which I have been known ever since."[250]

Some planters acknowledged that the African at large would use his original name instead of the Anglicized name given him. Some Africans left before the planter named them. "They were brought from Charlestown a day or two before they went away, one not named and can speak no English," wrote one planter describing an African couple. Henry Laurens said his slave's name was John "but he will readily answer to the name of Footabea." If the jailer could not find out the captive's name he could ask whether the captive knew the names of other blacks who lived with him. "Bristol or Mandingo can't tell his master's name but says he has Negroes named Issac, Apollo and Sam." The names of blacks on the slave ship were important. Cato and Marmadoe said "they both belong to one Johnson in the Indian Land, that their Master has a Negro Wench named Betty, and that she came out of the same ship with them." The keeper asked some captives whether their owner was alive: "A New Negro who spoke no English, Mandingo born, by what can be learnt his name is but his mistress is alive."[251]

The jailer, a relentless interrogator, demanded answers to his questions, but probably could not understand the African captive. Without the "workhouse Negro" the jailer would have had a difficult time locating this fugitive's owner. "By what I can learn by the Work House Negro who can talk with him, his master has two plantations. That in one he came from the Driver's name is Robin and other driver's name is Scripio and that another Negro runaway with him whose name was Sampson and have been out since the

---

[250]Gustavus Vassa, *The Life of Olaudah Equiano or Gustavus Vassa* (London, 1789), 76.

[251]*South Carolina Gazette*, August 23, 1760, March 3, 1759, June 26, 1762.

planting of corn."[252]

Expected to be trustworthy, the workhouse black basically determined whether the captured black would be returned to his proper owner. Yet in the long run the "Workhouse Negro," still a slave, sometimes harbored the same dreams as other blacks. In 1757, Christopher Holson, the keeper, offered a five pound reward for the capture of Frank who was "very well known in Charlestown as he lives so long at the workhouse to the warden of which he belongs to."[253]

Whether it was the gaoler or the workhouse black who interrogated them, some captured fugitives remained defiant. The jailer reported in 1753 that a "thin lean New Negro wench, cannot and won't tell her master's name." Could anyone blame them? Six months later an African with "several marks of the whip on his back, and either cannot or will not speak any English" was brought to jail. Cato, who could "not tell his master's name," had a "blotch under his breast by a bullet."[254] Some Africans might not have been maltreated in America, but in their homeland. Jalinka had "a scar in his upper lip occassioned by a knife in his own country." Prince, a Mandingo, has his "left hand burnt with fire in his own country."[255]

White men inflicted some of the pain. Jeffrey, an Angolan who, "cannot tell his master's name," reported the jailer, "had his left arm broke by some white person." Belfast, another African, "has the mark of a shot on his left thigh which he says was done by his master."[256] Could Cato, Prince, Jeffrey and Belfast and countless others be blamed for having a sudden loss of memory? Who could

---

[252]Ibid., October 30, 1762.

[253]*South Carolina Country Journal*, January 6, 1757.

[254]*South Carolina Gazette*, February 10, 1753, July 4, 1761, August 26, 1764, September 7, 1764.

[255]Ibid., August 26, 1764, September 7, 1764.

[256]Ibid., June 30, 1759; *South Carolina Country Journal*, August 18, 1767.

blame an African who had when "taken up a large Iron Chain, shakle and padlock on his right leg," and who would "confess neither his own nor his master's name," for choosing to remain silent?[257]

Some captives did not remain silent; they tried to be helpful. Lymus, a Callabrar, spoke a little broken English but could not remember his owner's name "but says he is a lusty man with a big belly, and the driver's name is Caesar." Lymus said his partner, who was also imprisoned, was named Jumper. The jailer reported Jumper's "actions in jumping and tumbling which he showed in the house since he has been with me."[258]

If the fugitive refused to cooperate, the jailer himself would suffer, for the jailer laid out the monies to the captor first. By 1740 the fugitive expenses were: five shillings for admittance, six pence for each day the fugitive stayed in jail, three shillings six pence for the advertisement, five shillings for printing, six pence for food, five shillings for bringing the fugitive to the owner and twenty shillings for the captor's reward. Some planters wanted the fugitives whipped, or branded, or maimed; others requested the fugitive's ears or testicles to be chopped off; and others asked to have their slaves killed, which 'services' cost anywhere from five shillings to five pounds.[259]

If the planter failed to claim his fugitive, the jailer lost money, hence the Assembly permitted the jailer to sell the planter's fugitive after eighteen months to pay for the expenses. "Whereas a Negro man slave named Rente," wrote one jailer, had been "detained in the Work House in Charlestown from the third day of July 1753," it was only in May 1757 that the jailer offered Rente for sale.[260] Yet one jailer "deliberately" concealed a fugitive from the owner. Thomas Benfield told the Assembly that the Provost Marshall, the jailer in the 1730's, had deliberately kept his woman

---

[257]*South Carolina Gazette*, June 6, 1741.

[258]*South Carolina Country Journal*, April 29, 1766.

[259]Cooper and McCord, *South Carolina Statutes*, 361.

[260]*South Carolina Gazette*, April 28, 1757.

fugitive in jail for some ten months. The "woman was born in South Carolina and spoke good English," claimed Benfield, and "she might have been made to declare the name of her Master had proper measures been taken for that purpose by the Provost Marshall." The woman fugitive "had great Liberty in the Prison, lived in great Plenty and done much work with her Needle and kept in constant communication with County Negroes who have furnished her with Rice and other Provisions." The Marshall returned the slave.[261]

The fugitive laws, drafted by some of the leading minds in the colony, could have never been enforced without the cooperation of the lowest ranking members of the legal hierarchy: the faceless gaolkeeper and his black assistants, the watchman on the beat, the patrolman on the prowl, not to mention the local white citizenry and the blacks and the Indians themselves, many of whom were armed with muskets, whips and irons. But it seems that no matter how intricate the machinery of control, no matter how harsh the laws, some blacks continued to make escape attempts.

---

[261]*Par. Trans.*, Box 1, Folder 6, 5.

CHAPTER V
WHY THEY RAN AWAY

To ask why the fugitive slave or servant absconded seems to ask the obvious, but since lack of opportunity prevented most fugitives from writing about their experiences, it is to the testimony of the planter that we must turn, and especially to those very newspaper advertisements which purport to explain why the fugitive left. In 1785, a planter printed a fugitive advertisement in a Maryland paper describing a servant named William Tompkins who was "artful, capable of forming a plausible story," had "several sores on his legs, owing to his being in irons the most of his passage having strove to prevail on the rest of the servants to take the vessel to themselves."[262] The planter failed to tell what sparked the escape, but Tompkin's past insurrectionary activities showed discontent with servitude long before reaching America.

The servants made several attempts to seize servant ships. In 1788, the *Maryland Gazette* reported that a ship "left Dublin with a few passengers, indentured servants and 93 convicts, but a short time after the ship left land the captain was informed of a design among the convicts to rise and take possession of the ship." Thirty-five years earlier, in 1753, the *Pennsylvania Gazette* wrote: "we have a report that a vessel with servants from Ireland, is on a shore near Capees and that the servants had mutiny and killed all the crew, except the Captain but we cannot learn the Particulars."[263]

The *Pennsylvania Gazette* reported in 1751 that six English convicts sentenced to fourteen years of servitude in Virginia "rose at Sea, shot the Capt., overcamed and confined the Seamen, and kept Possession of the vessel for 19 days" before they abandoned the ship and were later captured. And in 1773: "we hear that a Brig, from Dublin for Baltimore, with one Hundred and fifty indentured Servants and Convicts on board, is ashore near the Mouth of York River; and that a Boat which went to their

---

[262]Baltimore, *Maryland Journal and Baltimore Advertiser*, October 7, 1785.

[263]*Maryland Gazette*, May 13, 1788; *Pennsylvania Gazette*, June 21, 1753.

Assistance was seized by about thirty of the People, who went ashore in her." The authorities captured five servants including one woman but "the rest have found Means to make their Escape from the Vessel."[264]

Once in America merchants advertised and sold the servants to the highest bidder. In 1768, the *Pennsylvania Gazette* reported the arrival at Market Street, a ship called the Wharf of the <u>Snow-Buna</u> – carrying a "number of likely and English and Welsh servants chiefly brought up to farming business, and four tradesmen, some women and boys all in good health."[265] William Green in 1774, an English convict servant, recalled that, en route to Maryland:

> We were put all on shore in couples, chained together and drove in lots like oxen or sheep, till we come to a town called *Fike* where there was a great number of men and women, young and old, come to see us; they search us there as the dealers in horses to these animals in this country, by looking at our teeth, viewing our limbs, to see if they are sound and fit for their labour, and if they approve of us after asking our trades and names, and what crimes we have been guilty of to bring us to that shame, the bargain is made.[266]

As soon as the servant ship touched shore, according to William Eddis, a surveyor, living in Annapolis, Maryland, "planters, mechanics, and others repair on board; the adventurers of both sexes are exposed to view, and very few are happy enough to make their own stipulations, some very extraordinary qualifications being absolutely requisite to obtain this distinction; and even when this is obtained the advantages are no means equivalent to their

---

[264]*Pennsylvania Gazette*, May 9, 1751, February 10, 1773.

[265]Ibid., October 13, 1768.

[266]William Green, *The Suffering of William Green: Being a Sorrowful Account* (London, 1774), 5, 6.

sanguine expectation."[267] John Harrower, a white servant, who lived in Virginia, worked as a tutor. In his journal he noted in 1774 that "two Soul Drivers," colonists who "go on board all ships who have in either Servants or Convicts and buy sometimes the whole and sometimes a parcell of them as they can agree, and their they drive them through the Country like a parcell of sheep until they can sell them to advantage, but all went away without buying any."[268] The servants resented this. In 1774, a merchant named Moffman of Baltimore purchased a "parcel of convicts in order to dispose of them to his advantage, all of which he sold before he reached Frederickstown except four men." When one servant complained "he was too much fatigued to go any further, they therefore all rested on an old tree, and after a short time Moffman told them they must proceed on their journey and they refused and they immediately threw him backwards over a tree, dragged him four steps into the woods and cut his throat from ear to ear." The servants escaped.[269]

Once sold, the servant was expected to accept the planter's authority. In Westover, wealthy Virginia planter William Byrd II told a neighbor, Mary Jeffreys Dunn, about Incendia, a "homely, middle aged" woman whom he had allowed to live in his house because her husband had "forsaken" her. While Byrd was away, the woman ordered a servant weaver to sew clothes for her. He refused, claiming Byrd permitted him to clothe the servants only. Incendia called him a "saucy rascal for disputing her commands, and assur'd him she had a great mind to break his head." Byrd came home, found the servant's work unfinished, and "therefore brandisht a good cudget over the waver's head protesting I wou'd break his bones if he did not explain what disturb him?"

In New England the servant could confide in secret about his

---

[267]William Eddis, *Letters From America*, Aubrey C. Land, ed. (Cambridge, Mass., 1792, 1969), 40.

[268]John Harrower, *The Journal of John Harrower: An Indentured Servant in the Colony of Virginia, 1773-1776*, ed., Fritz Kredel (New York, 1963), 39.

[269]*Maryland Gazette*, June 6, 1774.

grievance with the town minister, though it might be fruitless. Benjamin Wadsworth, a Puritan minister, told servants that "God bids you to obey your master with heart and good will." Minister Samuel Willard felt it was a violation of the fifth commandment if a servant "neglected his duty." "When a servant," preached Wadsworth, "ranaway from his master or mistress, and quit and forsaked their Service," this was "a very great wickedness for it is indirectly contrary to those commands of God." New England ministers expected servants to obey, to be faithful and to be reverent; they expected the planter to be humane and responsive to God's laws. Willard spoke out against "Extreme Rigour" and warned masters "not to make *Asses* of our Servants whilst they may be treated as *Men*. They must avoid all Cruelty, both in words and blows and rather keep within the bounds of severity, than go beyond the limits of it."[270]

The maltreated servant could also turn to the local court for redress. The Salem Quarterly Court in 1650 heard Arthur Carey, a servant, charge George Keaser, his owner, with "cruelty and unreasonably correcting him." The court ordered Carey discharged and Keaser whipped.[271] In 1624, witnesses told the Council in Virginia that fugitive servant Elizabeth Abbot who had "divers tymes run Awaye and both layne in the woods some tymes 8 or 10 dyes together" had been lashed at least five hundred times; Elias Hinton had been beaten to death with a rake. A sheriff in Maryland, in March, 1662, found Pope Alvey's fugitive servant, Alice Sandford, her "body beaten to jelly." Alvey had called the woman a "Damn whoare," and whipped her to death for not walking home fast enough. The authorities burned Alvey's hands

---

[270]Benjamin Wadsworth, *A Well Ordered Family* (Boston, 1712, 1719), 114; Samuel Willard, *A Complete Body of Divinity* (Boston, 1726), 615-616.

[271]*Records and Files of The Quarterly Courts of Essex County* (Salem, Mass., 1911), I: 6.

with an iron.[272]

If the servant's life was endangered, why migrate to the American colonies at all? Had word not reached the local citizenry in England and Ireland about the conditions in America? The *South Carolina Gazette* reported in 1732 that Robert Sinclair's servant had "willfully drowned himself in Black River" after he had been "in the Province but a few weeks, and it is imagined that his being put to work, which was what it seems, he had not been used to, induced him to dispose of himself."[273] In 1747 the *Maryland Gazette* reported the drowning of Elisha Williams, a fugitive from Annapolis. The inquest showed the "too often rigorous usage and ill treatment of Masters to Servants whereby it is very often happen, that such ill treatment was the cause of many Servants making an end of themselve one way or another." And in 1753 in New Jersey, "a Servant man was found hanging in the Woods in New Township Gloucester county; which tis thought, has hung there since Sept. last when he runaway from his master."[274]

Some servants expected to be treated fairly in America, complete their time and start life anew. Idle though they might have been, it was these lofty dreams that lured Thomas Hellier of Dorsetshire, England to America and to his untimely death. The twenty-eight year old Hellier, no one's fool, had a first rate education, a stationer's trade, and fifty acres of land, but he squandered his money in local bars. Tired of being broke and of ducking his creditors, Hellier fell in with a seafaring man who offered to ship him to Virginia to work as an indentured servant. Hellier said that, "I had heard so bad a character of that Country, that I dreaded going thither," because he "abhorred the Ax and the Haw" and he told the contracting agent that he would only work as a "Merchants Accompts, and such Employments to which I had been

[272]McIlwain, *Minutes of the Council and General Court of Colonial Virginia, 1622-1632, 1670-1676*, 22-24; *Arch. Md.*, XLIX: 49, 167, 304-313.

[273]*South Carolina Gazette*, July 15, 1732.

[274]*Maryland Gazette*, August 4, 1747; *Pennsylvania Gazette*, January 16, 1753.

bred." The agent promised Hellier all that he asked and by 1677 the Dorset man was in Virginia working for "Cutbeard Williamson living at a Plantation call'd Hard Labour" located in Westover Parish in Charles City.[275]

"Williams promised me," said the newly arrived servant, that "I should be employed in Teaching his Children, and not be set to any laborious work, unless necessity did compel now and then, meerly for a short spurt." Because of the lack of food and clothes and because the "labour at the Howe was very irksome" and because Williams' wife had angered him with her "Taunts and bitter Flouts," Thomas Hellier absconded. When lawmakers captured him three weeks later, Williams forgave his servant, but the taunts returned. Hellier hacked both Williams and his wife to death and fled on horseback armed with his master's gun. Captured a few days later, Hellier confessed, and the authorities hanged him in 1678.[276]

Hellier's plight so affected an Anglican minister named Paul Williams that he penned a forty page pamphlet in 1680, entitled the *Vain Prodigal Life and Tragical Penitent Death of Thomas Hellier*. Reverend Williams talked glowingly of Virginia:

> it self a very fertil, good, pleasant Country abounding with the manifold Blessings of luxuriant Nature, the only Region of all under the Sun to enrich laborious, painful, industrious poor-men. So that many, who in *England* and many other Parts of the World are unable to get their Bread, may in this Region live comfortably and happy; the native Riches of the soil bountifully requiting each industrious person labour with a yearly plentiful product.[277]

Yet, he advised the ambitious servant to use caution, and "who

---

[275]T. H. Breen, James H. Lewis and Keith Schlesinger, eds., "Motive for Murder: A Servant's Life in Virginia, 1678," *William and Mary Quarterly*, 3rd Series, 40 (January 1983), 106-120.

[276]Ibid., 112-113.

[277]Ibid., 117.

know themselves unable to labour "not" to come over Servants at all; unless they can before-hand on infallible grounds assure themselves, that they shall be consigned to some truely generous-spirited Gentleman of real repute, good quality, and true worth who will infallibly deal so indulgently and favourably by them, as to employ them in such concerns, which their former Education hath most properly fitted them for." He warned servants that "tis more for the interest of *Virginia* to have their Servants to chop Logs lustily, than to chop Logic, Handling the Howe proves here far better Musick then the Hoghboy."[278]

Williams expressed concern about the planter who purchased servants "incapable of hard labour, or by Education totally averse to the same; pretending they will employ the said Servants in concerns suitable to their Strength, or Education, or both." And after these servants were "fast bound" to the planter and even after the servant "put forth his utmost ability, the planter still curs'd, bann'd, swore at, trampled under foot, and perpetually tormented with abusive Usage," those servants who could not reach his "expectations."[279]

John Barnes was another servant who migrated to America. Barnes, of Newark, New Jersey, was born in Lancashire, England. Barnes' parents were "mean poor people who died when he was young," and since Barnes himself had "no learning," he was bound as a laborer until age twenty-four. In and out of the Queen's army and between enlistments Barnes turned to stealing. Found guilty of theft, Barnes decided to indenture himself to a planter in Maryland for six to seven years. He served three years before he absconded with a servant woman to Philadelphia and to New Jersey where he resumed stealing for which the authorities hanged him in 1738.[280]

Hellier made a calculated decision and failed; Barnes might have been a victim of ignorance and poverty. Whatever the case, both

---

[278]Ibid., 119.

[279]Ibid., 120.

[280]*Pennsylvania Gazette*, December 14, 1738, *Virginia Gazette* (Parks), July 6, 1739.

had the fleeting belief that indentured servitude offered opportunity enough. Others might collapse of disease or hard work or fall victim to planter abuse, turn to drink, lose their mind, or kill themselves. For the survivors, life existed after indentured servitude. In fact, in seventeenth-century Maryland, the ambitious servant had a slim chance of becoming a sheriff, juror, justice of the peace or councilman. Some obtained enough status to be called mister, gentlemen or esquire. And some, too, had accumulated anywhere between fifty and four thousand acres of land after completing their indenture obligation.[281]

These servants worked the crops, plied their trades from dawn to dusk, six days a week with one objective in their mind – to complete their time. They did have hope, but as the French traveler Moreau St. Mery wrote in the 1790's, the servants in Philadelphia "are usually so unhappy as indentured servants that they never draw a happy breath until they know the joy of being their own masters." He added: "Manual labor is too well paid in the United States for any man to think that he wouldn't find it

---

[281]Russell R. Menard, "From Servant to Freeholder: Status Mobility and Property Accumulation in Seventeenth-Century Maryland," *William and Mary Quarterly*, 3rd Series, 30 (1973), 37-64; Lorena S. Walsh, "Servitude and Opportunity in Charles County, Maryland, 1658-1705, in *Law, Society, and Politics in Early Maryland*, Aubrey C. Land, Lois Green Carr, and Edward C. Papenfuse, eds. (Baltimore, 1977); Lois G. Carr and Russell R. Menard, "Immigration and Opportunity: The Freedman in Early Colonial Maryland," in *The Chesapeake in the Seventeenth Century: Essays on Anglo-American Society*, Thad W. Tate and David L. Ammerman, eds. (Chapel Hill, N.C., 1979), 206-209; Anita H. Rutman, "Still Planting the Seeds of Hope: The Recent Literature of the Early Chesapeake Region," *The Virginia Magazine of History and Biography*, 95 (January 1987), 3-24; Lorena S. Walsh, "Staying Put or Getting Out: Findings for Charles County, Maryland, 1650-1720, *William and Mary Quarterly*, 3rd Series, 44 (January 1987), 89-103.

more profitable to be free."[282]

Most servants voluntarily migrated to America, for they were an ambitious lot, ambitious enough to contract out their labor for a period of anywhere between four and seven years in return for a paid passage, including food, clothing and shelter during their indentured time. They were also ambitious enough to stay the course despite the fact that in the early beginnings of Virginia and Maryland, over 80% of the white men died in their early forties. Half the newly born died at birth and dysentery, typhoid fever, measles and smallpox frequently raged out of control. Doctors, ministers and women were scarce. Everything was scarce except work and tobacco leaves and short-tempered labor-hungry planters attempting to extend the servant's work commitments indefinitely.[283]

In 1666, a posse captured fugitive Japeheth Griphen of Maryland. His master said "Welcome home Runaway" and Griphen replied that he "did not runaway but went away." In Griphen's case his owner refused to sign an indentured contract though the lawmakers had passed laws requiring planters to bring servants without indentures to local county courts to verify ages and enter them into a "book of Record." Griphen's owner had purchased him from a storekeeper who told him he could make Griphen work "as long as he pleased either for 12, 14 or 20 years," which caused the Charles County court to order Griphen to "be free" and the owner "to pay him his corn and Cloathes with charges and costs of suit" which amounted to 420 pounds of tobacco or at least one year of

---

[282]*Moreau De St. Mery's American Journal, 1793-1798*, Kenneth Roberts and Anna Roberts, eds. (Garden City, New York, 1947), 295.

[283]*Seventeenth Century America: Essays in Colonial History*, James Morton Smith, ed. (Chapel Hill, 1959), 63-89; Welsey Frank Craven, *Red, White and Black: The Seventeenth Century Virginian* (Charlottesville, 1971), 20-29; Morgan, *American Slavery, American Freedom*, 126-129; Oscar and Mary R. Handlin, "Origins of the Southern Labor System," in *Colonial American Essays in Politics and Social Development*, 3rd edition, Stanley N. Katz and John M. Murrin, eds. (New York, 1983), 231-255.

servant wages.[284]

Why work anywhere between four to seven years for nothing save for the bare necessities? Why not disappear without a trace? Take someone's completed contract of indenture, go to another country, colony or county, change your name, your dress, and even your trade and pocket your own earnings? Patrick Sheeren "will set up school" said one master "as he followed that business when he went away before." John Shippley took with him "a set of shoemaker's tools and he will pass for a shoemaker as he can make a pretty good shoe." And Edward Mitchen intended "to set up a person where he is not known and gather people together to hear him read or sing psalms."[285] The act – setting up business, or seeking wage paying employment – defines the cause or reason why a servant made off, whether the planter acknowledged it or not.

Not every white servant sailed to America voluntarily; England sent convict servants to America as punishment for felonies committed in their homeland. The British authorities thought they were offering these servants a bargain by sending them to America for a period of seven years for property offenses and fourteen years for murder. Previously, one out of six convicts had been executed in England for felonies. The British benefitted because, as one writer said in 1731, it resulted in: "Draining the nation of its offensive rubbish without taking away their lives." During the period between 1718, the beginning of the convict trade, and 1775 when the trade ended, the British alone sent 30,000 convicts to America. Between 1718 and 1773 some 50,000 convicts from all parts of Europe sailed to America, 66% of whom were placed in Chesapeake.[286]

---

[284]*Arch. Md.*, LX: 46, 47.

[285]*Pennsylvania Gazette*, May 1, 1766, November 29, 1780.

[286]Kenneth Morgan, "The Organization of the Convict Trade to Maryland: Stevenson, Randolph & Cheston, 1768-1775," *William and Mary Quarterly*, 3rd Series, 42 (1985), 184-185; Roger A. Ekirch, "Bound for America: A Profile of British Convicts Transported to the Colonies, 1718-1775," *William and Mary*

During 1745-1774 the fugitive advertisements in the *Maryland Gazette* described 944 servants, of whom 452, or 48%, were convicts. Ninety-eight percent of these convicts were men. In a letter to the *Pennsylvania Gazette*, in 1751, one writer complained in 1751 about "the three hundred to four hundred felons" that were imported to that colony and that though "some few may possibly have been transported for small Matters or thro false Accusions, but most well deserve Hanging at home," and that "we have now no occasion for imported thieves in America, as the Breed seems to thrive upon us." During the 1750's the *Maryland Gazette* kept close watch on the fugitive convicts, especially the violent escapees. Daniel Sullivan ("An Irishman, about 23 Years of Age, who had been twice convicted into this Country") was tried for the murder of Donald McKennia in Baltimore County, and hung in chains. The Maryland authorities hung a convict servant in Elk Ridge for killing two of his master's children. In 1754, the Maryland paper reported that "John Orrick apprehended John Oulion (a Convict Servant, who has ran away from the Baltimore Iron Works, and bound him) after carrying him some Time, unbound him to let him eat" and the servant "stabb'd Mr. Orrick in the Breast" and made off.[287]

Some servants appeared to have been convicted of flimsy offenses. The *London Magazine* in 1736 told how lawyer Henry Justice, who was convicted of a felony for taking books and "Several Tracts cut out of Books" from Trinity College, Cambridge, asked the court "that he might not be sent Aboard, which would be a great Injury to his children, and prevent the University's recovering many of their Books, which he had caused to be carried to Holland." The court ordered him to be transported to America and if he tried "to return to Great Britain or Ireland during that Time, he would be tried for a 'Felony without Benefit of Clergy'." Richard Kibble of Virginia, an English convict, "made his Escape

Quarterly, 3rd Series, 42 (April 1985), 187; *London Magazine*, 5 (April, 1736), A. Roger Ekirch, *Bound for America: The Transportation of British Convicts to the Colonies: 1718-1775* (Oxford, 1987), 1-3.

[287]*Pennsylvania Gazette*, May 9, 1751.

home and was convicted again this year upon Six new Indictments and staid with his Master but three days before he went off again."[288]

Another group of servants had been kidnapped or enticed away and carried to America. On May 9, 1645, the House of Parliament flayed the "divers of lews Persons to go up and down the City of London, and elsewhere and in a most barbarous and wicked Manner steal away many little children." Thomas Smith of Oldstreete, of Middlesex, accused John Chetrost and his wife Christinia of "inticing away his servant, Katherine Penn, the said Christinia by promising her to help her to a service where she should have six pounds sterling per annum, but hee and his wife conveyed her into a shipp to sell her to a merchant to be transported beyond sea, as the said Katherine affirmeth." Hester Lambert fingered James Buckle as having 'unlawfully conveyed' her to a ship called the 'Augustine' in order to transport her for sale in Virginia, "without her consent and against her will." And William Stowne, "by flattering and great promises," had been successful in transporting George Creech and Thomas Riddle, to Virginia," the one being an apprentice and the other to Virginia without the consent of their parents." The court acknowledged "it was to their great loss and grief."[289]

The blacks did not voluntarily sail to America, for when the European traders came to African shores, they came not with an indentured contract but with the musket, the cutlass, the rope, and the branding iron. Alvaro Vasquez, a Portuguese, in the middle of the fifteenth century, wrote: "Let each one run as fast as he can, and so let us stoutly fall upon them and since we are not able to make captive of the young men, yet let us seize upon the old men, the women, and the little children." Defenders were "slain without pity." The Moors caught off guard "like unwary people" by the Portuguese, were thrown into confusion. They fought back, then retreated. "And others who were bold and light footed, trusting in

---

[288]*Pennsylvania Gazette*, May 9, 1751.

[289]*Virginia Gazette*, November 19, 1736; Peter Wilson Coldham, "The Spiriting of London Children to Virginia," 83 (July 1975); *The Virginia Magazine of History and Biography*, 280-287.

their fleetness, escaped through all."[290]

One ship's surgeon, James Arnold, who served on board an African slave ship called *Ruby*, reported that the "slaves that were brought to the *Ruby*, reached there from various causes. Most of them were bought at fairs, by traders, who brought them to the coast, but many were kidnapped as opportunity offered, and others were sold for debt or for adultery, either real or falsely charged." Others, having been enticed to the vessel were there seized and confined.[291]

Once apprehended, the captors tied the blacks or chained them together and forced them into ships. But there was resistance. Captain Philips, a slave trader, recalled this experience in the 1780's: "The Negroes are so wilful and loth to leave their own country, that they have often leap'd out of the canoes, boat and ship, into the sea, and kept under water til they drowned...; they have a more dreadful apprehension of Barbados than we can have of hell... We had about 12 Negroes did wilfully drown themselves, and others starved themselves to death."[292]

Some narratives survive of how the kidnapped Africans experienced their journey to America. Olaudah Equiano or Gustavus Vassa, the "son of an Ibo tribal elder," from the nation of Benin, en route to a plantation in Virginia in 1746, who had never before seen a white man, found himself on slave ship full of white men with different complexions, different "hair" and different "languages," white men standing next to a "large furnace of copper boiling," and whites standing guard over "a multitude of black people of every description chained together, every one of their

---

[290]*Documents Illustrative of the History of the Slave Trade to America*, Elizabeth Donnan, ed. (4 vols., Washington, D.C., 1930-1935), I: 34.

[291]*Slaves Ships and Slaving*, George F. Dow, comp. (Port Washington, New York. 1927, 1969), 173.

[292]Quoted in William D. Piersen, "White Cannibals, Black Martyrs: Fear, Depression and Religious Faith as Causes of Suicide Among New Slaves," *Journal of Negro History*, 62 (April 1977), 147-159.

countenances expressing dejection and sorrow." Olaudah "fell
motionless on the deck and fainted." When he awoke he asked the
other blacks if he were not to be "eaten by those white men with
horrible looks, red faces and long hair." In 1766, a slave ship en
route to North Carolina from Antigua, carrying at least thirty
blacks, lost its sails and was left to the "mercy of the sea" for
fifteen weeks and with no food for forty days. The restless seamen
began "eating one of the dead Negroe children which so
exasperated the Negroes they fell on the crew."[293]

Slave trader John Newton saw black women and girls taken on
board ships "naked, trembling, terrified, perhaps almost exhausted
with cold, fatigue, and hunger;" and how they were "often exposed
to the wanton madness of white savages," and "how the prey was
divided upon the spot and only reserved till opportunity offers."[294]
He had heard about a "shipmate in a long boat who purchased a
young woman with a fine child, of about a year old, in her arms."
When night fell, the baby began to cry, whereupon the sailor "rose
in great anger, and swore, that if the child did not cease making
such noise, he would presently silence it." The child cried on. The
man "tore the child from the mother, and threw it into the sea."[295]

After the slave ship docked, the planter waited anxiously.
Alexander Falconbridge called the sales process the "scramble"
because the merchants placed blacks in a yard and at a signal the
planters burst into the yard to "seize such of the Negroes as they
can conveniently lay hold of with their hands. Others, being
prepared with several handkerchiefs tied together, encircle with
these as many as they are able while others by means of a rope,
effect the same purpose."[296]

Is it then not understandable why "four new Negro Men, lately

---

[293]*Africa Remembered: Narratives by West Africans From the Era
of the Slave Trade*, Philip D. Curtin, ed. (Madison, 1969), 92-94.

[294]John Newton, *The Journal of a Slave Trader, 1750-1754*
(London, 1952), 104.

[295]Ibid.

[296]Dow, *Slave Ships and Slaving*, 152.

purchased of Brailsford & Chapman," a slavetrading company from South Carolina, had escaped from a newly arrived cargo, according to an advertisement in that colony's local paper? Is it not understandable, too, that these African fugitives "will keep together and make toward the seacoast."[297]

The slave had no indenture contract or court privileges: he was absolute property. What kind of food he ate and where he ate were determined by the owner. What kind of clothes he wore, where he lived, and what kind of work he did and how long he worked was determined, too, by the owner. Englishman Peter Gordon, an early immigrant to Georgia, the first Chief Baliff of Savannah, supported the introduction of slavery into Georgia, for when a black "becomes your sole property," an owner can "train him up in what manner you think either to the field or house." He did not like white servants. Their "time is so short," they could not stand the heat and they are "generally the very scumn and refuse of mankind."[298]

Pastor Johann Bolzius of Salzburg, Austria, another migrant to Georgia in 1733, opposed slavery, large plantations and gang labor. Give him a few acres of land, some hardy farmers, skilled labor and God would see him through, and for two decades Bolzius and his slave opponents had it their way: No slaves in Georgia. When the blacks arrived, Reverend Bolzius kept his European contacts informed. He tried to answer all his correspondents' questions in a questionnaire, which comprised sixty-seven questions in all. Questions nine, ten, and eleven were direct. "About how costly is a Negro man, and a Negro woman?"; "Whether these people [blacks] are as false, malicious, and terrible as they are described;" and "How many Negroes are necessary for the cultivation of a well-appointed plantation of about 1,000 acres?"[299]

---

[297]*South Carolina Gazette*, August 26, 1765.

[298]*The Journal of Peter Gordon, 1732-1735*, E. Merton Coulter, ed. (Athens, 1983), 56-57.

[299]"Johann Martin Bolzius Answers a Questionnaire on Carolina and Georgia," *William and Mary Quarterly*, 3rd Series, Klaus G. Loewald, Beverly Starika, and Paul S. Taylor, trans. and

"A faithful and sincere Negro is a very rare thing," Bolzius maintained, "but they do exist, particularly with masters who know how to treat them reasonably and in a Christian way." He acknowledged that "Eternal Slavery to them as to all people is an unbearable yoke, and very harsh treatment as regards food and work exasperates then greatly." He noted that "the upkeep of the Negros is cut very sparse." The Salzburger — after he recited his grace — ate salable rice, cheese, potatoes, eggs, squash, cabbage and lettuce and washed it down with milk, beer or rum. The black ate unsalable cracked rice, unsalted corn, and Indian beans, washed down with water. The Salzburger never complained of a meat shortage. Bolzius said, "they usually slaughtered oxen and pigs in the autumn and at the beginning of winter, when they are fat, and the meat keeps well." Other meat was also readily available: "geese, ducks, calcutta chickens, sheep, lambs, calves..." Meat was a rarity for the black, save for the loyal black, but the slaves "love to eat meat, and sometimes roast mice or steal meat."[300]

Bolzius spoke little about the Salzburger's clothes, but the white free women in Charlestown wore fashionable caps, stomachers, silk gowns, leather gloves, fans, velvet masks and umbrellas. White freemen wore long overcoats, beaver hats, silk shirts, leather boots, and fluffy white wigs. Generally, blacks received a blanket and a pair of shoes on a yearly basis. The material called "Negro cloth" was the "coarsest" of all cloths. In the summer the blacks "go naked, except that the men cover their shame with a cloth rag which hangs around a strap tied around the body. The women have petticoats; and the upper body is bare." Housing cost nothing because blacks lived in huts — two persons to a hut. The only cost was the nails. The black's yearly upkeep amounted to two pounds and two shillings.[301]

Another form of maltreatment experienced by blacks and a reason for their flights, an issue not touched upon by Bolzius, was the sale of blacks. These sales undermined relationships between

---

eds., 14 (1957), 221, 233.

[300]Ibid., 229, 233, 235, 236.

[301]Ibid., 236, 256, 257.

mother and child, wife and husband, brother and sister, causing a
great deal of grief. Olaudah recalled that he had six brothers and
one sister and "as I was youngest of the sons, I became, of course,
the greatest favorite with my mother, and was always with her; and
she used to take particular pains to form my mind." After the
African slavers snatched him up at age eleven with his young
sister, Olaudah and his sister never saw their parents again.
Olaudah Equiano remembered not only the breakup of his own
family, but that of others as well: "I remember in the vessel in
which I was brought over, in the men's compartment, there were
several brothers, who in the sale, were sold in different lots; and
it was very moving on this occasion to see and hear their cries at
parting."[302]

The planter sold anybody: man, woman or child. It might be for
money. One planter in South Carolina was selling a twenty year
old black man "for no reason but for want of money." Another
planter in South Carolina, in 1797, advertised a "young Negro girl
about 14 years old," because she was too "young for the use of
family." And a fourteen year old "Negro boy" found himself being
sold because his owner said he was not "able to look after him
owing to age and being unwell."[303]

The planter sold away the rebellious or "incorrigible" fugitive. In
a letter to Edward & John Mayne & Co., a merchant company
located in Portugal, Robert Pringle, a South Carolina slavetrader,
complained about Esther, his female slave who had a "practice of
goeing frequently to her Father and Mother, who Live at a
Plantation I an Concern'd in about Twenty Miles from Town from
Whence there was no Restraining her from Running away there,
and staying every now and then, which determin'd me to send her
off and hope may sell her to good advantage." Pringle shipped
Esther to Lisbon, Portugal in 1740. George Washington, in 1766,
sent Tom, a black, a "Rogue and a Runaway" to the West Indies.
And Henry Laurens sold a black named Sampson, and promised

---

[302]Curtin, *Africa Remembered*, 97.

[303]Charlestown, *City Gazette and Daily Advertiser*, August 1,
October 17, 1795.

he would not "keep a runaway."[304]   The planter who wished to unload an unwanted slave had to convince the buyer that the slave was not a fugitive. In 1799, the *City Gazette* in South Carolina ran an advertisement describing a black woman and three children who were up for sale. The woman would wash, iron, and cook and she was "no runaway."[305]

Some planters broke up families without giving a reason. In Maryland, in 1779, one seller offered "a healthy honest mulatto woman about twenty-three years of age with two fine girls her children." The woman was to be sold with or without her children to any person in Annapolis, Baltimoretown, or in the neighborhood of either. In New Jersey, in 1784, a "healthy likely Negro wench" was offered for sale "with or without child."[306]

To stop the breaking of a union, one black woman threatened to kill herself. In May 1784, a Scottish factor, Alexander Hamilton of Maryland, who worked for a Glasgow firm in Piscataway, sent Harry, a slave, to pick up a black woman and her five children from her owner and escort her to Gideon Smith, her new owner. The woman balked despite Harry's attempt to "coax her to come." She threatened "to destroy herself," if she was separated from her husband who was not part of the sale. Hamilton felt that "The Girl is a fool, with so many children she ought to be thankfull in having a master who will take care of her & children."[307]

Slaves threatened to escape. John Hanson, a Continental

---

[304]*The LetterBook of Robert Pringle*, Walter B. Edgar, ed. (2 vols., Columbia, 1972), I: 247; Fitzpatrick, *Wash. Writings*, III: 437; Rodgers, *Papers of Henry Laurens*, III: 261.

[305]Charlestown, *City Gazette and Daily Advertiser*, September 20, 1787, September 24, 1795, 1799.

[306]*Maryland Gazette*, October 29, 1779; *New Jersey Gazette*, February 24, 1768.

[307]David C. Skaggs, and Richard K. MacMaster, eds., "Post-Revolutionary Letters of Alexander Hamilton, Piscataway Merchant, Part I, January-June, 1784," *Maryland Historical Magazine*, 63 (March 1968), 47-48.

Congress president, placed an advertisement in the *Maryland Gazette* on August 30, 1781, describing a thirty-five year old black shoemaker, Ned Barnes, who probably "has a pass and intends to join the British troops." A letter from Hanson to Doctor Philip Thomas, his son-in-law and the manager of his plantation, noted Barnes' capture in January 1782 and that Barnes belonged to the Hanson estate but that another neighboring planter owned Barnes' wife. Hanson asked Bonds to continue Barnes' employment "while his wife continues at home." Hanson asserted: "I supposed there will be no danger of his making a second attempt to get off. You may let him know that his pardon depends upon his future behavior, that if he behaves well and endeavors to make amends for his past conduct I will when I return home purchase his wife if her master will set a reasonable price." Barnes escaped again. In April of 1782, Hanson told Bonds "it is a little unlikely that Ned went off again before you received my letter; perhaps had he known that I had consented to sell him it might have prevented it."[308]

Some fugitives, however, made off to provoke a sale. In 1746 Thomas Radcliffe of South Carolina maintained that Abram, "a tall well set fellow," made off "in Hopes that I should sell him." The reason for Abram's tactic can be explained in an advertisement that Radcliffe published five years later describing Abram's second escape. Abram's former master, Thomas Butler, had a plantation outside of Charlestown and "he has a wife there: And I am insensible of any other cause of his absenting from me then to be sold." Another planter from Virginia offered ten pistoles for a "Negro then named Joe who formerly belonged and was coachman to Mr. Belfield, of Richmond County." Joe had escaped three times in the past and the planter said "I have great Reason to believe, that he is privately encouraged to run away, and then harboured and concealed, that I may be induced to sell him, having had

---

[308]*Maryland Gazette*, August 30, 1781; John Hanson to Doctor Bond, January 29, March 5, and April 27, 1782; *John Hanson Collection* (Maryland Historical Society); Ralph B. Levering, "John Hanson, Public Servant," *Maryland Historical Magazine*, 71 (Summer 1976), 131.

several Offers made me for him since he went off."[309]

Why sever a tie when it caused grief, demoralization, anger and might even goad the black or servant to escape? Was it an irrational or delusionary act or was it a practical need to protect an investment? Whatever the reason, it made little sense for a planter in Virginia to track down Peter, a black fugitive, "who was not long since brought from North Carolina, where he has been about four years as a runaway, and where it is said he has a wife and children." Bob, a twenty-six year old black sailor of the same colony was "lately brought from Hartford county in North Carolina where he has been harboured for three years by one Van Pelt." He "has got a wife there" reported the planter. A black fugitive named Violet, of Perth Amboy, New Jersey, reported missing in 1771, had escaped in 1762, and was recaptured in 1764 in Fredericktown, Maryland and placed in jail. She escaped in May of 1771, to where it was noted "she has three children."[310]

When the planter did acknowledge that the black went away because of the sale of a family member he reported it matter of factly in his fugitive advertisement. Cuffee "now runaway, occasion'd by his wife and chil'd being sold [from him] the property of Catherine Cattrell," reported printer Peter Timothy. Tom, a twenty-three year old mulatto from Virginia supposedly fled to "South Carolina, as his wife was sold to a gentleman there a few months ago; and my refusing to sell him is the only occasion of running away" reported the planter.[311]

Statistically it is impossible to know how many fugitive men or women made off because of forced family breakups, mainly because the advertisements rarely mentioned the reason for an escape. Of the thirteen fugitive notices in the Virginia gazettes describing separated slave unions, none specifically said that family breakup

[309]*South Carolina Gazette*, March 24, 1746, March 4, 1751; *Virginia Gazette* (Parks), September 5, 1745.

[310]*Virginia Gazette* (Purdie, Dixon), January 1, 1766, May 2, 1766, April 16, 1767.

[311]*South Carolina Gazette*, March 13, 1749, *Virginia Gazette* (Purdie), August 21, 1778.

was the primary cause for flight. The planter was interested in the whereabouts of the slave, not in the reasons behind the escape. In 1746, Harry, of Jamestown, Virginia, who formerly lived in Richmond County, had escaped. The planter thought that this black man had "gone to Richmond County, where he has a Wife." The reason for flight? "As he runaway without any Cause, I desire he be punish'd by Whipping, as the Law directs." By permitting the black to visit his wife, the planter could keep the slave union alive, but it could also tempt a slave to escape. Harry's trek to Richmond County amounted to a distance of some 125 miles. Why would the planter expend so much energy in apprehending a fugitive?[312]

It appears that the planter regarded the sales or breakup of families as a matter of business which brooked no sentiment. Charles Ball, the noted fugitive from Maryland, remembered that in 1785, at an early age, his mother's master died. Because the dead man had outstanding debts, Ball's family was sold: "My mother had several children, my brothers and sisters, and we were all sold on the same day to different purchasers. Our new master took us away, and I never saw my mother, nor any of my brothers and sisters afterwards." Ball's mother did "entreat" the planter not to break up her family and begged to keep Charles but the slavedriver "gave her two or three heavy blows on the shoulders with his raw hide" and dragged her away.[313]

Because Daniel Jenifer Adams of Maryland owed George Washington money and desired to satisfy his debts, he turned over his properties to the General in 1775. These included a slave who, according to Adams, had "declar'd Several times that he will loose his life, or had rather Submit to Death then go to Virginia to leave his Wife & Children."[314] Despite Adams' appeals to General

---

[312]*Virginia Gazette* (Parks), March 20, 1746.

[313]Charles Ball, *Fifty Years in Chains* (New York, 1970), 16-17.

[314]Quoted in Jean Lee Butenhoff, "The Problem of Slave Community in the Eighteenth-Century Chesapeake," *William and Mary Quarterly*, 3rd Series, 43 (July 1986), 356-357; "Another Slave Auction at Wilmington, 1783," in *The North Carolina Experience:*

Washington, Lund Washington brought the slave to Mount Vernon.

The planter exercised his authority so capriciously, so irrationally, that he literally left the black or servant little choice but to attempt escape. In an article entitled "A Merciless Planter, and Two Generous Negroes," *The London Magazine* tried to show how the planter's shortsightedness could be disastrous. A Virginia planter with a "large Number of Slaves" had used them with the utmost Cruelty, whipping and torturing them for the slightest Faults." A slave named Arthur escaped, made it to the "Mountain Indians" only to be recaptured and was "immediately ordered to receive 300 Lashes stark naked which were to be given by his Fellow Slaves among whom happened to be a New Negro purchased by the Planter the Day Before." Arthur and the 'New Negro' had been close friends in Africa. In fact Arthur had saved his friend's life so it was understandable why the "New Negro" had "threw himself at the Planter's feet with Tears, beseeching him, in the most moving Manner, to spare his friend, or, at least suffer him the Punishment in his Room, protesting he would rather die ten thousand Deaths then lift his hand against him.

The planter threatened to lash the New Negro if he did not whip Arthur. He refused. The planter, then, ordered Arthur to whip his friend. He, too, refused to. Arthur "stabb'd the planter in the Heart and stabb'd himself as well." [315]

Why would a planter provoke Abraham Byfield, a thirty year old Irish Servant, who was a "SchoolMaster" for a "short time" by trying to "for his bad behavior turn him to plantation work?" Was he deliberately trying to humiliate him by arbitrarily changing his occupation? And there was one black fugitive who had "been used as waiting-man till about two years ago, but" the planter said "when, for his misdeeds in risling when aboard, I was obliged to

---

An Interpretive and Documentary History, Lindley S. Butler and Alan P. Watson, eds. (Chapel Hill, 1984), 204-205.

[315]*London Magazine*, 4 (Sept., 1945), 495-496.

turn him to labour."[316]

Why would a planter expect a captured black or servant to rest easily under his domination after having been at large for a decade? Hercules, age fifty, "6 feet tall, raw boned well made" had left Maryland and probably made his way to Chester County, Pennsylvania "having been brought home from thence 3 months ago, after an absence of 10 years." Why would a planter expect a fugitive who had gone off several times to stay put? Jackson of Maryland, age thirty, clad in irons, according to his owner had escaped forty-three times.[317]

For the planter who thought the fugitive had been "treated well" it probably was difficult to understand why a fugitive would escape. Three English servants of Cecil County, Maryland made off in 1766. "They all runaway last year, but not together, were brought home at considerable Expense and were forgiven on Promising of Amendment," reported a planter in his advertisement. "As they have gone off without the least Cause of Complaint, have lived extremely well, and have behaved with the greatest ingratitude, and it is hoped every Person will, as far as it lies in their Power, hinder their getting off," concluded the planter.[318]

The shrewd planter who understood the danger of discontent hammered out an agreement with the black or white servant promising that he would cut down maltreatment if the laborer would work hard and not malinger, stage work slowdowns, engage in sabotage or arson, commit suicide, escape, or, worst of all, plot insurrection. In 1773, wealthy planter Henry Laurens, who blamed the escape of his nine slaves on overseer maltreatment, tried to solve the problem by offering to reduce the blacks' workload because he believed that "those poor creatures look up to their Master as their Father, their Guardian, a Protector and whom

---

[316]Baltimore, *Maryland Journal and Baltimore Advertiser,* September 1, 1771, January 19, 1790.

[317]*Maryland Gazette,* August 20, 1761; Baltimore, *Maryland Journal and Baltimore Advertiser,* July 21, 1788.

[318]*Maryland Gazette,* May 8, 1766.

there is a reciprocal obligation upon the Master."[319]

The planter who saw himself as a father or protector and the planter who worked out individual agreements with blacks to increase productivity probably also had difficulty in understanding why the black escaped. Isaac, "a stout well looking fellow" from North Carolina, was a blacksmith and "pretty apt at the burners," but he was "a noted runaway and is light branded on each cheek A." His owner, who trusted him enough to let him work alone in the blacksmith shop, claimed that Isaac's "situation in his servile state, could not have been more comfortable than it had been in the point of diet, lodgings and clothing."[320] The owner wanted him back dead or alive.

James Habersham, governor of Georgia, owner of some five hundred slaves, and a slavetrader, appears to someone who might have understood why blacks escaped. He wrote to merchant William Knox in England in 1772 of the "dreadful shreiks" of a boy slave who had been bitten by a rabid dog and that the slave's suffering made it difficult to "hold up my Head." But when a fugitive slave named Daniel, a minister, had been asked to preach to blacks as well as whites in Charlestown and remarked that "God would send Deliverance to the Negroes, from the power of their masters as he freed the children of Israel from Egyptian Bondage," Habersham called it "wrong, and he thereby shewed his Ignorance and Folly."[321]

If the fugitive was scheduled to be executed, the planter cared even less about the reason for the escape. Sam, a "mulatto man slave," escaped from the *Sloop Tryal* in Rappahannock River, Virginia in 1771 and the planter said: "His Thefts were certainly the Cause of his Flight, to avoid the Gallows; for he was never punished whilst with me, nor ever complained, neither had he any Cause to be dissatisfied at his Treatment." What planter cared about a reason for flight if the fugitive stabbed his overseer.

---

[319]Rogers, *Papers of Laurens*, VIII: 527.

[320]New Bern, *North Carolina Gazette*, February 25, 1767.

[321]"The Letters of Hon. James Habersham," *Collections of the Georgia Historical Society*, VI: 243-244.

Burton, who was also from Virginia, was "taken up some Time ago, and made his Escape by cutting his Overseer in several Places with a knife."[322]

However, by not paying close attention to the cause of flight, by not listening to the slight murmur of dissatisfaction, the planter often unwittingly fanned the flames of discontent. In June of 1741, John Garnier of South Carolina published a fugitive advertisement describing two black men, Boatswain and Scipo, who were "very well known in Charlestown." For two months neither Garnier nor the *South Carolina Gazette* mentioned the fugitives' whereabouts. But in August of that year the authorities had captured Boatswain as well as a black woman named Kate and accused them both of trying to burn down Charlestown. Threatened with death, Kate had fingered Boatswain as her accomplice. The authorities pardoned Kate; they burned Boatswain alive, but not before he blurted out that he "looked upon every White Man he should meet as his declared Enemy." The *South Carolina Gazette* criticized Boatswain's "sottish wicked Heart."[323]

The fugitive who killed a planter often received colony-wide attention, but the reason for the slaying rarely came to light. Merchant Charles Purrey had been found stabbed to death in July 1754 in Port Royal, South Carolina. The authorities hanged two brothers and their sister for the slaying. One brother admitted that "he and 8 other Negroes were to have been concerned in the murder of two other Gentlemen at Beaufort" on the night after Purrey's death. These blacks "were to have taken over a schooner in the Harbor belonging to Mr. Smith" and make "their way for St. Augustine."[324]

In 1768, the *South Carolina Gazette* reported the capture of a famous black fugitive: "We hear that the most desperate villain the Negro Cain, who attacked and dangerously wounded his master, Mr. Issac McPherson, and several of his family in the year 1764 and made his escape has been lately taken in the woods by the

---

[322]*Virginia Gazette* (Purdie, Dixon), March 7, April 15, 1771.

[323]*South Carolina Gazette*, June 25, 1741, August 15, 1742.

[324]Ibid., July 25, 1754.

Cherokee Indians and delivered up to Matthew Keough." The gazette did not mention why Cain attacked his owner.[325]

To draw attention to his plight, one servant from Maryland "went into his Master's House with Ax in his Hand, determin'd to kill his Mistress, but changing his Purpose in seeing, as he express it, how'd innocent she look'd, he had his left-hand on a Block, cut it off, and threw it at her, now make me work if you can." After being at large begging and telling the public he lost his hand in an accident, a servant, according to a *Pennsylvania Gazette* editor, had "in a fit of Laziness cut off his Hand in Baltimore County, to incapacitate him from Working, was lately found dead on the Road; near Susquehanna, it having mortifi'd, and he perish'd for Nobody would give him any Relief."[326]

The fugitive, particularly the black, had a number of reasons for escaping, even if the planter did not openly acknowledge it. Examples abound in the fugitive notices of blacks and sometimes servants who had been whipped about the face, the neck, the chest, and the legs, whipped so severely that it left deep lacerations. Quamay of Virginia had "two Lumps on his left shoulder Blade, occasioned by a whip and one on his right shoulder." Sarah Davis, a white servant, had "many scars on her Back occasioned by severe whippings from her former master." One planter described a black named Harry as having "his back much furrow'd by whippings." In the planter's eyes these forms of maltreatment were nothing more than "marks" of punishment. George, a black, "had several marks of punishment on his back" according to a South Carolina advertisement.[327]

Edward Kimber, an English writer, visited America in 1745 and 1746. In Maryland he saw a slave beaten for so long with a "Cowskin" and "large Cane" that the black remained without sense and motion. The slave lived but remained a "Spectacle of Horror to his Death." One overseer said, while lashing a black woman,

---

[325]Ibid., January 18, 1768.

[326]*Pennsylvania Gazette*, May 9, November 7, 1751.

[327]*Virginia Gazette* (Purdie, Dixon), July 22, 1773; *Pennsylvania Gazette*, May 4, 1757; *Maryland Gazette*, June 6, 1765.

"G-d d-mn you, when you go to Hell, I wish G-d would d-mn me, that I might follow you with the Cowskin there."[328]

To the planter, whipping might have been a form of "correction," but to the blacks it was a combination of torture and humiliation. Moses Grandy remembered black men trying to help their wives in the field in order to shield them from the whip. But Grandy declared: "with his hardest labor, he often cannot save her from being flogged, and he is obliged to stand and see it; he is liable to see her taken home at night, stripped naked, and whipped before all the men." Women who had "recently gave birth and their breast were fulled with milk" could not always keep up. Grandy had seen the overseer "beat them with rawhide, so that blood and milk flew mingled from their breasts."[329]

Moses Grandy remembered pregnant women "large in the family way" being "flogged with the whip, or beat with the paddle which has holes in it, at every hole comes a blister. One of my sisters was so severely punished in this way, that labor was brought on, and the child was born in the field. This very overseer Mr. Brooks killed in this manner a girl named Mary; her father and mother were in the field at the time."[330]

Could anyone blame the fugitive for absconding or for stabbing, poisoning, or shooting the planter? Is it any wonder that the scowling fugitive arsonist Boatswain looked upon "every white man he should meet as his declared Enemy." One planter in South Carolina admitted as much. Planter William Roberts reported in his advertisement that "one of his outhouses was broken open and one of his Negro wenches named Tena, was carried off by a Negro

---

[328]"Eighteenth Century Maryland as Portrayed in the Itinerant Observations of Edward Kimber," *Maryland Historical Magazine*, 51 (1956), 328-329. See *London Magazine*, 14 (1745), 395-396, 549-552, 602-604, 40 (1746), 125-128, 248, 321-330, 572-573, 620-624; "Observations in Several Voyages and Travels in America," *William and Mary College Historical Magazine*, 1st Series, 15 (1907), 143-159, 215-225.

[329]Grandy, *Narrative of the Life of Moses Grandy*, 17-18.

[330]Ibid.

named Toby." Tena was captured, and although Toby remained at large, he later "came around to this Place on Thursday with intention (from exceeding good grounds) to take away the life of the Subscriber." Robert's fugitive advertisement was silent about the reason for Toby's anger, but one cannot discount the question of sexual abuse as a reason for flight.[331]

No planter could be expected to admit in his fugitive advertisement that he sexually abused a servant or slave or that a fugitive had fled because she refused or no longer wanted to have an affair with him. The Maryland court records show that the female servant had good reasons to abscond. In June of 1658 Arthur Turner of Maryland refused his servant Lucie Stratton, "her corne and clothes," and Lucie took him to court. At Charles County Court, Stratton's witness, Mr. Christopher Russel, swore that Turner came to his house, stayed the night, and before he left asked him "whether you can instruct me with the law" for "Turner had a child layed to his charge." Russel said this happened before any law had provided for such cases, and therefore according to usual custom, "the woman's oath would stand good against him." Finally Turner blurted out, "he could have her [Lucie Stratton] as well as ever he did his own wife, and that it was by her faithful promise to be his wife that made him act what he did." Russel and Turner rode to Lucie's house the next morning where Russel heard Turner ask Lucie to be his wife. She refused and accused Turner of being "a very lustful man." Turner demanded of her, "who was the most lustful shee or hee seeing thou camest to the bed when I was in bed and put thy hand under the cloathes and took me by the private parts." The court found Turner guilty of having illicit relations with Lucie Stratton and of fathering her baby.[332]

"Clapped up in jail" in June of 1663, was Master Jacob Lumbroso, a doctor accused of having gotten his maid, Elizabeth Wild, pregnant. He denied it, but witnesses swore he had forced the maid "to take a physic which caused a thing to come from her in the chamber pot which the doctor, her master, threw it out of doors." The jury found him guilty. Not satisfied with Elizabeth,

---

[331]*South Carolina County Journal*, July 18, 1775.

[332]*Arch. Md.*, LIII: 28-29, 528; XLI: 291-294.

Lumbroso moved on to his neighbor's wife, also indentured to him. John Gould, the servant's husband, told the court that Lumbroso asked his consent to "ly with my wife" in exchange for half of Lumbroso's "boat land and hogs and all that he had." Gould's wife said Lumbroso asked her "to be his whoore," threw her into the bed and embraced her. Had Lumbroso "any shame" asked Margaret Gould and "hee sayd to mee that hee did not and that he would show me scripture for it."[333]

The courts at least made an attempt to protect the unwilling white servant women; the black woman had either to rely on her wits or the black community or even another planter to ward off sexual abuse. She could not cry rape. How can property be raped? Bolzius, in 1742, had traveled to Charlestown, South Carolina and he reported that the "Europeans commit dreadful excesses with the Negro girls, as a result of which one sees many half-white children running around." Ebenezer Hazard, postal surveyor, had been in South Carolina in 1778 and he noted that the "number of Mulattos in the four southernmost states is a clear proof of a viciated taste in their inhabitants."[334]

Shortly after the Revolutionary War, George Washington had a number of distinguished guests over to his house at Mount Vernon for a gathering. One of the company was Frederick Wilhelm Baron Von Steuben, the Prussian army veteran, who was instrumental in whipping the American army into a disciplined body. Steuben brought along William North, his restless aide who said, 'Would you believe it. I have not humped a single mulatto since I been here.' In 1765 the *Georgia Gazette* reported that an overseer "infected every Negro wench on the plantation with a foul

---

[333]Ibid., LVIII: 550-557.

[334]George Fennick Jones, ed., "John Martin Bolzius' Trip to Charlestown, October 1742," *South Carolina Historical Magazine*, 82 (April 1981), 101; H. Roy Merrens, ed., "A View of Coastal South Carolina in 1778: The Journal of Ebenezer Hazard," *South Carolina Historical Magazine*, 73 (October 1972), 190.

inveterate and highly virulent disease."³³⁵ The abuse of women, whether prevalent or not, undoubtedly helped shape the attitudes of both the slave and the servant towards escape.

Sexual abuse and the black male's sexuality cannot be separated from the fugitive's reason for flight. Reverend Bolzius had seen the blacks "go naked except that men covered their shame with a cloth rag which hangs around a strap tied around the body." Hazard said: "The Virginians even in the city, do not pay proper attention to Decency in The Appearance of their Negroes: I have seen Boys of 10 & 12 Years of Age going through the Streets quite naked, & others with only Part of a Shirt hanging Part of the Way down their Backs. This is so common a sight that even the Ladies do not appear shocked at it."³³⁶

Should the women have been shocked? Lieutenant William Feitman of the First Pennsylvania Regiment had eaten at the Virginia dinner tables: "I am surprised this does not hurt the feelings of the fair Sex to see young boys of about Fourteen and Fifteen years old to Attend them. These whole nakedness Expos'd and I can Assure you it would Surprise a person to see these d_ __d black boys how well they are hung."³³⁷

Black teenagers busily astir, bustling through the dinner tables with their penises peeking through their undershirts; black men, sweating with their bodies covered by cloth only; and black women, working by their men wearing petticoats with their breasts bare, and black children running naked – all these show a society shot through with black sexuality, sexuality that could be contained by the symbolic act of castration. In 1757, "Jack, between 35 and 40 years of age, formerly belonging to Mr. John Brailsford," escaped

---

³³⁵Quoted in James T. Flexner, *George Washington and the New Nation*, 1783-1793 (Boston, Toronto, 1969-1970) 29; Savannah, *Georgia Gazette*, July 26, 1765.

³³⁶"Martin Bolzius Questionnaire," Loewald, Stariks, and Taylor, eds., 219-247; Fred Shelley, ed., "The Journal of Ebenezer Hazard in Virginia, 1777, *Virginia Magazine of History and Biography*, 62 (October 1954), 410.

³³⁷Quoted in Jordan, *White Over Black*, 159.

from his master in South Carolina who said that the Angolan fugitive "may be easily known upon close examination being castrated." "A Negro fellow," reported a jailer in Charlestown, "who calls himself Titus was born in Jamaica, said his master's name is Joseph Dobbins and lives at Round O, and that his master castrated him and another, but the other dying he ran away, he has on his neck an iron collar with his master's name on it and also an iron on each leg."[338] Statutory law ordering castration of the incorrigible fugitive had been on the books for almost a century in Virginia and South Carolina. But no fugitive white male servant, however incorrigible, would expect his testicles to be chopped off.

The fugitive had legitimate grievances; but what could the lone fugitive do to free his fellow laborers? Save for a war or general upheaval, fugitive flight was basically an individual act of resistance which paled beside the act of wholesale flight. During times of upheaval, times of restlessness, the black or the servant who would not ordinarily have dared to venture outside the plantation found himself on the run. At such times, the system which operated to deter flight was thrown in disarray. The informer, the captor, the gaoler, the sheriff, the patrol, the militia, even the planter himself, had other calls on his attention. Under these extraordinary circumstances, the number of fugitives increased immeasurably.

---

[338]*South Carolina Gazette*, April 14, 1757; *South Carolina Country Journal*, February 17, 1768.

CHAPTER VI
THE HARBORER

Fugitives generally escaped singly, and exhibited what Peter Wood calls a "singular act of self assertion." But without the harborers who provided the food, clothing and shelter, who filed off the chains, wrote the passes, and forged the indentures, who supplied the canoes, boats, and horses, who offered employment and who gave support and encouragement, fewer fugitives would have escaped. To go off alone hoping to live off the land was difficult. "George was for ten years a noted runaway, always in the woods and mostly naked, and now he has left that trade he is grown a sickly fellow," wrote Landon Carter. One jailer in South Carolina in 1765 reported the capture of Caesar, an "elderly Negro fellow of Angola country" who had "been in the woods these two years" and was "and is all in rags except a blue indigo cloth about his middle."[339]

By camping in the woods, swamps, caves or mountains, a fugitive risked getting lost, contracting frostbite or being struck by lightning. "A new Negro girl about 13 or 14 years of age," reported one planter of South Carolina, "was sent on shore at Hobacow out of the ship Elizabeth, Capt. McNeil, to Capt. Clement's *Lamprier* from whence she had either lost herself in the woods, or is taken away and harboured by some person or persons." In February 1739, a South Carolina captor reported that an Angolan fugitive woman's "Feet are very much frost bitten and for that Reason can't be sent to Goal." A North Carolina planter said that Frank had "by running away before, lost two of the little toes of his left foot, and part of the third one."[340] In January 1771, a South Carolina planter captured two Guineans, Pompey and Sambo "who spoke very little English." "By what I can learn" wrote the planter, "from a Guiney Fellow of mine, they have been run away ever since the Spring before last. They are entirely naked, and their

---

[339]Wood, *Black Majority*, 239; Carter, *Diary* I: 218; *South Carolina Gazette*, March 9, 1765.

[340]*South Carolina Gazette*, August 3, 1765, February 15, 1739; Fayetteville, *North Carolina Chronicle*, November 1, 1790.

Feet and Legs are swelled very much by lying in the Cold, on which Account I thought it would not be prudent to send them to the WorkHouse." A year later the *South Carolina Gazette* reported, "two runaway Negroes belonging to Mr. William Bampfield Sheltered themselves under a Tree during a thunderstorm and one was instantly struck dead with lightning and the other terribly scorched and hurt."[341]

Without help, a pregnant fugitive could not live in the woods for long. On June 3, 1741, a "Negro fellow" in South Carolina captured a "big belly'd runaway Negro woman" and placed her in jail. On August 5, the black woman "brought to Bed a Negro Girl in the Workhouse." Without help, disabled fugitives faced early capture. One white servant of Pennsylvania made off though he "walks as if he was blind." Caesar, a black cook from New England, had "both his legs cut off and walks on his knees." The jailer in Charlestown said "one old new Negro is deaf."[342] The sick, the mentally disabled, and the wounded needed help. On May 30, 1742, Ruth Wilcook, a Welsh white servant of South Carolina absconded and three weeks later a planter said she was "found on the Road near my Plantation, very ill of a Fever and has been taken Care of ever since." One jailer said Prince, a Guinean, "seems to be foolish." In his fugitive advertisement, Provost Marshal Rawlin Lowdnes said Mark and Luke, two Africans, had been shot: "One of them has a wound not quite well on one of his temples, and another occasioned by a shot on one of his buttocks," Marie, a seventeen year old Guinean woman who had "been very much whipt across the breast" and who had "an iron around her neck with three prongs to it, and a padlock" needed

---

[341]*South Carolina Country Journal*, January 1, 1771, June 16, 1772.

[342]*South Carolina Gazette*, June 7, August 5, 1741, August 23, 1771; *Pennsylvania Gazette*, July 18, 1754, October 28, 1759; *Boston Weekly News-Letter*, August 24, 1767.

assistance.[343]

Chained with irons, fugitives could not get far. One South Carolina planter said Abraham, a black, "had a Large clog or iron which had just [been] put on, in order to prevent him from escaping." How did the fugitives solve this problem? A twenty-six year old black named James had an "Iron Boot on his right Leg" but as he has "taken two Files with him may perhaps get it off." Prince, who was "under sentence of death did break and get off his irons and make his escape." But Will, a black fisherman, might have gotten his irons off "with the help of a blacksmith" who was probably a harborer.[344]

The harborer might shelter the helpless, but the planter himself despised the harborer. "Pests to Society," was how Brian Cape characterized the harborer or the "Stock of Relations" who "secreted" his slave named Betty in 1772 in South Carolina.[345] Malicious, evil minded, and villainous were other names used in the fugitive notices, but this never stopped the harborer.

The Virginia Assembly made the first official attempt in America to deter the giving of refuge. In March of 1642, the Assembly criticized "divers persons who entertained and enter into covenant with runaway servants and freeman who have formerly hired themselves to others to the great prejudice if not utter undoing of divers poor men, thereby also encouraging servants to run from their masters and obscure themselves in some remote plantation." The lawmaker forced the harborer to pay twenty pounds of tobacco for each night he sheltered the fugitive, but this appeared to be ineffective because the Acts of 1655, 1657, and 1666 pushed the fines to a high of sixty pounds before bottoming

---

[343]*South Carolina Gazette*, June 1, 28, 1742, July 5, 1782, July 6, 1765; *South Carolina Country Journal*, January 16, 1772, June 23, 1772.

[344]*South Carolina Gazette*, December 6, 1776; *South Carolina Country Journal*, June 10, 1766, July 14, 1767, March 21, 1769, November 13, 1770.

[345]*South Carolina Gazette*, April 2, 1772.

out at thirty pounds of tobacco a day, or a day's pay.[346]

The Virginia Assembly sought compensation for the lost labor costs; the Assembly in Maryland, in May of 1676, prescribing a fine of "five hundred pounds of Tobacco for every night or four & twenty hours that such person or persons shall give such Entertainment to such servant or servants" for the first harboring offense, tried to bankrupt the harborer. No wonder servant William Jackman of Maryland testified in Kent Count court in 1676 that his harborer, Ellis Humphrey, warned him, "If ever I did disclose it I should undoe him." Jackman had disclosed that Humphrey had "tould me he would give me one hundred pounds of Tobbi & he would sett me in the ready roade for way for New-york." Ten days of fugitive labor cost Humphrey 1,500 pounds of tobacco plus court expenses. By 1671, the Assembly had reduced the standard 1,500 pound tobacco fine to 500 pounds a night in Maryland. South Carolina, in 1737, had fined harborers twenty shillings a day; North Carolina, in 1741, had meted our forty shilling fines for each harboring offense. In the North the harboring fines for servants were lower. Pennsylvania imposed fines of twenty shillings a day. In New Jersey the fine was one dollar a day.[347]

For harboring blacks, the penalties were stiffer. In 1723, the Virginia Assembly slapped a fifteen shilling, or a one hundred and fifty pound tobacco fine on any white person, free Negro, Mulatto, or Indian harborer; failure to pay could result in twenty lashes, "well laid on." Maryland prescribed a five hundred pound tobacco fine for the black harborer in 1715. The Georgia white harborers, in 1770, paid "thirty shillings for the first day, and three shillings for every day such slave shall have been absent from his or her owner or employer." The free Negro, Mulatto, and Mustizoe could

---

[346]Hening, *Virginia Statues*, I: 253, 401, 440, II: 239.

[347]*Arch. Md.*, II: 524, LIV: 350-351; *South Carolina Gazette*, February 5, 1737; Clark, ed., *State Records, N.C.*, 194; *Laws of the Common Wealth of Pennsylvania* (Phil., 1810), I: 10; James T. Mitchell and Flanders, *The Statutes at Large of Pennsylvania from 1682-1801*, 79; *Laws of the State of New Jersey* (Trenton, 1821), 367-368.

receive "corporeal punishment, not extending to life or limb."[348]

South Carolina's harboring penalties, the harshest of all the colonies, prescribed forty lashes for the black harborer in 1712 and slapped a ten pound fine on the free black harborer for the first offense. If the free black lacked the money, he could be sold; the monies collected paid the fine. The harborer in that colony paid a five pound penalty to the informer for each day he employed a slave "without ticket from the owner of such a slave," or he had to turn over "the whole earning of a runaway slave" to the informer.[349]

The planter in South Carolina determined the amount received by the informer, although between 1732 and 1750, there was a standard statutory reward of five pounds. After 1750, the planter's fugitive advertisement listed rewards of anywhere from fifty to one hundred pounds for information that could convict the harborer; the black informer received less. The white informer's reward, greater than the captor's, averaged anywhere from five to ten pounds. In 1762, a planter describing a twenty-eight year old black woman named Mary offered "fifty pounds reward to any white person that will inform against any white person that may conceal or employ her, and thirty pounds to any Negro that will inform of her being concealed by any free Negro."[350]

The Northern colonies, too, prescribed harsher penalties for the black harborers. A convicted harborer in Rhode Island in 1703 paid four shillings a day and by 1750 that rose to fifty pounds or imprisonment. The free black harborer could also lose his house. Connecticut prescribed a twenty shilling fine; New Hampshire imposed the same fine and the slave received ten lashes.[351]

In South Carolina and Georgia the lawmakers saw harboring as a staging ground for insurrection. Patrols in the South searched "Negro houses" for clothes and "stolen" goods, guns and

---

[348]Hening, *Virginia Statutes*, IV: 29, 128-129; Candler, *Col. Recs. of Ga.*, XIX: 234.

[349]Cooper and McCord, eds., *Statutes S.C.*, VII: 402-405.

[350]*South Carolina Gazette*, February 20, 1762.

[351]Greene, *The Negro in Colonial New England*, 136-137.

ammunition and broke up "unlawful assemblies." South Carolina, in 1690, 1712, and 1740, passed laws giving army patrols the right to search "Negro houses." In Georgia in 1770, any slave caught in an "illegal meeting under pretense of feasting" could get up to twenty-five lashes.[352] The Commons House of Assembly empowered justices and constables to "search all suspected places for arms, ammunition or stolen goods, and to apprehend all such slaves as they shall suspect to be guilty of any crimes or offences whatsoever and to bring them to speedy trial."

The illegal relationship between the fugitive and the harborer was fragile. The timorous harborer, frightened by an irate owner, could jeopardize the fugitive's freedom. Henry Laurens wrote merchant Joseph Brown, a slave trader, on June 28, 1765, stating that a black fugitive named Sampson had been living in South Carolina "about 14 Months ago" before an overseer's maltreatment forced him to escape from Mepkin plantation. Sampson "fell in with a poor worthless fellow who entertained him near 8 Months. At length fearing an information from some of the neighborhood who had seen the Negroe working for him, he made a merit of his knavery & sends Sampson down to me." Sampson escaped again and returned to the harborer and Laurens said that the "knave who first harbour'd him heard that I was collecting evidence to found a prosecution against him for his first act, & therefore sent or caused him to be sent immediately to my plantation." Jack, a black fugitive from Chester, Pennsylvania, well known about that city, had gone to court in 1771 in quest of freedom "but being disappointed by his expectations he was sent home." He absconded. A white man named James Rigbe offered him a job in Maryland. Seven months later Rigbe, "finding he could no longer keep him again, without being put to trouble, or his ungenerous actions appearing in the public, he delivered him [Jack] up to his master."[353]

White men betrayed Jack and Sampson; a black man turned in Lydy. Landon Carter's diary entry of July 30, 1771 recorded that

---

[352]Cooper and McCord, *Statutes S.C.*, VIII: 353; Candler, *Col. Recs. of Ga.*, XIX: 216, 234.

[353]Rogers, IV: 645, *Pennsylvania Gazette*, September 5, 1771.

"It seems the Wench Lydy has been runaway for many days; and at last Mr. George at the Fork has been discovered to have had her in keeping in his room the whole time, for some days last week, and this morning as he found the wench was overheard in his room he brought her up pretending he had just catched her. An Old Son of a Bitch indeed."[354]

Harborers worried about the fugitive's exposing them, particularly the servant whose testimony carried weight in the courts. In 1657, servant Peter Underwood of Maryland confessed that he and another servant had been hidden by Abraham Holman and that "from time to time we desired to Come home to our masters; but the Said Holman neglected us therein and at all times when any Strangers Came to the house, the said Holman would hide us out of the way and not let of us be seen."[355]

Harborers also had to worry about the informer or the bounty hunter who apparently checked to see whether the harborer owned the fugitive, whether the fugitive had been hired out, or if he had a legitimate pass which allowed him to be out. A jailer in South Carolina reported the capture of a twenty year old Guinean woman named Nancy: "She had been in the possession of an old Negro who call himself *Free Peter*, 2 or 3 years, and pretends to own her as his property, but cannot show any title to her, and by all circumstances, it appears she is a runaway, and some other person property."[356]

Bounty hunters were often cautious. One planter gave an assurance in his fugitive advertisement "that no Persons may be afraid to take him, thinking the Property in Dispute" because "by examining the Records of the Court may be satisfied that I received £350 besides Costs of Suit for his being harbored before." If unmasked, informers risked attack; they had to be protected. "The informer's name will be kept secret if desired," promised one planter in his South Carolina fugitive advertisement. Another planter of the same colony promised the captor a thirty pound

---

[354]Carter, *Diary*, II: 601.

[355]*Arch. Md.*, X: 523-524.

[356]*South Carolina Country Journal*, July 27, 1773.

reward for Joe and the "same sum for discovery where he is harbored, if taken, and the person's name kept secret if desired."[357]

South Carolina planters seemed to be concerned enough about harborers to offer rewards for their conviction and to attack them in their fugitive advertisements. The Virginia, Maryland and North Carolina fugitive advertisements mentioned the harborer, now and then, but they appeared not to express alarm. Pennsylvania never highlighted the harborer role; indeed it was never even mentioned in the advertisements.

Who were these harborers and why did they risk stiff fines and even the loss of their freedom? The fugitive advertisement rarely named the harborer, only alluded to him. Therefore, it is difficult to pinpoint the harborer's identity and to reduce it to a statistic. January, according to one fugitive advertisement, was "supposed to either be harboured about Charlestown, where he has a sister and many acquaintances or at PonPon where he has a mother at the Rev. Mr. Baron's; or may be employed and concealed by some vile white person; he may deceive persons by saying he is free, or that he belongs to somebody else, or may be decoyed to the back settlements." The *South Carolina Gazette* owner Peter Timothy offered four dollars for the capture of Amy in June of 1766, after the black woman had been gone for three months. Was she "mending stockings at the Browns?" Was she with her "mother at the house of William Scott?" Was she with her "many acquaintances about town as well as some in the country"? Was she "in or near the town" of Charlestown? Before she absconded, Amy had been harbored "by free Negroes?" She had been at Doctor Oliphant's, Charles Biloct's, John Drayton's and Thomas Loughton Smith's kitchen. "No levity," wrote Timothy, "will be shown to whoever (white or black) shall be discovered to have harbored or employed her as I am determined to carry on the most severe prosecution against every one."[358]

The planters probably constituted the main group of harborers for they basically owned the food, clothes and shelter, and the means to turn harboring into a money-making venture. The owners

---

[357]*South Carolina Gazette*, June 2, 1766.

[358]*South Carolina Gazette*, November 14, 1761, June 2, 1766.

of fugitives in South Carolina made several complaints about other planters, especially backcountry planters who captured their fugitives and put them to work. In South Carolina the backcountry stood sixty miles beyond the coastal region and yet if a colonist hoped to make money by using slave labor to work the rice and indigo plantations, or if he chose to enter politics, practice law, or if he liked to dance, go to the horseraces or even to the library, the coastal region, especially Charlestown, not the back country, was the place to be. By the late 1760's, the backcountry area contained about thirty-five thousand or 75% of the white population in South Carolina. These colonists owned few slaves and owned small parcels of land, but as the backcountry planter began to grow tobacco and indigo, the demand for slaves rose in the 1760's. Where would they obtain the cheap labor?[359]

James Parsons published advertisements describing six fugitives in January 24, 1763. He concluded that "as it has lately become a pernicious custom for back-settlers when they meet with run away Negroes, and for some of the magistrates and others in the back parts of the country when such Negroes are brought to them to publish purposely blind advertisements for a short time of them, and afterwards keep them at work for themselves, instead of bringing or sending them according to the law, to the warden of the workhouse who would properly and for a proper time, advertise and describe them, and in whose possession losers would have an opportunity of suing and finding them."[360] Planters accused the backsettlers of enticing and then harboring their blacks in order to sell them. In South Carolina in 1763, Cyrus, a "Negro boy," made off and his owner offered a fifty pound reward for information concerning the fugitive "being harbored or entertained by a white person" and alluded to the "vile practice of encouraging Negroes to run away so that they may buy cheap." One slaveowner said his "Negroes are carried off by some Villains, about the said kitchen and harbored or disposed of in the backcountry of

---

[359]Rachel N. Klein, "Ordering the Backcountry: The South Carolina Regulation," *The William and Mary Quarterly*, 3rd Series, 38 (October 1981), 661-663.

[360]Ibid., October 24, 1761, January 29, 1763.

Georgia." The detection of the planters who harbored fugitives was difficult because their identities were rarely noted. One jailer reported the detention of a thirty-four year old African man "taken from one John Reynes, a notorious villain, which the justice imagines he stole from the lower settlements as he absented himself in being detected with the said Negroe and being out of this province."[361] How widespread this practice was is difficult to tell because only a few planters complained about it and the authorities did not keep an official count.

Several different ethnic groups harbored servants. A carpenter and a sadler, were "supposed to be going to the Congarees, or some Swiss Settlements." One Welsh servant of South Carolina made off in 1743 and the owner wrote: "It's imagined he is gone up the Path toward the Welsh settlement." One Dutch servant in 1753, "is presumed to be with a child and harbored by some of her country people in town." Elizabeth Ash, age seventeen, born in Ireland, was "supposed to be gone toward the Irish settlements in the back county." In Virginia, one planter took notice of the Irish harborer. John Lee, an Irishman, sped away by horse in 1737 and according to his master, Lee "was seized near the Ferry and it is suppose'd he was harbored by some of the Irish inhabitants in these parts and is since gone to New York." One owner in Pennsylvania predicted that "German servant John Christian, baker by trade, age 21, civil, well behaved fellow but adverse to servitude, and ready to embrace any scheme for obtaining liberty, expect to fix himself a place at some employment in a remote neighborhood of Germans in the state."[362]

How many fugitives found comfort with their countrymen or how many ethnic communities harbored servants cannot be determined from the surviving data in the fugitive notices. Whatever the case, neither the lawmaker in South Carolina, nor in Virginia and Pennsylvania enacted laws calling for military

---

[361]Ibid., September 10, 1763; *South Carolina Gazette Country Journal*, January 16, May 8, 1770.

[362]*South Carolina Gazette*, April 2, 1737, February 28, 1743, January 26, 1767, November 5, 1753; *Virginia Gazette*, March 3, 1737; *Pennsylvania Gazette*, November 2, 1772.

patrols to break into these harborer's homes to flush out the European fugitives. No angry editorials, and no indignant fugitive notices appeared in the local gazettes. While complaining about this practice, the authorities seem to wink at it.

Africans harbored their countrymen too. South Carolina was the one colony that took note of the practice. One planter described a fugitive, who happened to be an Angolan: "N.B. as there is abundance of Negroes in this Province of that Nation, he may chance to be harbour'd among some of them."[363] The planter mentioned nothing about the harboring activities of the Mandingos, Iboes, Guineans, or any other African nationalities.

Bermudians harbored their countrymen. In 1762, one planter suspected that his female black from Bermuda was harbored by her countrymen because "she has a large acquaintance amongst the Bermudian Negroes." Benabe and Caesar were "supposed to be harbored by some Jamaican Negroes in Charlestown."

Indians also harbored their countrymen. One advertisement on June 4, 1753 read: "A young Indian Fellow, about 20 years of age, who calls himself Jack, seems to understand something of the shoemaker's trade, pretends to come from the Catawba (which he calls his country) but can't speak a word of the language, and also pretends that he was never in the settlements; joined some Creek Indians about three years ago; and Smith's ferry is now in their nation and supposed to be a slave of some person at or near Pon Pon."[364]

Free blacks acted as harborers. One planter suspected that Dilch, "a tall black wench" in 1777 had been harbored, "by free Harry, among a pair of other free Negroes as she has been seen with them at different times at Mrs. Parker's plantation at Goose Creek." According to planter Anne Matthewes: "A Negro wench named Diana who took with her two children" had a "large acquaintance, particularly among the free Negroes, by some of whom she is supposed to be harboured." Slaves harbored fugitives, too. Kate's owner "suspected" that she was "secreted by a mulatto slave called Jenny (a Carpenter by Trade)" and it was "with the

---

[363]*South Carolina Gazette*, August 6, 1737.

[364]Ibid., June 4, 1753.

Assistance and contrivance of some other Slaves in the neighborhood where she was brought (who it seems she bragged) had promised to conceal her whenever she would runaway from me." Joe, "well known in Charlestown, was suppose to be harbored by some of Mr. Benjamin's Smith's Negroes" at his plantation.[365]

Relatives harbored each other. Some of South Carolina was "harbored by Jonathan Scott's Negroes where he had an aunt and several cousins." Mary of the same colony was "enticed away by her said mother, an Indian wench, named Sarah who lives at Thomas Fuller's Stono plantation, and where it is supposed that she is harboured and entertained by her said mother, or some other evil minded malicious person."[366]

Women harbored their male partners; men harbored their women. A North Carolina advertisement described a twenty-eight year old black named Jem, "a stout likely fellow" whose owner offered three pounds for him dead or alive. His owner said Jem "is supposed to be harboured or kept out by his Wife named Rachael." A Virginia advertisement described a black man who had been "seen frequently in Prince George and he is supported and concealed in that county by several Negro women whom he calls his "wives." According to another advertisement in that sale, a short thick yellowish wench had been "seen in company with Bilico, a fellow of Mr. Sanders', and is supposed harboured by him."[367]

Friends offered solace to a white butcher named George Allen of Maryland. "As he has some Friends in Philadelphia, it is likely he will endeavor to get to that Place," reported Allen's owner. Prostitutes harbored a black male "well known in Charlestown." He

---

[365]*South Carolina Gazette*, September 25, 1777; *South Carolina Gazette*, July 5, 1761, November 4, 1756, October 29, 1763.

[366]*South Carolina Country Journal*, October 20, 1767, January 21, 1772.

[367]New Bern, *North Carolina Gazette*, October 6, 1775, December 17, 1777, September 18, 1778; *Virginia Gazette*, October 24, 1774.

was "intimate with an abundance of black prostitutes and a roguish fellow."[368]

White women, now and then, harbored black men. A Pennsylvania advertisement reported that Friday, a black male, age twenty-two, was "harbored by some base white woman as he has contracted several intimacies with several of that sort lately." A South Carolina advertisement described a "mulatto fellow, named Caesar" who escaped in 1765 and "passes for a freeman, by the name of Brightwell; he has been harboured at Goose-creek by a Dutch woman near Charles Fauchereaud's Esq.; where he is supposed to be harboured."[369]

Quakers also provided asylum for blacks. "My Negro fellow Job," claimed a planter, "was one of the Negroes emancipated by the Quakers. And it is more than probable they wish to secret him."[370]

Indians harbored blacks, too. One planter said that Jack "speaks the Creek language tolerably well," and as he "used to be employed by the Creek Nation is supposed to be gone toward Augusta by the Indian land." "A Run-Away Negro man who says his name is Caesar, speaks very little English, Guinea born, is now in the Possession of an Indian in the Cherokee Nation" reported a planter in South Carolina. Indians harbored both servants and blacks. In 1655, a Maryland bounty hunter had been hired to retake a servant and Indian who found solace among the Catawba Indians. But he claimed "they would not come home saying they had rather live with the Pagans than come home to be starved for want of food, clothing, and have their brains beaten out."[371]

The Creek Indians, whether they were Upper Creek or Lower Creek, whether they lived in Florida, Georgia, or South Carolina,

---

[368]*Maryland Gazette*, August 4, 1753; *South Carolina Gazette*, November 14, 1761.

[369]*Pennsylvania Gazette*, August 10, 1763; *South Carolina Gazette*, July 8, 1765.

[370]*State Gazette North Carolina*, January 5, 1797.

[371]*South Carolina Country Journal*, October 4, 1768, October 2, 1770; *Arch. Md.*, X: 484.

probably caused confusion in the slave community. For though
they harbored blacks, they also turned fugitives over to their
owners in order to uphold the treaty agreements of 1717 and 1763.
And from time to time, the Creeks used fugitive slaves to work
their fields. Captain John Stuart, the Superintendent of Indian
Affairs, hired an agent named David Taitt to live among the
Creeks in order to learn their customs and to persuade the Creeks
to turn over several fugitive blacks to their owners.[372]

Why did the harborer offer refuge to the fugitive? Was it to
show concern for the fugitive's welfare, or was it merely a business
arrangement? If the harborer was a planter or business, then
harboring might have been a pragmatic arrangement. Steven
Hartley of South Carolina offered twenty pounds in 1750 for the
recapture of a twenty-eight year old black woman named Kate and
her son named Billy. "She has been frequently seen," reported
Hartley, "in and about Charles-town where she has gone about
washing by the name of Delia, and is suspected to be encouraged
and concealed by some white people, who have received wages of
her and others who have a desire to purchase her." Seven years
late, Kate, who was seven months pregnant, escaped with her
thirteen year old son named Billy, and her five year old daughter
named Alice. Her owner said of Kate: "tis probable she will get
into some of the Negro washing houses or kitchens, to be
employ'd in them."[373]

Free blacks employed fugitive labor. A forty-five year old
Angolan woman named Flora "used to be hired out as a washer
but since she went away has gone about the country within ten
miles of Charlestown selling cakes and pretending to have
permission from me and sometimes hires herself to free

---

[372]Daniel F. Littlefield, Jr., *African and Creeks: From the
Colonial Period to the Civil War* (Westport, 1979), 1-23; Martha
Condray Searcy, "The Introduction of African Slavery into the
Creek Indian Nation," *George Historical Quarterly; Travels in the
American Colonies*, Newton D. Mereness, ed. (New York, 1916),
540-541.

[373]*South Carolina Gazette*, Mary 21, 1750, October 13, 1757.

Negroes."[374]

Whoever harbored the fugitive stood to make money, especially if the fugitive was a craftsman. Bristol was at large in South Carolina in 1763, and his owner offered fifty pounds for his capture. Bristol was "well known in the southern and middle parts of the province as a remarkable good wheelwright, and used to work out with a monthly ticket," but his owner said someone "harboured, entertained and employed the said fellow without a ticket, by which I have lost about £300.[375]

A freeman might wish to protect a fugitive from abuse. Marylander Sarah Tailer came to Kent County Court on October 1, 1659, and told the judge about the "divers wronges and abuses given her by her Master & Mrs. Captain Thomas Bradnox and Mary his wife." One sympathetic witness noted that "he never saw Capt. Bradnox or his wife strike Servant Sarah Tailer with either Bulls pite or Rope but he said the said Sarah have a blacke place crosse one of her shoulders." Commissioner John Wickes admitted that Mrs. Mary Bradnox had "Broake the peace in strikeinge her servant before him being a maiestrate, and on the time when the said servant was there to brake her Complaint which the said Wickes could not in justice passe by or suffer, which was the slow or stroke with a ropes ende." Bradnox accused John Deer of harboring Sarah Tailer and Deer admitted "he had her under the bedd." The court found Deer guilty and forced him to ask Captain Thomas Bradnox "Forgivenesse in open Court and Promise never to commit the Like againe, And to pay Cost of suyt to the plaintiff." Tailer herself had to fall "on her Knees and ask forgiveness and promise amendment for the future." During the same court proceeding Bradnox accused John Smith of harboring Tailer. Smith claimed he "found her in the woods and brought her home to his owne house, but beinge weary that Eveninge he could not transporte her that night, but did intend next morninge to convey his master or the Constable or else to some Maiestrate."[376]

---

[374]Ibid., May 16, 1761.

[375]Ibid., December 17, 1763.

[376]*Arch. Md.*, LIV: 167-168.

Peter Manigault, a lawyer, a Speaker of the Commons House in South Carolina, and a plantation manager, wrote Ralph Izard, a wealthy absentee owner in the colony, about a fugitive, a black woman, who complained of "ill Usage from the Overseer." The Speaker sent the woman home only to see her return a few days later "whipped in a Manner cruel beyond Discription though big with Child." This time he kept the black woman at one of his plantations, at least until she recovered, and fearing that the "Ill Usage might be repeated."[377]

Whoever the harborer might be or whatever the motive, the fugitives could not expect the harborer to come to them. The harborer, low key and working behind the scenes, avoiding the arm of the law or the owner's wrath, was basically a receiver. Rarely did the planter complain in his advertisements about the harborer openly rescuing the black or servant. Two fugitive advertisements did show two black fugitive men making their way to a plantation and rescuing their mates. York and Billy of South Carolina escaped in 1767. "York had been taken up," the owner reported, "since he went away at or near Dr. Farrar's plantation at Santee, but got away in bringing down, and return to my plantation at PonPon and took away with him his wife named Sarah, and by information is now harbored above the Congarees."[378]

A white man named Peter Gossigon of Virginia apparently rescued two black men, Jack and Jacob, in 1771. According to the planter, Gossigon as "formerly a Skipper from this Shore, but lately Served on Board a Man of War's Tender may have carried him to the Western Shore." "My Slaves inform me," reported the planter, "he has been endeavoring to persuade them to go with him and he will free them; that the said Fellow went off with him; that he requested them to advise him how to rob me, and even told them he would make away with me if they should be detected add to this, that on my detecting him in a Matter where he was about to defraud me, he vowed he was determined to have

---

[377]Maurice A Clouse, ed., "The Letterbook of Peter Manigault, 1763-1773," *South Carolina Historical Magazine*, 70 (1969), 181-182.

[378]*South Carolina Country Journal*, May 13, 1776.

Satisfaction."[379]

Stratton might have been trying to settle a personal score or perhaps the planter was overreacting. Either way, it shows that some harborers would go to any lengths to assist a fugitive. As a rule, the harborer did not advocate, make plans or physically attack the fugitive's owner or destroy his property. What good did it do for a harborer to kill a planter or burn down the planter's house and risk exposing himself to the white community's wrath, especially if he already had his freedom? And if the employer showed interest in the fugitive's labor, why risk losing the business?

If anybody attacked the planter, it would be the black or servant, not the harborer, which means that the harborer had his limitations in providing assistance to fugitives. One harborer might offer employment, another shelter, food and clothing, and still another temporary protection. A fugitive, then, had to have the courage to abscond, and he also had to go out in broad daylight to work or to dance or to a funeral, and return back to his harboring site without being detected. The planter called this stratagem, "passing for free."

---

[379]*Virginia Gazette* (Purdie, Dixon), June 15, 1771.

CHAPTER VII
PASSING FOR FREE

The planter used the term "passing for free" to describe the fugitive who pretended to be a freeman in order to remain at large. This fugitive devised different forms of deception to outwit the captor: he changed his name or his clothes, cut his hair, feigned obsequiousness, pretended to be a planter, passed for white, professed to be an Indian or a Spaniard or a free mulatto. He also pretended to be crippled, insane, or sick; forged passes, filched indentures, appropriated emancipation certificates and pocketed army discharges. Passing for free called, too, for the fugitive's mastery of English or, at least, knowledge of its rudiments. How could a bondsman named Leeds, "of a black complexion" who was caught on board a ship in Charlestown trying to pass for a "free fellow under the name of Jack Lips,"[380] perform this simple deception had he not known how to speak English?

No matter how well an African or a new white spoke his native language it was useless if they were unable to persuade an American harborer to help them or convince a captor that they should not be jailed and returned to their owner. "A likely new Negro fellow of the Mundingo country" a planter in Virginia wrote, had "only landed in the country three days before his elopement, he could therefore have no particular route to prosecute, nor can he speak English sufficient to give any account of himself." A Dutch servant escaped and his owner maintained that this fugitive "can speak no English at all, being but two months in the country." A fugitive, a "New Negro Man Slave" recently imported, "cannot tell who he belongs to" and therefore, his master said, "he may be committed to Prison." The master also said that the "little Time I had him he went by the Name of David,tho he may not remember it." A new Negro woman named Statira, reported Provost Marshal Rawlin Lowdnes "cannot speak any word of English, nor even tell her own name." Servant Thomas Haggarty of Pennsylvania "talks very bad English and Scarcely

---

[380]*South Carolina Gazette*, August 29, 1763.

understands what is told to him."[381]

The fugitive could be a linguist and the planters still described the escapee's English skills. A German servant man, age twenty-eight, a tailor, could "speak several languages, his English is bad; he brags he can speak nine, but has been known to speak French, German, Spanish and the Portuguese." A Dutch servant "speaks no English but can speak several other languages such as the French and the Turkish." Pierro, a black, "speaks good English, French and Dutch." Emanuel "carried with him a Book or two" and "talks good English, and pretends to talk Spanish, and to be a Frenchman."[382]

The non-English speaking fugitive often needed an English speaking companion to steer him away from the suspicious captor. In South Carolina, three Guineans made off in July 1769. Toney and Marcellus "cannot speak any English" but Boston, age twenty-four, spoke "very good English, Spanish and Portuguese." The owner maintained that Boston, who is a "cunning, artful Fellow and has been in several different Parts of the World," enticed the others. Three Scottish servants of Virginia absconded in 1767 and William Nelson the "Ringleader writes a tolerable good Hand, and by his superior knowledge of the English tongue, tis imagine he will write Passes and act as a Speaker for the rest."[383]

A clothes change helped some fugitives pass for free. Irish servant Mary Connor, age twenty-three, "may possibly change her dress, as she said she would dress herself in man's clothes," wrote one planter. A black woman named Hannah of Pennsylvania was expected to "dress herself in man's clothes." Servant Dick Simon might "change his clothes and put on a woman's in order for

---

[381]*South Carolina Gazette*, August 29, 1763, May 19, 1759; *Pennsylvania Gazette*, October 27, 1763, September 29, 1764; *Virginia Gazette* (Hunter), November 14, 1751.

[382]*Pennsylvania Gazette*, April 11, 1754, October 3, 1771; *South Carolina Gazette*, April 26, 1740; *Virginia Gazette* (Hunter), June 10, 1775.

[383]*South Carolina Gazette*, August 3, 1769; *Maryland Gazette*, June 18, 1767.

better concealments as he did once before." Bob's "dress is of needless description as he has several suits of clothes and will change them at different times." How Bob, a black, obtained several sets of clothing is unclear, but he "had plenty of money with him; it is very probable he will buy some clothes," said the owner.[384]

Planters could easily identify the newly-imported fugitive slave or servant by examining his clothes. One planter from Maryland said that his servant "appears like a servant just come off the ship and had a bundle of old clothes with him." Referring to his fugitives, one planter maintained: "To those used to the smell of servants just from a ship they will be easily discovered unless they procured new clothes." A gaoler had an African in confinement who was "stark naked except a rag around his Middle by which it would seem as if he was just imported into the country."[385]

A white servant might don quality garments to imitate a free man. Henry Laurence would not be "suspected of being a servant" because of his "blue Thicket Coat and Breeches, red Jacket, check shirt, half worn beaver hat, good shoes, and buckles." Indentured servant Katy Norton was trying to pass for an "Honest woman" because she had stolen a fine cotton Chinz Gown, of a genteel Figure, with red, green, blue, and yellow flowers, a white gown, five skirts, with Robbins and the Sleeves, one white Apron, two check ditto, silk gauze cap, with broad lace, which she wears far back on her Head and a Black Peeling Bonnet, two black silk handkerchiefs, one Linen Ditto, white homespun thread stockings, new shoes, with brass square buckles set with stones."[386]

Genteel garments allowed some servants to pass as planters. John King "is too gentle dressed for a servant, but his capacity entitled him to that indulgence, provided his integrity was answerable. He has an affected swing in his Gait, and is very apt to intrude into Gentlemen's company especially of the mercantile

---

[384]*Pennsylvania Gazette*, October 27, 1763, February 2, 1769, February 24, 1772, January 26, 1785.

[385]*Maryland Gazette*, September 1, 1763, May 12, 1772.

[386]*Pennsylvania Gazette*, June 25, 1763.

class."[387] John Bowyer announced the capture of two blacks, Poll
and George and, "a Dutchman who pretended to be their master."
One advertisement noted that Richard White, a ditcher, "often
changed clothes with each other, with White passing the Master of
the Other."[388]

Servants trying to pass for freeman boasted about their past
exploits and achievements. James Murphy, a schoolmaster, whose
master said he was a "very proud fellow, loves drink and when
drunk is very impertinent and talkative, pretends much and knows
little," was an example of this. One planter stated that servant
Edward Carlow claimed to have "two Uncles in New London, both
Ministers, says he has a small Estate in Ireland," and is "well
beloved amongst the Women." William Daniel Angels "a
shoemaker by trade, an Englishman about 5 feet high, age 28,"
according to the advertisement describing him, was a "pert spoken,
squat made man, and likely to behave with a great deal of
assurance if examined." One Irishman "pretends to be a Conjuror
and brags much of his land and Negroes in Cecil or Kent City."[389]

Blacks who donned elegant garments risked drawing the captor's
attention. In 1735 South Carolina – the only colony to do so –
enacted a dress code for the slave: "Whereas many of the slaves,
for the procuring Whereof they use sinister and evil methods." The
lawmaker expected the black to wear "Negro cloth duffelds, coards
Kearsies, Osnabrings, blue linen, checked cotton, plaids, garlic or
calico." If the black wore a gentleman's clothes, the authorities
could "seize or take away" the clothes.[390]

One fifty year old Guinean fugitive in 1773 named Erskyne, a
black barber, disregarded that law. His owner, merchant Alexander

---

[387]*Maryland Gazette*, July 18, 1762.

[388]*Virginia Gazette* (Purdie, Dixon), December 23, 1768;
Pennsylvania Gazette, July 8, 1742.

[389]*Pennsylvania Gazette*, November 28, 1765; *Maryland Gazette*,
May 1, 1765.

[390]Cooper and McCord, *South Carolina Statutes*, VII: 396, 410;
Woods, *Black Majority*, 232.

Wylly, said: "As he has carried off all his Cloathes (some of which are really too good for any of his Colour) he probably may change his Dress, and Name, pass as a free Man, and endeavor to get off the Province in some Vessel."[391] Two weeks later, the Grand Jurors in Charlestown complained about "the Law for preventing the excessive costly Apparel of Negroes and other Slaves in the Province (especially in Charlestown) not being put in force."[392]

Color and exclusionary policies limited the range of deceptions the black could draw on. No black could pose as an army officer, or an assemblyman, or an aristocrat without arousing suspicion. A white fugitive named Edward Mitchen of Maryland intended to go to a place, "where he is not known and will set up a parson or preach, where he gathers people together to hear him read or sing psalms." Maryland servant John Chappel, age forty-three, "has been much used to the Seas, understands Navigation perfectly well, and has been a Captain of a Man of War, has a Register from the Admiralty at home, which makes him appear to have acted in that Capacity."[393] Could a black pass for such?

Black ministers did exist. Master John Hale's Pennsylvania advertisement reported missing "a Negro man Moses Grimes about 32 years of age, about 5 feet, 6 inches high, a yellowish complexion, the fore part of his head shaved, and is rather bald, he sometimes wears a wig, is very religious, preaches to his colour, walks before buriels and marries; he is very artful, pretends to be free." A Virginia advertisement, in 1767, described Jupiter as being "6 feet high, age 35 years of age, stout, very black, and had "several scars on his back from a severe whipping he lately had at Sussex court-house, having been tried there for stirring up the Negroes to an insurrection, being a great Newlight preacher." Primus of the same colony has been a "Preacher ever since he was sixteen Years of Age, and has done much Mischief in his Neighbourhood. I expect he will endeavour to pass for a Freeman and perhaps

---

[391]*South Carolina Gazette*, May 10, 1773.

[392]Ibid., May 24, 1773.

[393]*Maryland Gazette*, May 31, 1751; *Pennsylvania Gazette*, November 25, 1772.

change his name."[394] The Charlestown Grand Jurors of took no chances with black ministers. On March 27, 1775, they accused a Patrick Hinds of allowing them in his house where they "delivered doctrines to large numbers of Negroes; they are dangerous and subversive to the Peace and Safety and Tranquility of this Province."[395]

Like other blacks, the black doctor possessed little standing in the American colonies. Doctor Jacob Nicholas Schwatzkopff of South Carolina offered ten pounds in 1771 for Lempster – dead or alive – who was "well known in Town especially among the Negroes, being employed by them as a Doctor." Another planter wrote: "Harry age 45, pretends to be a kind of Doctor in the tooth drawing and bleeding ways." And "a Negro man named Simon, age about 40 years old, talks good English, can read and write, he is very slow in speech, pretending to be a great doctor and very religious and says he is a churchman."[396]

Caesar, a black doctor, knew about drugs: their composition, their pharmacological actions, and their contraindications. In 1750, the South Carolina assembly applauded his discovery of an antidote for poison, the local gazette extolled him, and the almanac highlighted his findings in its future publications. "Caesar's Cure," brought Caesar's freedom and a one hundred pound yearly stipend for life. So long as the discoveries benefitted the white colonist, the authorities expressed satisfaction, but as soon as it posed a threat to the colonists' security they retaliated. In 1751, the Assembly in South Carolina ordered the death penalty for any black who "shall teach or instruct another slave in the knowledge of any poisonous root, plant, herb or other poison whatsoever." No "physician apothecary or druggist" could employ a black where drugs were stored. And the black who administered drugs without

---

[394]*Virginia Gazette* (Purdie, Dixon), October 1, 1767, February 27, 1772.

[395]*South Carolina Gazette*, March 27, 1775.

[396]*South Carolina Gazette*, January 3, 1771; *Maryland Gazette*, August 21, 1771; *Pennsylvania Gazette*, February 4, 1768, September 11, 1780.

white supervision could expect fifty lashes.[397]

Enforcement was difficult. The *South Carolina Gazette* reported on January 17, 1761, that "the Negroes it seems have again begun the hellish practice of poison." The gazette said that the authorities executed two blacks in Waduelah Island for that "crime." A poisoned planter recovered with the help of "Caesar's anitidote." And this same paper wrote in 1769 that Dolly and Liverpoole, a black doctor, had been burnt alive for poisoning their master's child and trying to put the infant's father "out of the world the same way."[398]

The gazettes mention nothing about the servant preacher's insurrectionary activities, or the servant poisoners. Unlike the black doctor, if the servant could convince the public that he was a doctor, then the door to freedom swung open for him. In a previous escape, John Browder, a shoemaker, had been out for six months lurking from "one county to another" where he imposed upon "the country people" to harbor him, and to provide him "with their Vituals, Drink and Lodging by strange invented stories that he was a rich man's son in Philadelphia, and that he was obliged to abscond for a little time while his father made up some differences or trouble he was engaged in." Sometimes Browder said he was a "Doctor or Surgeon and by such pretences abused the credibility and good nature of honest and well receiving people." According to a planter who was a doctor himself, one Dutchman from Virginia "took with him a Case of Surgeon Needles, a Silver Probe and a Lancet. As he practiced Physic some Time at the said Willcuxen's and received Money of several of my Patients he may appear like a Gentlemen."[399]

The black who desired to pass for a gentleman had to have an appearance that resembled the white man. Harry of Annapolis, Maryland was "so fair as sometimes to be taken for a white man."

---

[397]*South Carolina Gazette*, May 9, 1750; Cooper and McCord, *South Carolina Statutes*, VII: 442-423; Woods, *Black Majority*, 289-290.

[398]*South Carolina Gazette*, January 17, 1761.

[399]*Maryland Gazette*, November 29, 1764.

Osbourn, wrote one planter, was "almost white enough to pass for a white man" said a planter in Maryland. A South Carolina advertisement said Delia, a mulatto, intended to "Pass for a white woman." And Jack a "light mulatto man (who may easily pass for a white man)" escaped from a planter in Virginia.[400]

The planter used the term "mulatto" to describe the black with partly white ancestry while reserving the term "mustee" to describe the Indian with partly white ancestry. Though both groups had white features, whites considered both the mulatto and the mustee a category of the Negro racial group. A planter said Otho, a "light Mulatto Fellow" had a "freckled face, light gray eyes, brown Hair tied behind, his under clothes very white."[401]

The fugitive advertisements showed that the mulatto as well as the mustee, who was mostly advertised in the South Carolina newspapers, rarely tried to pass for white. Of the eighty-six mulattoes advertised in the Virginia newspapers during the period between 1736 and 1780, two tried to pass for white. Of the forty mulattoes advertised in the Maryland newspapers during the period 1745-1780, planters reported none trying to pass for white. Of the 106 mustee fugitives listed in the local South Carolina newspapers, none were described as trying to pass for white.

A few mulattoes tried to pass for Indians or Spaniards. A New Jersey planter described a thirty-seven year old mulatto named Tom who "intends to cut his watchcoat, to make him Indian stockings, and to cut off his hair, and get a blanket, to pass for an Indian." "A tall thin Mulatto slave looks very much like an Indian," reported a Maryland planter and "will endeavor to pass for such when it suits him" had probably made it to the "Back Indians"

---

[400]*Maryland Gazette*, September 2, 1746; *Virginia Gazette or American Advertiser*, January 25, 1783; *South Carolina General Advertiser*, January 1, 1778, *Virginia Gazette* (Purdie, Dixon), September 27, 1770.

[401]*Virginia Gazette* (Purdie, Dixon), February 18, 1773; *Maryland Gazette*, September 18, 1783; Winthrop Jordan, "American Chiaroscuro: The Status and Definitions of Mulattoes in the British Colonies," *William and Mary Quarterly*, 2nd Series, 19 (April 1962), 183-187; Jordan, *White Over Black*, 167-168.

wearing an Indian "Match Coat."[402]

Like the white servant, the light complexioned black had the racial and the legal advantage over the dark skinned black. If the planter had to look twice at some blacks because they looked white in appearance, they also had to look twice at the laws concerning mulattoes who tried to outwit the captor by claiming they were legally freed by law. Dick "goes by the name of Jack Simpson, and has a forg'd Pass, pretending he has served as a Mulatto 31 Years, agreeable to the laws of this Colony," reported a planter in 1751 in his Maryland advertisement. John Randolf, a close kin to Thomas Jefferson, wrote of "a mulatto slave named Aaron who brought suit against my father (Henry Randolph) in the General Court for his Freedom, in the name of Aaron Griffin." He contined: "The suit was determined last October, twelve months ago in my father's favor, though the said Fellow may change his name and endeavor to pass for a freeman as many of his Color got their Freedom in that Court."[403]

The so-called mulatto who could trek to the local court to win his freedom had privileges, but the non-mulatto slave did not. To understand why, one has to examine Maryland and Virginia statutes. In 1662, the Assembly in Virginia declared that if "any English woman being free shall have a bastard child by a Negro or mulatto" she had to either pay a fifteen pound fine or labor five years for the church wardens and her "bastard shall be bound as a servant by the said Church wardens until he or she shall attain the age of thirty years." A servant woman in a similar situation gave five extra years of indenture time to the Church after she completed her indentured time. If the black child was "got by an Englishman upon a Negro woman should she be slave or free," this child could not later sue for his freedom because the law required him to follow "the condition of the mother."[404]

---

[402]*Pennsylvania Gazette*, May 9, 1751; *Virginia Gazette* (Purdie, Dixon), March 7, 1766; *Maryland Gazette*, May 21, 1752.

[403]*Virginia Gazette*, (Purdie, Dixon), January 10, 1771; *Maryland Gazette*, May 24, 1759.

[404]Henings, *Virginia Statutes*, II: 179.

In Maryland the Assembly in September 1664 claimed that "divers of freeborne English women forgettfull of their free condicon and to the disgrace of our Nation doe intermarry with Negroes Slaves." The Assembly forced a white woman of this character to "Serve the master of such slave dureing the life of her husband And that all the Issue of such freeborne woemen soe marryed shall be Slaves as their fathers were And Bee itt further that all the Issues of English or other freeborn women that have already marryed Negroes shall serve the Master of their Parents till they be thirty yeares of age and noe longer."[405]

The Assembly accused the planter, too, of "Instigation, Procurement, or Conievance" for his part in creating these interracial marriages and declared that the planters could lose "all their Claim and Title to the service" of such an indentured woman and that this servant's children could be set free and that he could be fined ten thousand pounds. Mary Peters, a servant or slave in possession of Mr. Carheny, had served eight years and she had enough. In 1692, she told the court in Maryland that the "illusion and instigation of her late master caused her to marry a christian Negro" and "was drawn into slavery" and now she "prays for her manumission."[406]

In 1692, the Maryland Assembly reduced the miscegenation penalties concerning the white woman, both free and bound. The "freeborn English white woman" who had "a child by a Negro" did not have to serve a lifetime of slavery, but had to "forfeit her freedom and become a servant during their term of seven years." The servant women had to serve their indentured time as well as seven more years. The person who forfeited his freedom during his natural life was the black freeman who married a white woman. The children of those unions had to serve twenty-one years of indentured servitude if the parents were married. If the child's mother was unmarried, he could expect to be a servant until he reached the age of thirty-one. No relief could the black child get if his mother was black and the father white; he remained a slave

---

[405]*Arch. Md.* I: 533-534.

[406]Ibid., VI: 204.

for life.[407]

Had constant pressure not been brought to bear on the planter, the offspring of these interracial unions would have remained enslaved during the eighteenth century. In 1770, William and Mary Butler, both slaves, went to court, claiming descent from Eleanor alias Irish Nell, a white woman who married a black man in 1681, at the behest of Lord Baltimore. They claimed, too, that Irish Nell, a domestic servant, as well as her offspring should have been freed by the 1681 Act. This Act, again, accused "diverse freeborn English or white women sometimes by the Instigation" of their owners of marrying black slaves. The owners, if proven guilty, lost "their Claims and Title to the service and servitude of any such freeborn woman." The servant woman was "absolutely discharge manumitted and made free Instantly upon her inter-marriage" and "All children of such freeborne women" were to be "manumitted and free." The 1770 Provincial Court freed the Butlers; the 1771 Court of Appeals reenslaved them. Even so, the 1770 court decision raised hopes and it provided another strategy for those trying to pass for free.[408]

On February 14, 1771, a planter published a fugitive advertisement in the *Maryland Gazette* describing a "Mulatto man slave who calls himself Stephen Butler who says he was a relation of Will and Moll Butler who were cleared at Provincial Court." He claimed that Stephen said he will not "serve nor has any mulatto a right to." In 1787, Mary, the daughter of William and Mary Butler, sued for freedom and won. In that year a mulatto named Stephen (probably the same black) was depicted as having, "changed his name and passes as a freeman in company with Nace Butler, as a kinsman, who has now a suit depending for his freedom."[409]

Because the planter issued no birth certificates or baptismal papers to blacks, the only way they could prove white descent was

---

[407]Ibid., VI: 204-206, XIII: 547-548.

[408]Ira Berlin, *Slaves Without Masters: The Free Negro in the Antebellum South* (New York, 1974), 33-34.

[409]*Maryland Gazette*, February 14, 1771, May 10, 1787.

by word of mouth, which seems to have carried some weight. The lawmakers permitted the black to attend the General Court in Annapolis, and to be represented by an attorney, though the planter himself could contest the freedom claims or prevent the claimant from going to court at all. One planter in August of 1789 was looking for Bess, a "bright Mulatto colour," age fifty, and her fifteen year old son: "It is suposed that they will make for Annapolis, as they pretend to be descendants of the famous *Nell Butler*." Another planter accused Ralph, a "Mulatto fellow," of being "under pretense of going to the general court in order to procure his freedom as one of the descendants of *Nell Butler*."[410]

These "escapes" to the General Court angered planter Edmund Plowden who placed a fugitive advertisement in the *Maryland Gazette* claiming that "George Butler is one of those who has petition the general court for freedom, whence he has but lately returned, and said the court set him free, and that Mr. Chase, his attorney told him he might go where he pleased, and work for what he could get." Plowden also claimed that he was "informed the Butler cause did not come on the last term and I ordered him into my service, and a complaint being made against him by his overseer, I had him corrected for his ill behavior." Because Plowden refused to acknowledge Butler's freedom and did not accept the court's decision, George Butler was forced to "pass for free" when he should have been legally set free. Plowden admitted that "George has an order of the court with him, signed by Mr. Gwinn, which I have no doubt he will produce if stopped by any person and show as a discharge from my service, as several of them have done the same."[411]

The Butler case paved the way for other successful freedom suits: Eleanor TooGood (1783), Anthony Boston (1793), Basil Shorter (1794), Robert Thomas (1794), Nathanial Allen (1793). And it paved the way for the fugitive who looked like a "mulatto" and who had a pass to use these names to elude the captor. Jack "may pass himself for one of the Thomas family of Negroes belonging to the said estate, who made pretensions to their

---

[410]Ibid.

[411]Ibid., August 13, 1789.

freedom, but the fallacy of his attempt may be easily detected as he is quite black whereas the Thomas family are all of the mulatto color" reported one planter. Ben, Phil, Jack and Mareen made off in December of 1791. "These persons," the owner reported, "affirmed the name of Boston, and have petitioned for their freedom at the last term of the general courts and have since absconded under the pretense they are free." A "Mulatto man slave, named George, but has taken the name of George TooGood" escaped in 1787 from Elk-Ridge, Maryland. And a "likely Negro man named Bill, about twenty-two years of age" escaped in 1792; his owner states that Bill "has petitioned for his freedom under the name of Bill Shorter."[412]

How many planters made mention of the Butler name in their ads? Of the 232 black fugitive advertisements published in the *Maryland Gazette* during 1771 and 1795, eight described blacks who intended to use the Butler name, one was expected to use the Thomas name, one the Too Good name and one the Boston name. If only eleven blacks intended to use these celebrated names, then perhaps the concern for them was of little consequence.

To pass for free some fugitives declined to change their names, rather they used the name of a planter who had manumitted his slaves. A twenty-seven year old black woman named Lucy of Maryland had told "people that she is free and was set free by one of the Hopkins as they had set many free."[413]

The white servant mastered this stratagem well. Convict servant Sarah Knox, her master warned, "will make a great many courtesies and is a very deceitful, bold insinuating woman, and a great liar." Robert McAnaly was an Irish servant with a "down look is apt to have a shaking in his voice and body when asked any questions." Simon Harding "is remarkable; he cannot look one in the face." And John Miligan "has a down look when spoken to, with often repeating of words, hat off, sticking his hair back and very complaisant, often repeating the word 'Sir'." Hugh Baker, "when spoke to is apt to move his head to and from, as well as keep his

---

[412]Berlin, *Slaves Without Masters*, 34; *Maryland Gazette*, June 6, 1793, January 18, 1798, December 22, 1771.

[413]Ibid., October 14, 1784.

body and feet in motion."[414]

Blacks, too, feigned obsequiousness. Dick, of Maryland, has a "down look, stutters much when quickly spoken to, has great emotion in attempting to speak and hardly able to pronounce one syllable." Aaron was "almost sure to smile when spoke to by a white person." Pompey was "very apt to wink his eyes quick, contract one corner of his mouth, and stammer in his speech when under apprehensions of fear." "A designing, cunning rogue," Sampson "though would often appear silly, or a fool, by which means he disguises himself." Some slaves and servants did not feign obsequiousness. Servant William Halton, a stocking weaver, had a "remarkable way of staring any person in the face that speaks to him." Ned, a black, age thirty-three, was "apt to give surly answers and in general a bold, obstinate fellow." And Jack, "a yellow country-born Negro Man was a "bold, fierce looking Fellow." Tom, a mulatto shoemaker had the "look of a rogue when sharply spoken to, and discovers a great deal of assurance and impudence in his conversation." And a Welsh servant "hath a great deal of Assurance."[415]

Why one fugitive slave named John "when speaking looks you full in the face," and James Ward, a "downlook" Irish servant could "hardly look a man in the face" was a matter of style and personality, as well as a matter of who the fugitive was trying to trick. Twenty-two year old convict servant Jacob Parrott was born in Devonshire, England and claimed he came from a family of gentlemen. His master, who acknowledged that Parrott was multiskilled, expected this fugitive from Maryland to "pretend to be a groom, coachman, gardener, barber, sawyer, shoemaker, etc" but, Parrott, was also "a lover of dancing, singing, carding, racing, cockfighting, etc" and would "cringe to those who he thinks his

---

[414]*Pennsylvania Gazette*, August 16, 1750, February 27, 1753, July 18, 1756, August 27, 1767, November 1, 1770.

[415]*Virginia Gazette* (Purdie, Dixon), April 25, 1766; *Pennsylvania Gazette*, October 11, 1767; *Virginia Gazette*, January 16, 1761; *Virginia Argus*, July 18, 1799; *Maryland Gazette*, December 6, 1764, January 15, 1775, September 1, 1777, March 15, 1794; *Pennsylvania Gazette*, April 30, 1729.

superiors, and abusive to others, in whose company he will brag, chatter, fight, curse, swear, etc."[416]

Some felt comfortable just telling a planter they were freemen. One black had "a great deal of assurance and good address and will use exertion to pass as freeman." In the summer of 1779, Sam, who was "very black" with a "proud lofty carriage" and an "impudent look" had left his owner in Maryland. He had "some good friend help him write a letter that he was going to a relation of mine." During his last escape Sam had passed for a freeman by the name of James Black and said he got his freedom by the death of an old Quaker. "In seaports," his master continued, "he said he was a seafaring cook." Sam, to pass for free, had to resort to a number of stratagems designed to keep his owner at bay, though his owner would often predict the very stratagem that Sam would draw on. But Sam never gave up: "He will tell so many pretty tales, that he will make any man believe he is a freeman, for he faced a man down that he was free who knew him well."[417]

Passing for free called for a fugitive to pretend almost anything. Aaron "pretends to be in Search of Horses, by which means he has got far up the Country on his way to the Mountains." John Wright, an Irish servant, "has a Way of putting his hand in Crooked form like if he has not the Use of it, and one of his Fellow Servants says he intends to travel as a Cripple till he gets quite away." Servant William Smith pretended he was "scalped by the Indians, who he says shot him in the roof of the mouth, where there is a hole, but not from a shot, but from a Canker." Servant Audrey Leavy, who "speaks very bad English," was seen going toward Philadelphia, and acted as a dumb man by using signs. Jack Ash, a black, who "to prevent any inquiry, and to favour his making escape out of the colony, as he might think I should suspect he had drowned himself." Jim, a black, would "curse anyone he is acquainted with, pretend to strip himself and make believe he will tear them to pieces but as soon as they come he will run." And there was a servant who "pretends she was with the

---

[416]*Pennsylvania Gazette*, September 27, 1759, May 28, 1752.

[417]Baltimore, *Maryland Journal Baltimore Advertiser*, August 6, 1779.

Indians as a prisoner for six years." One servant "pretended to be sick and asked leave to go to a doctor to get some medicines but never returned."[418]

Each encounter with a planter required an appropriate response, however ludicrous, that had to be believable. One owner in Maryland offered a six dollar reward for an English servant named John White who was "about five feet four inches high, brownish coloured hair, of a yellowish complexion, had a scar on one of his cheeks; who was by his thieving and running away has been kept a servant those ten years and scarcely work with his victuals at the best, for when he is affronted he will pretend to be sick or lame, and will not do anything for several days; he carried his arm in a sling for 3 or 4 weeks before he went away, and said it was dead, that he had no use of it when he thought nobody observed him. I think he will pass for an object of charity, and go begging." Another owner said convict servant John Williams "often Acts as a Beggar, and pretends that he has no Tongue, makes Signs to People that his Tongue was cut out by the Indians and other Harms done him by them, which is all false; he has a most excellent Tongue that he draws out of his throat when provoked, though it is probable he will leave off Begging when he thinks himself safe from his Master."[419]

Servants carrying indentured contracts or routine passes could discontinue the practice of putting the master on. No more exaggerated deferences, dissimulations, shams, or any other misrepresentations were necessary. If questioned, all the servant need do was to flash the proper papers allowing him to move freely; for the citizenry understood that once the servant completed his indenture time and once the planter turned over a signed indenture section to the servant then the two parties could go their separate ways. The servant could buy some land, set up a business or hire himself out and keep his wages, or even run for office. No more curfews, no more overseers and no more

---

[418]*Virginia Gazette* (Purdie, Dixon), October 6, 1762, February 11, 1768; *Pennsylvania Gazette*, September 27, 1750, May 28, 1752, September 19, 1766.

[419]*Pennsylvania Gazette*, November 3, 1763, March 10, 1773.

compulsory labor. The indenture contract was a valuable document, and the planter desired to keep it under lock and key to prevent a servant from taking it. Despite such precautions, James Reilly a weaver, age 30, "picked the lock of a little trunk and Stole his Indenture which was assigned over to me by Captain Pardue before three magistrates."[420]

Some servants took the indentures of other servants who had completed their time and then changed their names to fit the stolen indentures. English convict servant Joseph Holmes of Pennsylvania, his master asserted, would "change his name to that of William Yeats, having stolen a discharge given to me by the said Yeats." Richard Dowd of New Jersey "has got an indenture belonging to John Butch who served his time in Lancaster County and may therefore change his Name." The Patuxent Iron Works owners, Thomas Samuel and John Snowden accused convict servant Henry Glover, a blacksmith, of having an "old Indentured with a Discharge on the Back of it, signed by Christopher Lowdnes in the Year 1752, and has passed him the Name of the Person mentioned in the same Indentured (tho' what name it is we can't find out) by which Means he has deceived many who have questioned him."[421]

An indenture clearly stated the length of time a servant had to serve and if a servant took an indenture that showed that there was more time to serve then he had to be prepared to change the date. William Martin had "an indenture with him and he will probably alter the Date so that he may appear to be free. "One planter wrote that his servant has a "Note or Contract of mine with him, by which he pretends to be discharged from my Service, which is false, he not having comply'd with his Part, and has now Five Years to serve, besides Runaway-Time and Charges."[422]

One servant completed his indentured time, his owner certified

---

[420]*Pennsylvania Gazette*, September 19, 1742.

[421]Ibid., July 4, 1754; August 14, 1742; *Maryland Gazette*, September 3, 1766.

[422]*Pennsylvania Gazette*, June 19, 1746; *Maryland Gazette*, August 5, 1748.

the indentures, gave it to the servant but another planter hires this former servant unaware of the signed indenture contract from former master or not knowing that the servant intended to use that contract as a way to pass for free. "It is supposed," said one master, that Patrick Hopkins "has an old Indenture, whereby he was bound to his former masters, Andrew Bandy and Richard Bandy which 'tis likely he may produce in order to make people believe he is a freeman.[423]"

One servant completed his indentured time in his European homeland or in America, kept his indentured contract and used it to pass for free. Eighteen year old William Sheppard "served his time in Ireland to a weaver," claimed his owner, and "may have his indentures with him, with a clearance from his master in Ireland." Thomas Mason, "twenty-three years old, has been a servant before, and has his old indentures with him, which he will endeavor to pass."[424]

Unlike an indenture, a pass did not call for a black's discharge, nor did it call for him to go and leave when he decided to do so, but it did state the black's destination and how long he could remain at that site. A pass listed the slave's or servant's name, the planter's name, the date and the destination. In 1740 the South Carolina Assembly provided this model pass: "Permit the slave to be absent from Charlestown (or any other town, or if he lives in this country from – plantation/parish) for _____ days hours dated the day of _____ ."[425]

Blacks used these passes from their masters to pass for free. Titus, "if well examined," said owner Charles Atkins, "may impose on people with two or three Tickets, I have at several times given him to go to Mr. Thomas Farr's plantation at Stono, to which place he probably may now be gone. He has also others tickets from me to go to Mr. Farr's house in town where he hath a wife." Some wrote their own passes: "Peter has behaved badly about 7 or 8 years, but has not been much corrected; but by some means

---

[423]*Pennsylvania Gazette*, March 22, 1748.

[424]Ibid., April 24, 1755, September 11, 1766.

[425]Cooper and McCord, *South Carolina Statutes*, VII: 398.

learned to write a little and has frequently wrote passes for himnself and other Negroes to go a little distance, and I apprehensive he has now done the like again or got some person to write for him." Others wrote passes for blacks. The owner of Abraham expected him to "produce a false certification drawn up by some person." A black named Quaco, who called himself William Murray, according to one advertisement, "has a certificate of his being baptized, which he shows as a pass, and says he is a freeman." Frank had a free pass signed by David Stanley and John Dawson, both of whom have been "dead some years past." The servant used forged passes, as well as indentured contracts, to avoid recapture. One owner claimed that George Allen, a butcher, "writes a good hand and it's probable he has forged a pass." Peter, a black, could read and write, and may probably have a forged Pass."[426]

Fugitives used letters and emancipation certificates to avoid detection. One black woman of South Carolina "received a letter about a fortnight ago from Mr. Parks of Goose Creek, directed to the subscriber, which she procured under the pretense of going home and will probably make use of it as a ticket or pass."[427] Ann Griffith, a white servant, told her owner that "she was going to *Philadelphia* to her husband," but the owner claimed that "but she has none; and shewed a counterfeit Letter as if from him requesting her to come to him." One planter said his slave, Joe, age twenty-eight, formerly belonged to planter Walter Hopkins of New Kent City who freed all his slaves, including a thirty year old black named Joe. The author of the runaway advertisement had "good reason" to think that the said fugitive "will get the emancipated fellow's pass" since they had similar names.[428]

The Army discharge proved to be an important document for the fugitive. A planter in 1768 placed an advertisement in the

---

[426]*South Carolina American General Gazette*, September 30, 1774; *Virginia Gazette* (Purdie, Dixon), February 3, 1769; *Virginia Gazette* (Purdie, Dixon), February 21, 1771.

[427]*Maryland Gazette*, August 20, 1767.

[428]*Maryland Gazette*, April 18, 1780.

Maryland Gazette describing a forty year old Englishman who had been "shot through the left Leg when in the Service, as a Soldier, in one of the Regiments in the late Wars in *America*." The servant had a "discharge from the Regiment he served in, and a Discharge from the Hospital where the Cure of his Legs was effected, (which is now broke out again), he may probably make Use of the said Discharge to pass him off as a Freeman." One black from Maryland "pretends to have a Certificate for his Freedom, which it is supposed he had from one of the Sailors inboard the Vessel he run from." The Spaniards gave passes to black fugitives. Peter John of Maryland "has a Writing expressing his Freedom, given him by the Spaniards, by whom he was lately taken."[429]

Passing for free required that the fugitive break all ties of apparent trust, break any forms of understandings whether written or oral, ignore any duties or charges imposed in faith or confidence by the planter who would probably claim he was betrayed. "Ungrateful rogue," was how a Maryland master characterized Will, a blacksmith, barber and shoemaker. The master maintained that he had "manumitted [Will] some years past with a number of other slaves, who were free at different periods, and I am apprehensive he has got one of their discharges. He is not free by manumission till next Christmas, and from that time he was to serve me six months, by agreement, for the expences of a former elopement, about two years past, which cost upwards of Twenty Pounds."[430]

No mutual trust existed between a twenty year old shoemaker named James Hill of Pennsylvania and his master. Hill was "trusted by his master to go off to Cumberland County to Juniate River with an old sorrel mare, loaded with leather and new shoemaker tools which he has with him."[431]

A large number of Europeans came to America as Redemptioners, a name given to the European emigrant families

---

[429]Ibid., October 10, 1768, December 2, 1746, October 4, 1745.

[430]Baltimore, *Maryland Journal Baltimore Advertiser*, September 16, 1785.

[431]*Pennsylvania Gazette*, September 5, 1771.

who lacked all or part of the travel costs to America but worked out an agreement with the captain of the ship to pay the remaining monies within fourteen days after the ship docked in America. The servant left collateral on the ship before he left, collateral that might consist of household goods, chattel or even family members. One Dutch servant of Pennsylvania never came back: "He got liberty last in last August, to go for two weeks among the Dutch Calvinist clergy, to get as much money as wou'd free him, and tho' he has left his wife a bound servant, has not returned."[432]

Planters who permitted the servants or blacks to visit their friends and relatives expected them to return, not to abscond. One black man of Delaware had "liberty of his master to go and see his Friends at Philadelphia, to return in two or three days but it has now been about sixteen days" and the owner was concerned. Thirteen year old Catherine Elizabeth Ochlier of Pennsylvania had "liberty from her master to go and see her father named Jacob Ochlier, by trade a Butcher, who took her away and it supposed they gone to New York," said one planter.[433]

Some fugitives probably did not need a pass because over the years they became so well known the planter expected the captor to know the slave's name, master and occupation. Who in Charlestown did not know the "Negro Fellow named Pierro, but commonly stiles himself Peter, he is the Fellow who carried the *South Carolina Gazette* about this Town, and is very well known," according to Peter Timothy the owner of the *Gazette*? And who did not know Tom? This fugitive was "well known by almost every one in Charlestown being use to alter and chime the Bells of St. Philips Church." And lastly, who did not know John Mullan of New York City? "He has carried," said his owner, "the *New York Gazette and Weekly Mercury* to the Customers in part of this city for five years and is well known."[434]

---

[432]Ibid., December 19, 1754.

[433]Ibid., February 7, 1764, November 20, 1765.

[434]*South Carolina Gazette*, June 14, 1740, September 21, 1740; *New York Gazette and Weekly Mercury*, June 30, 1784.

Being well known and trying to pass for free might have undermined the fugitive's attempt to remain at large because sooner or later, a captor might spot him. On the other hand, the fugitive might be a well known slave or servant who was hired but probably knew exactly where to go for employment. In fact, the planter encouraged him to look for work as long as he brought home the proceeds. Elizabeth Smith of South Carolina complained that Lancaster, a black fugitive, "commonly known about Town for a *White Washer* and *Fisherman*, has of late imposed upon his Employers and defrauded me out of his Wages." Smith had asked the colonists "not to employ the said *Lancaster*, without first agreeing with me, or his producing a proper Ticket." Two weeks later Smith said: "I have formerly advertised all Persons not to employ my Negro man Lancaster in white washing or in any other kind of Work, whatever, but to little Purpose, once he constantly earns money which he loses either by Gaming or Spends money in the little Punch Houses, although he has been runaway for this Month past."[435] Smith had no one to blame but herself and her need for Lancaster's wages. She permitted Lancaster to go at large, gave him a pass, and allowed him to negotiate with the employers. In short, she set the stage for Lancaster's rebelliousness.

To capture the fugitive who intended to pass for free, the planter had to choose the fugitive's most identifiable characteristic, a characteristic that would be hard for a fugitive to change at will. The fugitive who worked for several years at the same occupation and in the same work area would have difficulty changing his field, therefore some planters mention how long a fugitive worked at his occupation as well as where he worked. Emanuel was "well known in Charlestown having been patron of a boat upwards twenty years." Sancho was also "well known in Charlestown as to want no description having for many years used to go in pilot boats." Two servants absconded from Richard Snowden's Pauxant ironworks in Maryland. Snowden thought: "they would pass for sailors because they have been brought up in that Employment."[436]

---

[435]*South Carolina Gazette*, January 1, 1741; *Virginia Gazette* (Parks), June 22, 1739.

[436]*Virginia Gazette* (Parks), April 6, 1739; *South Carolina*

To outwit the planters, some fugitives concealed their occupation. Master William Aylett purchased a servant from a ship captain, and said "I was told by the Captain I had him from, that he was reputed to be a Blacksmith, and I am persuaded he is one; but he has always deny'd it." Some fugitives pretended to be craftsmen. Servant George Walter of South Carolina "pretends to be a butcher and baker but can work hard at the plow."[437]

Certain telltale signs gave away the fugitive craftsmen. A convict servant escaped, but the apprehender would "know him to be a Taylor by the fore Finger of his left Hand being prick'd with the Needle." One butcher carried his "knife, Scabbard and Steel with him and the Fingers of his left Hand are crooked by the cut of a Butcher's knife."[438]

Fugitive craftsmen could be identified by the tools they carried with them. James McDaniel was a "Sailmaker by trade and has got his needles and palm with him." One servant "took with him a sett of shoemaker's tools; and it is suppose that he will pass for a shoemaker, as he can make a pretty good shoe." One servant "shaves very well and took a shaving Bason, and Razors, so tis likely he will pass for a Barber." A Negro man named Joe, forty-five years old" reported one planter "carries Razors combs and powder bag and is fond of acting as a barber." A few craftsmen gave themselves away by bragging. One barber was "fond of expressing his calling." Others had nervous quirks. James was "remarkable for chewing his tongue when in a hurry about piddling jobs."[439]

Whether the fugitive was a craftsman or not, the planter expected the fugitive to reveal his deception. But was this not

---

Gazette, May 29, 1755.

[437]*South Carolina Gazette*, January 15, 1741; *Virginia Gazette* (Parks), April 20, 1738.

[438]*Maryland Gazette*, August 6, 1761; *Pennsylvania Gazette*, November 5, 1765.

[439]*Pennsylvania Gazette*, October 3, 1777; *Maryland Gazette*, September 20, 1763, July 3, 1769.

mere conjecture? One servant had black hair and his owner "expected he has cut it off as he carried away a pair of scissors." But how can one know what the servant intended to do with the scissors? Daniel, a black, "would never own he was a servant that he intend to travel at night to make his escape more secure." And Joe, a black, of Maryland, "will never make his appearance in the daytime but travel and steal at night." How did the planter reach this conclusion? Surely the fugitive did not stop to tell the planter how he planned to pass for free.[440]

Some blacks and servants informed the planter about a fugitive's intentions. "I have been informed" wrote one Maryland planter, "by my servants there used to frequently talk by Philadelphia." Fifty year old Harry Spencer of Virginia, a black fugitive, had "run away some years ago from the late Col. Spotswood, and went to Carolina, where he staid a considerable time, it is seem he made off that way again by an account given by a slave belonging to Col. Spotswood's estate who he wanted to carry with him."[441]

Remembering the method and the route a fugitive used in preceding escapes helped a planter find the fugitive. One black fugitive named Billy was "lately brought from Carolina, where, by virtue of a forged pass that some good natured person had wrote for him, he had travelled without much interruption, and very possible may prevail on some other of his acquaintance to forge another." Bella "about two years ago absented herself from my service, and took in washing in Charlestown of which she is capable and passes as a free person," reported one planter.[442] For the "noted runaway," the planter tried to deter him from passing for free by branding him with the R, slicing off a piece of ear, cutting off his hair, putting him in irons and whipping him. Dick, a twenty-four year old mulatto, had "the letter R branded on the

---

[440]Ibid., October 3, 1775; Baltimore, *Maryland Journal Advertiser*, December 16, 1785.

[441]*Maryland Gazette*, March 21, 1765, *Virginia Gazette* (Purdie, Dixon), May 21, 1767.

[442]*Virginia Gazette* (Purdie, Dixon), August 4, 1768; *South Carolina American General Gazette*, April 17, 1776.

Right Cheek." One master expected two black men to "change their Names after they went away, but may be well known by the Brand which each of them have on their Right Breast U12.CE." Dick had "received Two remarkable Certificates; the first, stripes, by whipping, the other, having the Letter D branded on his A-sd." A black woman's "Hair was lately cut in a very irregular Manner, as a Punishment for Offenses and may now be easily discovered." Tom, a black, was "branded on each cheek, the brand very large, both ears cropt, his back very much scarred with the whip." Sabina, a black, had an "Iron chain and lock about her Neck."[443]

Some fugitives managed to overcome these hardships. A brand or any mark on the body made by a hot iron would eventually heal and wear off. Dorah, a black woman from South Carolina had "a brand upon her face but much wore out." Peter Holmes, a black, was "branded on the cheek with the letter R which is covered by his whiskers." Isaac, a black, had "a small iron collar which he wears under the collar of his shirt." An another black named Billy concealed his iron chain "by wrapping a cloth around it."[444] Peter had a "Cotton Pair of Breeches, laced on the Sides for Convenience of putting them on over his Irons." Master Sherwin said a "twenty-five year old Mulatto fellow escaped twice and when captured the second time he "branded him S on the cheek, and R on the other, though very probably he will endeavor to take them out."

Passing for free, to be sure, was an act, a skill, a battle of wits that showed how a fugitive could outwit, out-fox, out-think the ever suspicious planter if his performance was masterly enough. Passing for free was basically an individual act of resistance — one on one — but during times of upheaval and great unrest, thousands of blacks and servants made off, tossing aside the need to feign or to pretend or to deceive.

---

[443]*Virginia Gazette* (Dixon, Hunter), October 4, 1777; *South Carolina Gazette*, January 17, 1745; *Maryland Gazette*, August 6, 1767.

[444]*South Carolina Gazette*, September 6, 1748, September 12, 1771; *North Carolina Gazette*, February 12, 1794; *Virginia Gazette* (Parks), May 2, 1745; *Virginia Gazette* (Rind), May 9, 1771.

CHAPTER VIII
WHOLESALE FLIGHT
DURING THE COLONIAL WARS

The lone fugitive escape is an individualistic form of resistance; fugitive escapes that involved hundreds, sometimes thousands of indentured servants or slaves, enough fugitives to disrupt the daily activities of a county, city or colony can be called wholesale flight. Because of the ubiquitous informer, the ever vigilant overseer and the observant and attentive planter and because of the bleary eyed watchman who legged his nightly beat in the local cities and the patrol who trooped through the countryside, wholesale flight could hardly go unnoticed by the local authorities. For mass flight to occur a shift in power had to come about that loosened the planter's reins of authority. Such a shift took place during the colonial wars where the angry face of turmoil, armed conflict and violent disorder undermined the planter's authority. The first upheaval of this kind occurred in Pennsylvania and it helped trigger the flight of hundreds of fugitive servants.[446]

Neither the planter nor the indentured servant in Pennsylvania, that wayward Quaker colony, had met an earless man named Captain Edward Jenkins who claimed that the Spanish coast guard had chopped off his ear in 1731 simply because his British vessel was carrying contraband illegally taken from Porto Bello (Panama) a Spanish colony. They probably never knew this Englishman had carried his mutilated ear with him in 1738, when he testified before the House of Commons claiming that, "I committed my soul to God and my cause to my country." Despite Spain's reparation payment of $98,000 to England designed to sidestep the conflict, "the War of Jenkins Ear" broke out between these two nations in

---

[446]Blassingame, *Slave Community*, 207-208; Herbert Aptheker, *The American Negro Slave Revolts* (New York, 1943), 1-5.

October 1739.[447]

In America, the colonists called this war "the King George War" (1740-1748) because the King himself ordered the colonial governors from South Carolina to New Hampshire to raise enough troops to help capture Porto Bello and to occupy the Isthmus of Panama. The recruitment bore fruit; 3,600 colonists donned their uniforms, shouldered their knapsacks and snapped up their flintlocks hoping to find glory and fame and, in the case of servants, their freedom. Governor Thomas of Pennsylvania put eight hundred men in uniform during the first three months of 1740, three hundred, or 38%, of whom were fugitive servants, causing the planters to complain to their Quaker assemblymen who in turn laid their grievances before Governor Thomas. Speaker John Kinsey stated that the Quaker assemblymen opposed the "bearing of Arms or applying money to any such purposes" and they complained that "great Numbers of bought Servants belonging to the Inhabitants of this Province, encouraged to that purpose, had enlisted in the King's Service and were detained from their Masters, to their great Loss and to the injury of the Publick, which we thought called loudly upon us to endeavor to redress."[448]

Sixteen years later hundreds of America's able bodied men

---

[447]Robert Leckie, *The Wars of America* (New York, 1968, 1981), 31; Allan R. Millet and Peter Maslowski, *For The Common Defense: A Military History of the United States of America* (New York, 1984), 33-34; Douglas Edward Leach, *Arms For Empire: A Military History of the British Colonies in North America, 1607-1763* (New York, 1973), 208-209; Warren W. Hassler, Jr., *With Shield and Sword: American Military Affairs, Colonial Times to the Present* (Ames, Iowa, 1982), 8-9; William A. Foote, "The Pennsylvania Men of the American Regiment," *Pennsylvania Magazine of History and Biography*, 87 (1963), 36-37; Howard H. Peckman, *The Colonial Wars, 1689-1762* (Chicago, Ill., 1964), 1-10.

[448]Leach, *Arms For Empire*, 219; Chessman Abiah Herrick, *White Servitude in Pennsylvania: Indentured and Redemption Labor in Colony and Commonwealth* (New York, 1926, 1969), 235-236; *Colonial Records of Pennsylvania: Minutes of the Provincial Council of Pennsylvania*, IV: 435.

marched off to war again. The foes? France and her Indian allies. The Pennsylvania governor? Robert Hunter Morris. The assembly speaker? Issac Norris. The English Monarch? King George III. Again the ever resentful Quaker-controlled assembly denounced the servant recruitment. On February 13, 1756, speaker Issac Norris told the Assembly that "a great Number of bought Servants are lately inlisted by the Recruiting Officer now in this Province, and clandestinely or by open Force conveyed away to the very great Oppression of the said Masters, and Injury to the Province." Norris never mentioned how many servants escaped.[449]

The planters in 1740 and 1756 accused the recruiters and the governor of officially having instigated the wholesale flight, provided shelter, food and clothes, blocked the planters from recapturing the fugitives and offered hope that life would be better in the army. In fact, Governor Thomas opposed enlisting servants, and on April 14, 1749 he published a proclamation outlawing it. But speaker Kinsey said the governor had "taking some of them [white servants] by the Hand let them know they were freed from their former Masters, and were obliged to serve none but the King; that there was no Difference between himself and them, but he had better Clothes and Money in his Pocket, which he also let them know would be provided for them." The governor's actions apparently stirred the servants on. According to Kinsey, "Great Numbers of Servants applied to have their Names entered and they grew so tumultuous and disorderly that the Governor was put under the necessity of publishing the Proclamation he is pleased to mention, by which it was declared that the Contracts between Servants and Masters was not dissolved by the entering of their Names as before mentioned."[450]

Speaker Norris blamed General William Shirley, Commander of the British Armed Forces in North America, and his recruiting officers, for enlisting servants during the "Midst of Harvest or Seed Time" and for inciting the servants who are "not inlisted, since they must humor them in everything lest they should be provoked to inlist, which they daily threaten incase they are disobliged and

---

[449]Herrick, *Servitude in Pennsylvania; Col. Rec. of Penn.* VII: 37.

[450]*Col. Rec. of Penn.*, IV: 452-453.

grow idle, neglectful, insolent, and mutinous, and occasion many Disorders in the Families they belong to."[451]

General Shirley told Governor Morris in February 1756 that the "King has a Right to the Service of Indentured Servants as well as other Volunteers," that this "Liberty" made it easier for "him to fill his Majesty's Regiments much sooner and at less Expence to them." But Shirley knew that servant enlistment caused the planters great "Inconveniences and Hardships" even though he "disapproved of the practice."[452] In spite of the general's disapproval of servant recruitment, the practice continued. One planter from Philadelphia advertised for two convict servants in April 1756 named Edward Bradshaw and Joseph Thornton, claiming they fled "thro Chester on sunday 28th of March with a party of recruits."[453]

Between 1756 and 1759 in the *Pennsylvania Gazette* planters published 84 advertisements describing 95 servants and four blacks; three servants and one black headed toward the army. From 1739 to 1740 the planters published forty-six advertisements describing twenty-five servants and one black, none of whom they expected to enlist in the army. If the advertisements help little in determining how many fugitives joined the army, perhaps the planter thought it was futile to name the army recruiter as the harborer, especially if the army could not be compelled to return the servant. One planter issued a plea for his English servant named Henry Smith: "All recruiting captains are beggd not inlist him, and all masters of ships are forbid to carry him off."[454] Anywhere between 6,000 and 11,000 blacks lived in Pennsylvania in 1751, yet neither the planter nor the assembly seemed concerned about black flight, and made no effort to recruit black men. One advertisement in 1756 did describe Guy, a thirty year old mulatto slave and an "old

---

[451]Ibid., VII: 38.

[452]*Pennsylvania Archives*, 1st Ser. (12 vols., Phil., 1822-1856), II: 587-592.

[453]*Pennsylvania Gazette*, April 8, 1756.

[454]Ibid., August 28, 1755.

runaway," who "may follow the recruits."[455]

Maryland legislators complained about servant escapes, but it is difficult to tell whether the servants left en masse. Governor Horatio Sharpe's efforts to procure money and recruit soldiers to fight in the French and Indian War came to naught, for the freemen appeared uncertain about capturing Fort Duquesne, Fort Niagara and Crown Point. The freemen may have tarried, but the servants did not. In May 1755, General Edward Braddock, according to Governor Sharpe, "finding the Regiments incomplete gave Orders for Recruiting servants, though in vain endeavored to persuade them off from, representing the Mischief & Detriment that the Inhabitants must suffer from such a measure; the servants immediately flocked in to enlist, Convicts excepted, and their masters made innumerable applications to me for Relief which I was sorry to be unable to grant."[456] One hundred and eighty white colonists joined the army but neither Sharpe nor Braddock mentioned the number of servants who enlisted. Of the thirty-four fugitive advertisements describing white servants in the *Maryland Gazette* during this period, none mention any servants joining Braddock's regiments. Save for Maryland and Pennsylvania, none of the other colonies showed concern about the mass flight of servants or blacks at this time. South Carolina assemblymen did, however, worry about the blacks who made it to St. Augustine, but these daring escapes do not constitute mass flight. Like Pennsylvania, none of the colonies tried to recruit the blacks to fight in the King George War or the French and Indian War.[457]

Governor Thomas claimed that the war was based on "Principles of Right and Justice to obtain satisfaction for great injuries done

---

[455]Ibid., February 19, 1756.

[456]*Arch. Md.*, I: 204, 211; Arthur Meier Schlesinger, "Maryland's Share in the Last Intercolonial War," *Maryland Historical Society Magazine*, 7 (June 1912), 119-129; Paul H. Giddens, "The French and Indian War in Maryland, 1753 to 1756," *The Maryland Historical Magazine*, 30 (December 1935), 281-303.

[457]Benjamin Quarles, "The Colonial Militia and Negro Manpower," *Mississippi Valley Historical Magazine*, 45 (March 1949), 643-652; Edward R. Turner, *The Negro in Pennsylvania: Slavery, Servitude Freedom 1639-1861* (New York, 1911, 1969), 11, 12.

and secure our commerce in the West Indies," but, in reality the King George War was pointless for the indentured servant, who was eager to be freed from his contract, and never expected to be a dead freeman or mere canon fodder in the futherance of England's territorial gains. In 1741 up to 3,500 Americans, led by Admiral Edward Vernon, stormed the heavily fortified seaport of Cartagena, later named Columbia, but the Spaniards held fast. The English launched another attack, but yellow fever struck first sending about three thousand of the colonial soldiers to their graves.[458]

The servant who joined the army in 1755-1756, picked the worst time to be a conscript. Some two hundred Frenchmen and some six hundred Indians gave Major General Edward Braddock, an Englishman chosen to run the French out of North America, the worst thrashing of his sixty year old life. Of 1,459 Americans involved in that conflict, 977 were killed or wounded. Several battles and two years later the Commanding General Louis Joseph the Marquis de Montcalm headed a force of 3,000 Frenchmen and captured Fort Oswego on Lake Ontario and Fort William Henry on Lake George. Montcalm's forces captured 7,600 English prisoners.[459]

A decade after the French and Indian War, England went to war again. This time, the Americans did not have to enlist, for the English troops stationed in Boston in 1775 shot five Americans in trying to crush an uprising. One of the first to be slain was a forty-seven year old black named Crispus Attucks who himself had sought to gain his freedom from slavery by absconding from his master, – at least according to a fugitive advertisement published in the *Boston Gazette* in 1750:

RAN-away from his Master *William Brown* of *Framingham*,

---

[458]Leach, *Arms For Empire*, 217-218, 296-297; Hassler, Jr., *With Shield and Sword*, 9.

[459]Ibid., 384-389, 397-402; John Shy, "A new look at colonial militia," *William & Mary Quarterly*, 3rd Series, 20 (1963), 135-185; See Fred Anderson, *A People's Army: Massachusetts Soldiers and Society in the Seven Years War* (Chapel Hill, 1984).

on the 30th of Sept. last, a Mulatto Fellow, about 17 Years of Age, named *Crispus*, 6 Feet two Inches high, short curl'd Hair, his Knees nearer together than common; had on a light colour'd Bearskin Coat, plain brown Fustian Jacket, or brown all-Wool one, New Buckskin Breeches, blue Yarn Stockings, and a check'd woollen Shirt.

Whoever shall take up said Run-away, and convey him to his above said Master, shall have ten Pounds, old Tenor Reward, and all necessary Charges paid. And all Masters of Vessels and others, are hereby caution'd against concealing or carrying off said Servant on Penalty of the LAW. Boston, October 2, 1750.[460]

As the colonists and the British headed towards war, the threat of wholesale flight increased. In September 1775, two planters from Georgia told John Adams, "If 1000 regular Troops should land in Georgia and their commander be provided with Arms and Cloathes enough, and Proclaim Freedom to all the Negroes who would join his Camp, 20,000 Negroes would join it from the two Provinces in a fortnight."[461] This was no mere speculation. In an attempt to crush a colonial uprising in Williamsburg, and bring the "Colony to a propere sense of their duty to his Majesty's Crown" British governor John Murray Earl Dunmore of Virginia on November 7, 1775 "declared all indentured servants, Negroes or other (appertaining to Rebels) free that are able and wiling to

---

[460]Sidney Kaplan, *The Black Presence in the Era of the American Revolution 1770-1800* (Greenwich, Conn., 1973), 7; *Dictionary of American Negro Biography*, Rayford W. Logan and Michael R. Winston, eds. (New York, 1982), 18-19; Hiller B. Zabel, *The Boston Massacre* (New York, 1979), 3.

[461]John Adams, *Diary and Autobiography of John Adams*, Lyman H. Butterfield, ed. (4 vols., Cambridge, Mass., 1961), II: 182-183.

bear arms..." And come they did, between 800 and 1,000 blacks.[462]
"Slaves flocked to him [Dunmore] in abundance," acknowledged
Virginia Committee of Safety President Edmund Pendleton. In the
spring of 1776, William Eddis, the English traveler and surveyor,
said Dunmore's "measure of emancipating the Negroes has excited
a universal ferment" and that the "governor was speedily joined by
some hundreds of all complexions."[463]

In 1776, Colonel Landon Carter in his fugitive notice mocked
Phill, a black man for leaving his "plantation at Sabine Hall, about
six weeks ago, and really for nothing at all." "Had he been near
any vessel," and had he been "remarkable for enduring labour, I
should thought he was gone to increase the *black regiment* forming
in Norfolk harbour; but really he is too weakly and idle to be
desirous of going where he must work for his freedom, as it is
called." One planter in 1777 in Pennsylvania claimed that Cuff, an
active, "well-made fellow," had "changed his name," and that
"Negroes in general think that Lord Dunmore is contending for
their liberty; it is not improbable that said Negroe is in his march
to join his Lordship's own black regiment."[464]

Dunmore's proclamation provided the black and the servant with
another way to pass for free; that moved the authorities in
Virginia to denounce Dunmore. George Washington saw him as
an "arch traitor to the rights of humanity" and thought that he
"should be instantly crushed if it takes the force of the whole army
to do it; otherwise like a snowball rolling his army will get size."

---

[462]Benjamin Quarles, *The Negro in the American Revolution*
(Chapel Hill, 1961), 19, 31; *Black Mosaic: Essays in Afro-American
History and Historiography* (Amherst, 1988), 35-47; *American
Archives: A Documentary History of the English Colonies in North
America*, 4th Ser., 3 (Washington, 1849), III: 1385.

[463]*Edmund Pendleton to Richard Henry Lee*, November 27, 1775;
Force, *American Archives: A Documentary History of the American
Colonies*, 4th Ser., 5, III: 202-222; William Eddis, *Comprising
Occurrences from 1769-1777 Inclusive* (London), 281.

[464]*Virginia Gazette* (Purdie), April 5, 1776; *Pennsylvania Gazette*,
January 3, 1777.

The *Virginia Gazette* called Dunmore's proclamation "an evil declaration" and predicted: "Masters will be provoked to severity if their slaves desert them."[465]

Did the white servant join Dunmore's army? One master described a servant named Thomas Daley of Pennsylvania whom he expected "to make for Dunmore as he came from that way and is a great Tory." Few advertisements described the servants heading toward Dunmore's camp, and neither the *Virginia Gazette* nor the Virginia Safety Committee nor any other governmental authority threatened the servant who fled to the English camp. Two English servants from Pennsylvania will "join the king's forces when opportunity serves," claimed one planter. Daniel Slude of Maryland fled to "Boston to General Gage who he understands will protect all servants who come to him." Sarah Craig, about five feet high, planned "to go over to the English army which she is very fond of."[466]

Neither the *Virginia Gazette*, the Virginia Safety Committee, nor General Washington expressed concern about the servant who headed toward the American recruiter. English traveler and diarist Nicholas Cresswell, on December 14, 1776, recorded, "Great Numbers of recruiting parties are out to raise men but can scarcely get a man by any means though the bounty is £12," for no one "will enlist if they can avoid it." Servants and convicts remained available, but "these will desert at the first opportunity." Three months later in Leesburg, Virginia, Cresswell saw a "review of Captain Johnston's Company" whom he called "a set of rascally convicts mostly servants just purchased from their masters."[467]

Planters warned recruiters against enlisting servants. In 1776, one planter of Pennsylvania "Suspected his two Irish servants will try to enlist and make for the camp," and that "all officers are

---

[465]Fitzpatrick, *The Writings of George Washington*, IV: 67; *Virginia Gazette*, November 17, 1775.

[466]*Pennsylvania Gazette*, August 21, 1776; *Maryland Gazette*, July 13, 1775, August 1, 1776.

[467]Nicholas Cresswell, *The Journal of Nicholas Cresswell*, 1774-1777 (New York, 1924), 176, 186.

forewarned not to enlist them." Another planter there asked
recruiters to take notice of the "Resolve of the Honorable
Congress which forbids taking servants in the American forces."
Still another planter tried to sell his servant to an enlistment
officer: "If any officer has enlisted him, his master will sell him
reasonable."[468] Pennsylvania's Council of Safety on September 19,
1776 declared that servants could not be "enlisted for the Flying
Camp of the state, without the Consent of their Masters in writing
and that all who enlisted heretofore, shall be discharged on the
application of their Masters for that Purpose." Delaware, New
Jersey, and New York also prohibited recruitment of servants, but
it appears the authorities did not enforce the laws.[469]

The Cumberland County Committee, eight months later, held a
meeting in Shippensburg, Pennsylvania and "Resolved that all
Apprentices and servants are the Property of their masters and
mistresses, and every mode of depriving such masters and
mistresses of their Property is a Violation of the Rights of
mankind, contrary to the Constitution and Laws of this State, the
Resolves of the Honorable Continental Congress, and an offence
against the Peace of the good People of this State, except the
consent of the masters and mistresses, in their proper persons, or
by their Representatives in General Assembly met, shall be first
had and obtained."[470] The committee asked the soldiers to return
all enlisted servants to the planters, called on the freemen to assist
in capturing the fugitives, placing them in jail or delivering them
to their owners, and bid the gaolers to escort them home.[471]

In Georgia, on January 2, 1776, Captain William Manson
complained to the Council of Safety that "several of his indentured

---

[468]*Pennsylvania Gazette*, August 7, 1776, March 13, February
12, 1777; Quarles, *The Negro in the American Revolution*, 23;
William Miller, "The Effects of the American Revolution on
Indentured Servitude," *Pennsylvania History*, 7 (July 1940), 131-141.

[469]*Pennsylvania Colonial Records*, XI: 7.

[470]*Pennsylvania Archives*, 1st Ser., V: 340.

[471]Ibid.

servants had been enticed from him and enlisted into the provincial service of South Carolina, to his great loss and damage." The Council hauled recruiter John Spencer into a hearing and ordered him to return the servants because it was not "warranted by the honorable Continental Congress."[472]

How the servant himself felt about going to war is difficult to ascertain because first hand testimony is scarce. Johann Carl Buettner, an indentured servant and a fledgling medical surgeon, recalled in his *Narrative* that he had wandered into a Lutheran church in Philadelphia and heard Major Van Ortendorff, a French and Indian War veteran, encourage the male members of the congregation to join the American army using thirteen acres of free land as an inducement. After receiving twenty dollars, Buettner enlisted and Abraham Eldrige his master, a militia lieutenant himself, "was very happy on the following day, when he saw me in the blue uniform with green collar and cuffs, and wished me good luck in my new profession." Eldrige demanded Buettner pay him "every month for twenty months one pound sterling" and the servant "consented." Buettner claimed the "service of this corps was very hard." He lived in huts, not tents, had stale beef, stole cattle to eat, and "patrolled all night long." Six months later Buettner escaped, joined the Hessian troops, divulged valuable military information and swore allegiance to King George the Third.[473]

Between April and June 1775, the Americans relied on Blacks such as Peter Salem and Salem Poor, to beat back the British at Bunker Hill, Great Bridge, Lexington and Concord; yet, by July 10, 1775, Army Adjutant General Horatio Gates stopped the enlistment of deserters, blacks and vagabonds. Similar decrees followed from the Army Council of War in Cambridge on October 8th, and the Quartermaster General on October 31, 1775, including virtually all the New England states. But as the war wore on and the casualties began to mount, New England began in 1777

---

[472]*Collections of Georgia Historical Society*, I: 5, 26.

[473]Johann Carl Buettner, *Narrative of John Carl Buettner in the American Revolution* (New York, 1915), 39-48.

to enlist blacks.[474]

In June 1777, Lieutenant Frederick Mackenzie, a British officer stationed in Rhode Island, had heard from the Negro Spies that the American Rebels "find it so difficult to raise men for the Continental Army, that they inlist Negroes, for where their owners receive a bounty of 180 Dollars, and half their pay; and the Negro get the other half and a promise of freedom at the end of three years." French General Compte de Rochembeau's aide-de-camp, Baron Ludwig Von Closen, noted in his journal in July 1781, at a military camp in White Plains, New York that "I had a chance to see the American army, man for man. It was really painful to see those brave men, almost naked, some with trousers and little linen jackets most of them without stockings but would you believe it, very cheerful and healthy in appearance. A quarter of them were Negroes, merry confident and sturdy."[475] The Southern states, save Maryland, continued their exclusionary policies, probably because it endangered their wealth. In December 1780, Joseph Jones, a member of the House of Burgesses in Virginia, wrote James Madison decrying black enlistment and calling "unjust sacrificing of the property of a part of the community to the exoneration of the rest."[476] Racial attitudes slowed black enlistment. Alexander Hamilton in 1779 told John Jay that "the contempt we have been taught to entertain for the blacks, makes us fancy many things that are founded in neither reason nor experience; and an unwillingness to part with property of so valuable a kind will furnish a thousand arguments to show the impracticability of a pernicious tendency of

---

[474]Quarles, *The Negro in the American Revolution*, 15.

[475]Frederick Mackenzie, *The Diary of Frederick Mackenzie* (2 vols., Cambridge, Mass., 1930) I: 145; *The Revolutionary Journal of Baron Ludwig Von Closen*, Evelyn M. Acomb, ed. (Chapel Hill, 1958), 89, 92, 107.

[476]"Joseph Jones to Worthing C. Ford," *The Letters of Joseph Jones of Virginia, 1777-1787* (Washington, 1889), 63.

a scheme which requires such sacrifice."[477]

Virginia permitted free blacks to enlist by May of 1777, but planters claimed, "Several Negro slaves have deserted from their masters, and under pretense of being free men have enlisted as soldiers." The lawmakers in Virginia asked the recruiters to enlist only those blacks who displayed certificates of freedom; this did not stop George Cook, age twenty-six, who escaped in 1777. Cook's owner claimed: "My Negroes tell me he some time ago applied to a recruiting officer to enlist as a soldier expecting the country could free him from his master." George and Tull, two blacks, aged twenty-three and twenty-seven respectively, made off in 1781. Tull intended to "enlist in the service or join a regiment."[478]

The Americans might not have understood the black's military usefulness, but the British certainly understood the importance of the black conscript. General Henry Clinton's forces, employing hit and run tactics, had laid waste to the Northeast seaport and in 1779 he and General Lord Cornwallis plotted to sack the city of Charleston. Not lost was the fact thousands of able-bodied slaves lived in that city. General Clinton in 1779 issued a Proclamation giving "notice that all Negroes taken in Arms, or upon any military Duty, shall be purchased for a stated price; the Money to be paid to the Captors." He forbade anyone to "sell or claim Right over any Negroe, the Property of a Rebel, who may take refuge with any part of this Army and I do promise to every Negroe who shall desert the Rebel Standard full Security to follow within these Lines any occupation which he shall think proper."[479]

Had the British not issued freedom proclamations, the blacks would have flocked to them anyway. On September 5, 1777

---

[477]*The Papers of Alexander Hamilton*, Harold C. Syrett and Jacob E. Cooke, eds. (27 vols., New York, 1966-1987), II: 67, 68.

[478]"Conscription, Revolutionary Virginia: The Case of Culpepper County, 1780-1781," *Virginia Magazine and Historical Biography*, 91, 1275.

[479]Hening, ed., *Statutes of Virginia*, IX: 27, 268, 289; *Virginia Gazette*, September 11, 1777.

Governor Patrick Henry told the Council that "many Negroes have deserted their Masters in the Counties of Northampton and Accomack on the Easternshore, and have joined the Enemy; and that there is good reason to apprehend many more may follow their Example & be Instruments in the Hands of our Enemies." On January 26, 1781 planter Robert Armstrong of St. Mary's, Maryland, complained to Governor Thomas Lee that many Negroes "have gone from this neighborhood since the time the enemy anchored off St. Mary's." Dick Barnes also told Lee about "the Negroes going to the Enemy and that the greatest part of them in the County would join the British."[480] The British torched George Washington's house, razed his plantation, and took nineteen slaves.[481]

A month later Jean Blair, the wife of merchant George Blair of North Carolina, wrote Hannah Iredell claiming that "All my Brothers' Negroes at Booth except two fellows are determined to go to them — British — even old Affra [.] N. Hill lost twenty in two nights."[482]

For the fugitive hidden on the British ship, the Captain permitted the planter under a "flag of truce" to apply for his slave. In 1778, Major Thomas Smith of Gloucester County petitioned the Virginia Council to allow him to apply to the Commanding Officer either at York or Hampton to make "application for thirteen slaves" which "he has lost."[483]

The Americans tried to stop the blacks from joining the British.

---

[480]H.R. McIlwaine, ed., *Official Letters of Governors of Virginia*, I: 184-185; *Arch. Md.*, LVII: 39, 148.

[481]Quoted in Leslie A. Fishel, Jr. and Benjamin Quarles, *The Black American: A Documentary History* (Glenview Illinois, 1967-1968), 57. See *Royal Gazette* Rivington's, New York, July 3, 1779, 31.

[482]Don Higginbotham, ed., *The Papers of James Iredell* (2 vols., Raleigh, 1976), II: 239.

[483]McIlwaine and Hall, eds., *Journal of the Council of the State of Virginia*, II.

The Georgia Council recommended that "some guards be stationed in Savannah River to prevent Negroes from going down to Cockspur." The Maryland Council ordered John Thomas to take a "company to Cedar Point or Susquehana River in the Lower parts of St. Mary's county and guard the shores from thence to the River Potomac to prevent any servants or Negroes from going on board the Fowey ship of War." In early 1777, the Virginia Navy Board placed guards on the Wicomico, Potomac, Rappahannock, and Upper Chesapeake Bay to prevent slave flight.[484] Complaining about the blacks leaving Northampton and Accomack counties on Virginia's eastern coast to join the British, Governor Patrick Henry ordered that restive blacks "be removed from the eastern coast counties to the interior of the state" in September 1777.[485]

President Henry Laurens of the South Carolina Council of Safety accused Lord Campbell of "harboring and protecting Negroes on Sullivan's Island, from whence those villains made nightly sallies and committed robberies and depredations on the sea-coast of Christ Church." He dispatched fifty-four foot rangers to the island who "burned the house where the banditti were often lodged, fought off four Negroes, killed three or four and also took white prisoners." He intended to "humble" the blacks and "Mortify" Lord Campbell.[486] So long as the British kept burning houses and crops, scattering livestock, abducting civilians and occupying the colonies themselves, the planters could do little to stop the mass flight. In early 1781, Joseph Jones felt if the British "do us any injury it must be by plundering private persons of their property along the shores and receiving the Negros who may runaway and join them." To stop the wholesale flight of slaves, the Americans needed to defeat the British troops; this happened on October 17,

---

[484]*The Revolutionary Records of the State of Georgia*, I: 184; *Arch. Md.*, XL: 511, 517; William B. Clark, ed., *Naval Records*, V: 741; *Official Letters of Governor of Virginia*, I: 184-185.

[485]*South Carolina Historical Magazine*, 7 (1904), 304.

[486]"Joseph Jones to James Madison," January 17, 1781, *James Madison Papers*, William T. Hutchinson and William M. E. Rachel, eds., II (16 vols. Chicago 1962-1972), 289.

1781, when the American and French forces forced Lord Cornwallis' 8,077 man army to surrender at Yorktown, Virginia. Because the British forces continued to occupy Charleston, Savannah, Wilmington, and New York, and because Spain, France's ally, wanted to fight on to regain lost territory, the hostilities wore on. Fearful that France or Spain would make a separate peace with Britain, America itself made peace on November 30, 1782, calling it a preliminary treaty until both France and Spain agreed to sign, which took place on January 20, 1783. The war was over. Now began, in earnest, the campaign to reenslave the thousands of blacks liberated during its course.[487]

---

[487]R. Arthur Bowler, *Logistics and the Failure of the British Army in America, 1775-1783* (Princeton, 1975), 67, 69; Francis W. Greene, *The Revolutionary War and the Military Policy of the U.S.* (New York, 1911), 278; Henry B. Carrington, *Battles of the American Revolution, 1775-1781* (New York, 1876, 1968), 643; Samuel Flagg Bemis, *Jay's Treaty: A Study in Commercial Diplomacy* (Westport, 1962); Edmund S. Morgan, *The Birth of the Republic, 1763-1787* (Chicago, 1956), 448.

CHAPTER IX
REENSLAVEMENT

During the Revolutionary War the planter chased down, captured and reenslaved thousands of blacks who had escaped from their owners, but because he unwittingly or calculatedly used self-serving phrases to describe the mass abduction it is even more difficult at times to understand what the planter was up to, and it is difficult to understand what the blacks felt. On April 6, 1779, General William Moultrie, who would come in to possession of 352 slaves and 10,800 acres of land in 1790, wrote Colonel Charles Cotesworth Pinckney complaining about the blacks who made it to the British ships at Yamassee Bluff, opposite Abercorne: "A great number of Negroes in this part of the country got over to them, in spite of our care; it seemed absolutely necessary, therefore, to run some risk to remove them from thence."[488] The phrase "got over to them" apparently means escape, and "remove from thence" probably means to board the ships and abduct the fugitives.

The Executive Council Board in Savannah, Georgia met on July 15, 1782 and stated that:

> WHEREAS, there is a great reason to believe that numbers of Negroes and other property, belonging to the good people of this land the United States are now secreted in and about the Town and Garrison of Savannah to their great injury & prejudice.

It therefore becomes a duty indispensable on us to take every

---

[488]William Moultrie, *Memoirs of the American Revolution* (2 vols., New York, 1802, 1968), I: 364; Walter B. Edgar, ed. *Biographical Directory of the South Carolina House of Representatives* (4 vols., Columbia, South Carolina, 1974-1984), II: 485-488.

means in our power to detect such abominable proceedings and prevent those abuses, if possible, in future. Therefore, RESOLVED, Messrs Joseph Clay, James Habersham, John Habersham, John Houston, William Le Conte, John Wereat, William O'Bryan, John Kean, Peter Deveaux, Thomas Stone, Peter Taarling, and Joseph Woodruff Esquires do take into their immediate possession and custody all suspected property of whatever kind soever, and give public notice of the same, by advertisement, in order that the inhabitants may apply for, and after proof being made, obtain such property as they are or may be justly entitled to.[489]

Neither Georgia's Executive Board nor General Moultrie mentioned that they intended to reenslave the masses of liberated blacks, but that is precisely the action they contemplated.

One of these "good people" was Joseph Clay, the colony's Paymaster, a Continental Congress delegate, a leading slavetrader, and related to the Habershams who were also planters and slavetraders. Clay said a "Negro fellow belon'g to me Named Chance, by trade a Cooper, Run away & went on board" a British "Men off War" in late 1778 and made it to Florida. Clay had "been told several of the Negro's that were carried away by the Man of War at the same time have been sent back to their Owners" and he asked about "two other Negroes who were carried away at the same time" and continued: "if they could be sent back I should be very glad."[490]

The planter also used phrases such as "carried away," "my Negroes" or "plunderers" to show that he had been victimized or

[489]*The Revolutionary Records of the State of Georgia*, II: 341. See Jack P. Green, "Slavery or Independence," Some Reflections on the Relationship Among Liberty, Black Bondage and Equality in Revolutionary South Carolina," *South Carolina Historical Magazine*, 80 (1979), 193-214.

[490]"Letters of Joseph Clay Merchant of Savannah, 1776-1793," *Collections of the Georgia Historical Society* (1913), VIII: 99; *Dictionary of American Biography*, M. Dumas Malone, ed. (11 vols., New York, 1930), IV: 179-180.

to gain sympathy. On May 22, 1781, General Isaac Huger, owner of 113 slaves and 10,644 acres of land and other properties in South Carolina, wrote Robert Morris, son of Lewis Morris, the Signer of the Declaration of Independence and said that "All my Negroes below are taken by the Enemy – furniture stock & c – am informed are destroyed – I have not, nor cannot procure a White Man to take charge of my Negroes to Virginia, and greatly perplex'd for the want of Horses, the Enemy having taken all my Horses from this place; however flatter myself I shall be able to move part of my Negroes the 25th."[491]

The planter saw the British army as being the devil incarnate. Angry because the British had burned houses and "carried away Negroes," Governor John Mathews of South Carolina, owner of 241 slaves, in a letter to Arthur Middleton, a signer of the Declaration of Independence, and a member of the Jacksonborough Assembly, criticized the British in 1782: "Of all the insatiable Devils that were ever let loose to torment Mankind, the British army – especially in this Country – must bear away the bays."[492]

Another "devil" was Lord Cornwallis. Governor Edward Rutledge, the South Carolina governor, owner of 55 slaves, and 4,369 acres, and a war prisoner, contended that Cornwallis should not be exchanged for another prisoner and that he should have been "held a Prisoner for Life as a Rascal, & the World should have known that he was precluded from the Benefits of Freedom, because he was a monster & Enemy to Humanity." Yet in 1779, General Benjamin Lincoln informed William Moultrie that 1,782 blacks had been "taken" apparently by the British and "many of them I hear are the property of his excellency Governor

---

[491]"Revolutionary Letters," *The South Carolina Historical and Genealogical Magazine*, 38 (July 1937), 78; Edgar, *Biographical Directory of the South Carolina House of Representatives*, II: 343-344.

[492]Joseph W. Barnwell, ed., "The Correspondence of Hon. Arthur Middleton, Signer of the Declaration of Independence," *The South Carolina Historical and Genealogical Magazine*, 27 (1926), 71.

Rutledge."[493]

Why did the planters rail at the British for "plundering" when they themselves "carried away Negroes." Governor James Wright from Georgia, owner of 500 slaves and eleven plantations, complained to Lord Germain, England's Secretary of State, that "we are in a Truly Grievous Situation, and Continually Harrassed and Plundered by Party's of Rebels. The Americans Burned and Destroyed 7 of my Barns with rice, and did me other Damage to the Amount of at least £8,000 Sterling and they shot 4 of my Negroes dead, and wounded 3 more, one of which it is thought will dye and how many they have carried off with them, it is not yet in my power to say with certainty."[494] General Francis Marion of South Carolina, better known as the "Swamp Fox," told Captain John Postell, in January 1781, that "You must take such Negroes for the boats as belong to those persons who may be with the enemy, or from those estates which the enemy think forfeited. Gen. Greene is in want of a number of Negroes — say fifty — for the use of the army."[495]

Whether loyalist or patriot, the planter had no qualms about returning the blacks to slavery. Even if the loyalists deserted the American army and openly joined the British or the Germans, they still retained the right to retake the blacks. General Riedesel, a German commander, and his wife, Friederlike Charlotte (Von Massow) Riedesel, had packed and prepared to leave the United

---

[493]Moultrie, *American Memoirs*, I: 453; "Correspondence of Arthur Middleton," *South Carolina Historical and Genealogical Magazine*, 27 (1926), 15.

[494]James Wright, "Letters from Sir James Wright," *Georgia Historical Society*, 2 (1878), 281; William Grief, *Georgia Through Two Centuries*, E. Merton Coulter, ed. (2 vols., New York, 1965), I: 64.

[495]William Dobein James, *A Sketch of the Life of Brig. Gen. Francis Marion* (Charlestown, S.C., 1948), 14 (1821, 1982), 14-15; George W. Kyte, "Francis Marion As An Intelligence Officer," *South Carolina Historical Magazine*, 77 (1976), 224. See Hugh Rankin, *Francis Marion: The Swamp Fox* (New York, 1973).

States for Canada in 1783. They had harbored a young black named Phyllis and another black couple and they, too, awaited departure; but a loyalist planter had "arrived with the order that the Negroes be returned to him" recalled Riedesel's wife in her memoirs. "Since they were much attached to us, and this man was also an evil master, who had treated them badly, the horror and lamentation of these poor people were extremely great." Phyllis "fainted" and asked the Riedesels to purchase them but the German couple could not afford to buy them as a group, as demanded by the planter.[496]

To stop the loyalists from seizing them, some blacks went to court. In 1784, Ned Griffin, a slave, told the North Carolina General Assembly that "before the Battle of Gilford, a certain William Kitchen then in the Service of this Countrey as Soldier Deserted from his line which he was Turned in to the Continental Service to serve as the Law Directs." Kitchen made a deal with Griffin, his slave, to "enter into the Continental Service in said Kitchen's Behalf and was Received by Colo: James Armstrong at Martinborough as a free Man." Ned Griffin served the time, received his discharge, and claimed he was "Seized upon by said Kitchen and Sold to a Certain Abner Roberson who now holds me as a Servant." Griffin felt that by "Contact and merit he is Intitled to his Freedom."[497]

Another black who served in the American revolutionary army found himself reenslaved. James Roberts, a black soldier, penned a narrative depicting his experiences after the war. Born a slave to a planter in Maryland named Francis De Shields, Roberts stated that he fought with De Shields "through the whole course of the Revolutionary War. At the battle of White Haven, I fought in Washington's army, after that at the battle of Roanoke river." Roberts saw action at "Ragged Point, on Dorset county river, next Vienna Ferry, thence to Cambridge" and was at Yorktown when

---

[496]*Baroness Von Riedesel and the American Revolution: Journal and Correspondence of a Tour of Duty*, 1776-1783, Marvin L. Brown, Jr., ed., trans. (1965), 112-113.

[497]*A Documentary History of the Negro People in the United States*, Herbert Aptheker, ed. (5 vols., New York, 1971), I: 13-14.

Cornwallis surrendered. Five years after Washington became President, De Shields died in Philadelphia. Roberts said that he could have made off with his planter's carriage and six horses and about four thousand dollars, but "honor, justice and the hope of being set free, with my wife and four little ones, prompted me to return home." Roberts rode home only to be "sold to William Ward, separated from my wife and children, taken to New Orleans, and sold at auction sale to Calvin Smith, a planter in Louisiana, for fifteen hundred dollars." Smith flogged him (thirty-nine lashes), before the soldier performed a "stroke of work," and took Robert's army clothes. No wonder Roberts called America an "ungrateful illiberal country to me and my race."[498]

Jupiter Hammon, a black poet who himself "did not wish to be free" and preferred that the "young Negroes" be free, did understand that "Liberty is a great thing. We may know from our own feelings and we may likewise judge so from the conduct of the white people in the late war. How much money has been spent, and how many lives have been lost to defend their liberty! I must say that I have hoped that God would open their eyes, when they were so much engaged for liberty, to think of the state of the poor blacks, and to pity us."[499]

Neither pity nor liberty did the black expect and if it came, it would come mostly from their efforts alone, as was the case during the 1781 Yorktown campaign, a campaign that was the turning point of the war. Lord Cornwallis slipped out of Wilmington, North Carolina on April 12, 1781 and forty-three days later he marched into Petersburg, Virginia with about seven thousand troops, thereby paving the way for black wholesale flight.[500]

Regimental surgeon, owner of eleven slaves and 900 acres of

---

[498]James Roberts, *The Narrative of James Roberts, Soldier in the Revolutionary War, and at the Battle of New Orleans* (Hattiesburg, 1945), 10-11.

[499]Oscar Wegelin, *Jupiter Hammon, American Negro Poet; Selections From His Writings and Bibliography* (Freeport, N.Y. 1970), 27.

[500]Quarles, *The Negro in the American Revolution*, 140.

land in Richmond, Scottish born Dr. Robert Honyman witnessed
the black escapes and the planter's determination to block these
escapes in eastern Virginia in 1781. According to Honyman,
"Numbers of Negroes in the lower parts went off to them [the
British], whom they received, but I have not heard that they took
any from their owners." On May 11, Honyman wrote that the
British were "carrying off vast numbers of Negroes, Horses and
Cattle" and that the "infatuation of these poor creatures was
amazing: they flocked to the Enemy from all quarters, even from
very remote parts, & numbers were sent back exceedingly
mortified, not being fit for their purpose, as old men, women &
children." What was a planter to do if they "lost 30, 40, 50, 60, 70
Negroes" or if they found some "plantations entirely cleared, & not
a single Negro remained?" Some planters tried to "bring their
Negroes up the Country & some succeeded, but from others the
slaves went off by the way & went to the Enemy."[501]

Captain Johann Ewald, a Hessian, who had fought alongside
Cornwallis at Yorktown, claimed that "well over four thousand
Negroes of both sexes and ages" followed the British troops, but
he depicted them as a "horde" and "swarm of locusts" who "looked
rather like monkeys." He claims these "people were given their
freedom by the army because it was actually thought to punish the
rich, rebellious-minded inhabitants of Carolina and Virginia." But
as the Franco-American siege tightened, Ewald "drove back to the
enemy all of our black friends, whom we had taken along to
despoil the countryside. We had used them to good advantage and
set them free, and now with fear and trembling they had to face
the reward of their cruel masters."[502]

British asylum, though not the Garden of Eden, might have
been a better place than a rice field. But Cornwallis, like the

[501]Richard K. MacMaster, ed., "News of the Yorktown
Campaign: The Journal of Dr. Robert Honyman, April 17-
November 25, 1781," *The Virginia Magazine of History and
Biography*, 79 (October 1971), 394.

[502]*Captain Johann Ewald, Diary of the American War: A Hessian
Journal*, Joseph P. Tustin, ed. (New Haven, London, 1979), 305,
335.

planter, had "regulations concerning Horses and Negroes." On February 19, 1781, he permitted each Quarter master to have "Eight Negroes to Assist him in receiving provisions and other Regimental Business." He also ordered "Each Negro to have a Ticket with his Masters Name Signed by the Commanding Officers of the Corps or the Head of the Department to which he belongs." Blacks could not go where they chose for the Deputy Provost Marshal had received orders to "Seize & detain every Negroe who has not a Ticket agreeable to the above Order." Cornwallis did not tolerate "Negroes Stragling from the Line of March, plundering & Using Violence to the Inhabitants." Indeed, Cornwallis ordered his law officers to "Execute on the Spot any Negro Who is found quitting the Line of March in search of plunder." He ordered that "no Negroe shall be Suffred to Carry Arms on any pretense" and violators could expect to be "punished on the Spot."[503]

Baron Von Closen, an aide-de-camp to Comte de Rochambeau, appeared to be concerned about the horrors of the war at Yorktown: "I will never forget how frightful and disturbing was the appearance of the City of York, from the fortifications on the crest to the strand below. One could not take some three steps without running into some great holes made by bombs, white or Negroes arms or legs or some bits of uniforms."[504]

The blacks in Eastern Virginia probably knew that on October 19, 1781, Cornwallis had surrendered and they would have to face a gang of angry planters who kept one eye on the British and the other on them. Angriest of all was George Washington. On April 21, 1781 the British had ransacked his home in Mount Vernon, liberated sixteen slaves and sailed away with them. His nephew, Lund Washington, served the British soldiers refreshments hoping

---

[503]A.R. Newsome, "A British Orderly Book, 1780-1781," *The North Carolina Historical Review*, 9 (1932), 276, 296, 370; R. Arthur Bowler, *Logistics and the Failure of the British Army in America*, 1775-1783 (Princeton, NJ., 1975), 86-87.

[504]Baron Ludwig Von Closen, *The Revolutionary Journal of Baron Ludwig Von Closen, 1780-1783*, Evelyn M. Acomb, ed. (Chapel Hill, 1958), 155; Arnold Whitridge, *Rochambeau* (New York, 1965), 82, 92, 111, 112.

they would return the "blacks,"[505] but that ploy failed. According to Lund Washington, these blacks made off:

> Peter, an old man. Lewis. an old man. Frank. an old man. Frederick. a man about 45 years old, an overseer and valuable. Gunner, a man about 45 years olds; valuable, a Brickmaker. Harry. a man about 40 years old, valuable, a Horseler. Tom, a man about 20 years old, stout and Healthy. Sambo. a man about 20 years old, stout and Healthy. Thomas. a lad about 17 years old, House Servant. Peter. a lad about 15 years old, very likely. Stephen. a man about 20 years old, a cooper by trade. James. a man about 25 years old, stout and Healthy. Watty, a man about 20 years old, by trade a weaver. Daniel. a man about 19 years old, very likely. Lucy, a woman about 20 years old, Esther. a woman about 18 years old. Deborah. a woman about 16 years old. 'A later note adds:' "Frederick, Frank, Gunner, Sambo, Thomas recovered in Philadelphia. Lucy, Esther were recovered after the siege of York. The Genl. pd. salvage on Tom, in Philadelphia but I cannot tell what it was. I pd. 12 Dollars expense on him from Philadelphia here. LUND WASHINGTON."[506]

John Parke Curtis, owner of 10,000 acres of land and some three hundred blacks, and General Washington's stepson, asked Martha Washington on October 12, 1781 to tell Lund Washington that "I have made every possible Enquiry after his Negroes, but have not seen any belonging to him the General or myself. I have heard that Ned is in York, old Joe Packer is in this Neighbourhood tho I have not been able to see him. His wife is dead, and I feared that most who left us are not existing. The Mortality that has taken place among the wretches is really incredible. I have seen numbers lying dead in the Woods, and many so exhausted that

---

[505]John C. Fitzpatrick, *The Writings of George Washington: From the Original Manuscript Sources, 1745-1799* (39 vols., Washington, 1938-1944), XXII: 15.

[506]Ibid., XXII: 14

they cannot walk."[507]

Marquis de Lafayette, too, had received word of the slave escapes at Mount Vernon and told Washington that "When the ennemy came to your house many Negroes deserted to them:" and that he too was "unhappy" about Lund's behavior. In Washington's eyes the British were nothing more than "plundering Scoundrels" and his nephew's obsequiousness was "exceedingly ill-judged," but he admitted that "until the arrival of superior naval force, I have little thought of it ending in the loss of all my Negroes."[508]

With Cornwallis in prison, Washington resumed tracking down the blacks. He ordered evacuation superintendent David Ross, owner of 300 slaves, and 101,430 acres of land, that blacks be turned over to their owners and that the "Negroes that have been retaken, from whatever State, whose Owners do not appear, should all be treated in the same Manner and sent into the Country to work for their Victuals and Cloathes, and Advertised in the states they came from." About the white servants, Washington said nothing, though indentured servitude had not been abolished. The local planter too, showed little concern about tracking down the indentured servant; for the fugitive notices describing them virtually stopped appearing in the colonial newspapers.[509]

With General Washington bearing down on them, the black refugees headed for the military transports in the York river, but Washington wrote on October 25, 1781 that "many Negroes and Mulattoes the property of Citizens of these States have concealed themselves on board the Ships in the harbor; that some still continue to attach themselves to British officers and that others have attempted to impose themselves upon the officers of the French and American Armies as Freemen and to make their

---

[507]Billy J. Harbin, "Letters from John Parke Curtis to George and Martha Washington, 1778-1781," *William and Mary Quarterly*, 3rd Ser., 43 (April 1986), 292.

[508]Louis Gottschalk, *The Letters of Lafayette to Washington, 1777-1799* (New York, 1944), 187; Fitzpatrick, *Wash. Writings*, XXII: 14, XXIII: 23.

[509]Fitzpatrick, *Wash. Writings*, XXIII: 262.

escapes in that manner." The general ordered the officer to halt this practice and "deliver" the blacks to the "Guards" at York and Gloucester counties.[510]

How many French soldiers obeyed Washington's order is hard to tell, but some complied. On July 20, 1782, one jailer said: "Taken by permission from the French army a Negro man named Ned." The next week in Hanover jail three blacks, one of whom was a woman with a two year old, had "come from French Camp" and in that September Mary Ann came to "Dumfries with the French troops."[511]

From Philadelphia, General Washington asked French General Comte De Grasse on February 6, 1782 to turn over five blacks who belonged to a Colonel Fitzhugh of Maryland. The British took "forty of his most valuable Slaves," but "Five of those people, in endeavoring to make their escape from York, were taken in the Bay and put on Board the Magnanime; No person appearing, with proper authority, to claim them, they were unavoidably carried off with the Fleet to the West Indies." Washington mailed him the slave's descriptions and promised to pay expenses.[512]

The Marquis de Lafayette rode to Richmond to aid the Virginia militia headed by Colonel Josiah Parker in the summer of 1781. Parker informed the French commander about his movements at Portsmouth while waiting to trap Cornwallis, and told Lafayette about "Col deBoses Hessian Battallion accompanyed by a vast Concourse of runaway Negroes... now on board their shiping in Elizabeth River," as well as "A number of Negroes... left dead & dying with the Small pox." Yet the French general, working hand in hand with the planter, wrote in August 1781 to Virginia Governor Thomas Nelson, owner of 384 slaves: "I Beg leave again to Mention to your Excellency and Council the Proposition Concerning Negroes and Horses taken from the Ennemy. Perhaps it would Be well to Return Negroes to the owners provided they pay Half the value in Hard Money. Some premium Might Be

---

[510]Ibid., XXIII: 264-265.

[511]*Virginia Gazette or American Advertiser*, July 20, 27, 1782.

[512]Fitzpatrick, *Wash. Writings*, XXIII: 488-489.

Given to Encourage the taking of Negroes Going into the British lines."[513]

The French soldier was not always completely forthcoming in helping the planter. The sixty year old Edmund Pendleton, the President of the Supreme Court of Appeals, and his nephew Edmund Pendleton, Jr. discovered this in August 1782. The nephew's slave named Bob, age twenty-two, in his third escape attempt, took a horse, probably changed his clothes and ducked into the French lines, hoping to find solace or a job in that camp. Pendleton Sr. called on James Madison to help him retrieve the black and Madison, writing from Philadelphia on August 6th of 1782, said he had given "due attention to his request." Bob did find a servant job in a French camp in Baltimore, but Pendleton Sr., who received word about Bob's whereabouts, dispatched an overseer to escort the fugitive to Virginia. Under a government order, the French detained the overseer until Pendleton Jr. paid twenty dollars for Bob's upkeep. Pendleton, writing from Virginia, told Madison that he had "never heard of such an Order, but if there was such, I am persuaded it related only to those taken from the British at the siege of York, and not to such as run away and join them on their March, & are encouraged to do so by their secreting & Protecting them from their Masters." After Pendleton paid the fees, the French handed Bob over to the overseer, but the slave, "tied & handcuffd," escaped and intended to "practice every Stratagem to conceal himself by denying his Master's name, & changing his own & his dialect; but the marks on his shoulder cannot be removed." Last word was that Bob had been "confined in the Baltimore goal."[514]

---

[513]*Lafayette in the Age of the American Revolution: Selected Letters and Papers, 1776-1790*, Stanley J. Idzerda, ed. (5 vols., Ithaca, London, 1981), IV: 314, 334; Idzerda, *Lafayette in the American Revolution*, IV: 314.

[514]*The Letters and Papers of Edmund Pendleton, 1734-1803*, David John Mays, ed. (2 vols., Charlottesville, 1967) II: 402; *The Papers of James Madison*, William T. Hutchinson and William M.E. Rachal et al., eds. (14 vols. to date, Chicago, Illinois, 1962), V: 27, 63, 96, 97, 109.

Where could the Yorktown fugitives go if not to the French? German troops harbored blacks. George was "seen in York, after the capitulation of Cornwallis, to pass through Williamsburg and Fredericksburg, and I am informed was secreted by a Lieutenant in a Capt. Van Hair's company of Hessian troops from which circumstances I am convinced he must still be either at Winchester or Frederick-Town Maryland."[515] It appears that the blacks continued to seek asylum within the British lines, at least according to the ninety-six fugitive advertisements in the *Virginia Gazette* during the period between 1782 and 1783. The advertisements described 96 black men, 16 black women, and 3 white servants. Thirty blacks made off to the British, 2 to the Americans and 1 to the French. The jailer notices during that period described 32 black men, 6 black women and two white servants. Of the 9 that had their capture sites mentioned, 8 were in the British hands, 5 with the French and one was holed up in the woods. Clearly the British held sway, although the planter kept the pressure on the blacks who hoped to escape. One jailer wrote: "captured at the end of siege of York, a boat with one British soldier and seven Negroes making their escape to New York.[516]

Some blacks lost hope at least temporarily. Kate, a black woman, had been with the "British in Gloucester, but according to the planter, she "returned home of own accord, and went off again." "A Negro fellow named Anthony" was with the British in York during the siege, and after the surrender, returned home. His owner expected him to return to York and "pass for a freeman." Because abuse lurked in the shadows, why take the risk? Molly had "four horse locks fastened on her legs when she went away." Daniel, age twenty-three, had "several large bumps like warts, occasioned by whipping." Twenty-six year old Kate had "many

---

[515]*Virginia Gazette and American Advertiser*, February 9, 1782. See George Fennick Jones, *The Black Hessians in South Carolina and Other Colonies*, 83 (1982), 292-293.

[516]*Virginia Gazette or American Advertiser*, November 16, 1782; Sylvia R. Frey, "Between Slavery and Freedom: Virginia Blacks in the American Revolution," *Journal of Southern History*, 49 (August 1983), 375-398.

scarjas about her neck and breast, and her back will prove her to be an old offender," and Mose's "back [was] much scarred by whipping." Dead or alive notices found their way into the *Virginia Gazette*. Master John Holt offered five pounds for a black named George or ten pounds "for his head separated from his body." The blacks, according to the revolutionary planter advertisements, were the same old "incorrigible," "villainous," outlaws.[517]

Before Washington had locked up the British soldiers in the Yorktown prison camps and General Clinton had retreated to New York, and because Washington had ordered the Continental army to kick the fugitives out of their lines, wrest them from their harboring berths, and return them to their owners, the black's opportunity to escape diminished as time wore on. Clinton instructed General Alexander Leslie to protect the remaining strongholds in the South, but it was too late for Marquis Rockingham's ministry replaced Lord North's and Shelburne, Rockingham's new secretary of state, dismissed Clinton and brought on General Guy Carleton. By May 5th of 1782, Carleton entered New York, armed with orders to withdraw the British troops as well as provide shipping accommodations for the loyalists and the liberated blacks.[518]

Carleton chose Savannah as the first departure site. The Georgia Assembly complained about the "considerable number of Negroes within the British lines which are to be carried out of State by the Present Possessors," but of the 5,254 blacks who left the state 1,786 went to East Florida and 1,568 to Jamaica during July and December 1782. Charlestown was the next embarkation site. Governor John Matthews expected Leslie to ship out the remaining 4,575 troops and the 4,230 white loyalists, but not the 5,327 self-liberated blacks. Moultrie, had heard that when "the evacuation of Charlestown drew near, it was apprehended that the

---

[517]*Virginia Gazette of American Advertiser*, April 26, June 8, 22, 28, July 12, 13, August 9, 1782.

[518]Eldon Jones, "The British Withdrawal from the South, 1781-1785," in *The Revolutionary War in the South - Power, Conflict, and Leadership: Essays in Honor of John Richard Alden*, W. Robert Higgins, ed. (Durham, NC, 1979), 264.

British army would carry off some thousands of Negroes which were within their lines." But because Matthews threatened to seize the British debts and cancel estates reserved for marriage settlements, Leslie was given pause. In October 1782, Matthews and Leslie agreed that "all slaves of the citizens of South Carolina, now in the power of the honorable Lieutenant General Leslie shall be restored to their former owners, as far as practical, except such slaves as may have rendered themselves particularly obnoxious on account of their attachment and services to the British troops, and such as have specific promises of freedom."[519]

No one consulted the blacks about the agreement, even though the planters promised to forgive them for assisting the British. Could the planters trust Governor Matthews, a man who would own 206 slaves and 806 acres of land by 1790? Could they trust his two commissioners, Benjamin Guerard and Edward Rutledge, both slated to be future governors in that state and both expected to possess hundreds of acres of land and hundreds of slaves in the years ahead? Matthews trusted the planters enough to provide a site — Elliot's plantation — for planters to come and claim their slaves. To put the planters at ease, Mathews told General Leslie: "As the Inhabitants will be daily coming down to receive their Negroes, I shall expect that they will not be liable to attack by your armed Parties but free egress and regress given to them for the above purpose."[520]

Blacks jumped on board the British transports heading to St. Augustine, but the American commissioners "searched the Fleet" and found 136 black escapees. Without Leslie's permission, the navy commander refused to release the blacks. Leslie was not to be found at home, nor did he answer his letters and when he was found Mathews complained about a "glaring infraction of the Spirit of the Treaty," and said he would have "nothing further to do in

---

[519]Quarles, *The Negro in the American Revolution*, 163; Moultrie, *Memoirs*, II: 344, 345; *Colonial Office Papers, Class 5, American and West Indies*, British Public Record Office.

[520]Moultrie, *Memoirs*, II: 345; Jerome Nadelhaft, "Ending South Carolina's War: Two 1782 Agreements Favoring the Planters," *South Carolina Historical Magazine*, 80 (1979), 50-64.

the business." Leslie apparently never intended to turn the blacks over to the Americans, because he had written to Carleton on October 18, 1782, about the "impossibility of delivering up under any stipulation a certain description of Negroes, who having claimed our protection have borne arms in our services or otherwise rendered themselves more peculiarly obnoxious of their former masters." By December 14, 1782, some 2,664 blacks sailed to Jamaica and 2,000 others to East Florida, and a couple hundred to St. Lucia, Halifax, England and New York. New York remained the last port to be evacuated by the British, a port packed with thousands of blacks anxiously awaiting asylum, many of whom had fled from the rice and indigo plantations of the state of South Carolina. It was the last port in which the Americans would have the opportunity to board the British transports and yank the self-liberated blacks from the ships and hand them over to their owners.[521]

To stop Carleton, to stop the black exodus, the planter needed someone skillful to reverse the English government's policy of harbouring blacks. Benjamin Franklin seems to have been that man, although if it was left up to him, he would have resigned in 1781, at age 75, as America's first French minister. But if any one knew the dark side of diplomacy and its endless intrigues, deceptions and treacheries, Franklin surely did. A diplomat of first rank, Franklin hammered out two friendship treaties with France on February 6, 1778, called the Amity and Commerce and an Agreement of Alliance in case war broke out between England and France. That Congress chose Franklin as one of the plenipotentiaries to negotiate peace with England in 1781 when his natural habitat was France, seems strange. Congress chose Franklin and John Jay of New York to represent the middle states, the New England area, and Thomas Jefferson of Virginia and Henry Laurens of South Carolina the southern sector. But Jefferson bowed out because his wife was ill and the British caught Laurens with a pouch of classified documents on a ship heading toward Holland, and threw him in the Tower of London. Who, then,

---

[521]Quarles, *The Negro in the American Revolution*, 162-165; *Alexander Leslie's Letter Book*, New York Public Library, November 18, 1782, 156-163.

would represent the South? Who would help reenslave the blacks?[522]

Franklin took on this task. On November 26, 1782, he met with Richard Oswald, a British peace commissioner, and handed him a Congressional letter dated September 10, 1782, maintaining that "thousands of Slaves, and other property to a very great amount, have been carried off or destroyed by the Enemy," and that restitution for the loyalists was out of the question for now. In that same month, Franklin presented a Pennsylvania Bill entitled "An act for procuring an estimate of the damages sustained by the inhabitants of Pennsylvania, from the Troops and adherents of the King of Great Britain during the present war." One enactment mentioned that "all losses of Negroe or Mulatto slaves and servants, who have been deluded, and carried away by the enemies of the United States, and have not been recovered or recompensed shall be comprehended within the accounts and estimate aforesaid."

Benjamin Franklin chose the right person to whom to pour out his complaints about fugitive slaves, for Oswald, the one eyed Scot, was himself a wealthy slave trader and owned thousands of acres of land in East Florida. It seems strange that Franklin, a man who would be the nominal head of the Pennsylvania Society for Promoting the Abolition of Slavery in 1789, would confide in a slavetrader about fugitive blacks. Yet Franklin, as printer of the *Pennsylvania Gazette,* published notices of the sales of blacks in

---

[522]Samuel Flagg Bemis, *The Diplomacy of the American Revolution* (New York, 1935); *A Diplomatic History of the United States, 5th Edition* (New York, 1965), 31; Donald L. Robinson, *Slavery in the Structure of American Politics: 1765-1820* (New York, 1971), 122-125; Eldon Jones, "The British Withdrawal From the South, 1781-1785," in W. Robert Higgins, ed., *The Revolutionary War in the South: Power, Conflict and Leadership: Essays in Honor of John Richard Alden,* 261; Quarles, *The American Revolution,* 163, 167; Esmond Wright, *Franklin of Philadelphia* (Cambridge, London, 1986), 299-315; Charles R. Ritcheson, "To an Astonishing Degree Unfit for the Task?," in Ronald Hoffman and Peter J. Albert, eds., *Peace and the Peacemakers, The Treaty of 1783* (Charlottesville, 1985); Richard Morris, *The British Peacemakers: The Great Powers and American Independence,* 70-100.

that newspaper. His father or his brother sold slaves out of their home. Franklin himself, as well as his daughter and son, owned slaves.[523]

England and America signed the "Provisional Articles" at Paris on November 30, 1782, to be effective on January 20, 1783. The draft of the treaty consisted of eight articles. The first two acknowledged territorial limitations – southern Canada to Florida and the Atlantic to the Mississippi; the third, the granting of fishing rights in the waters near Newfoundland, Labrador and Nova Scotia; the fourth, that creditors could collect their debts, a demand pushed by the British merchants who accused the planters of owing them millions of dollars; the fifth, the restitution of loyalist property; the sixth, the end of the prosecution of war participants and the confiscation of their land with amnesty for civilian prisoners; the seventh, the release of American prisoners and the withdrawal of British "armies, garrisons and fleets without destroying any Negroes or other property" and, the eighth, that the Mississippi waterway "shall forever remain free and open to the subjects of Great Britain and the citizens of the United States."[524]

The Seventh Article, designed to prevent the British from transporting thousands of blacks from the United States, ran into difficulties. Seven months before the Paris Treaty took effect, Guy Carleton, British Superintendent of North American operations,

---

[523]Morris, *The Peacemakers*, 461-465; Samuel Flagg Bemis, *A Diplomatic History of the United States*, 5th ed. (New York, 1936, 1942, 1950, 1955, 1965), 59-60; Albert H. Smyth, ed., *The Writings of Benjamin Franklin*, VI: 622-624; Claude-Anne Lopez and Eugenia W. Herbert, *The Private Franklin: The Man and His Family* (New York, 1975), 291-302; J. Leitch Wright, "British East Florida: Loyalist Bastion" in *Eighteenth Century Florida: The Impact of the American Revolution*, Samuel Proctor, ed. (Gainesville, Florida, 1978), 6; Ronald W. Clark, *Benjamin Franklin: A Biography* (New York, 1983), 414; Thomas Fleming, *The Man Who Dared Lightning: A New Look at Benjamin Franklin* (New York, 1971), 442-446; David Freeman Hawke, *Franklin* (New York, 1976), 301-302; Carl Van Doren, *Benjamin Franklin* (New York, 1938), 129.

[524]Morris, *The Peacemakers*, 461-465.

met with General Washington on May 6, 1783, in Georgetown, New York and said: the "Negroes who came into the British lines under the Proclamation of his Predecessors in Command" were not considered property but freemen" and that "delivering up the Negroes to their former Masters, would be delivering them up some to possibly Execution or severe Punishment which in his Opinion would be a dishonorable Violation of the public faith pledged to the Negroes in the Proclamation."[525]

Carleton kept a count of each black who came aboard the transports. His commissioners, during the withdrawal from New York harbor, questioned each black about his name, age, master's name and residence, skill and destination; how freed; and how he made it to New York. Once a black showed proper freedom certification, he went aboard the ship. Washington said the slaves changed their names and went undetected; Carleton believed a freed black had no need for name concealment. On May 12, 1783, Sir Guy Carleton wrote George Washington reiterating the specific measures "taken for the evacuation of this place" in order to "lessen mistakes or misconstruction." He spoke, too, about the "Negroes who had been declared free previous to my arrival. As I had no right to deprive them of that liberty I found them possessed of, an accurate register was taken of every circumstance respecting them so as to serve as a record of the name of the original proprietor of the Negro and as a rule by which to judge of his value." This would "prevent all fraud" and the planters could "trace" their slaves for future compensation. Again Carleton stated that "The Negroes in question I have already said, I found free when I arrived at New York. I had therefore no right, as I thought to prevent their going to any part of the world they thought proper."[526]

An examination of the "Book of Negroes registered and certified after having been inspected by the commissioners appointed" by General Carleton shows that blacks hardly needed to change their names or even their former master's name for the inspectors to

---

[525]Fitzpatrick, *Wash. Writings,* XXVI: 403, 404.

[526]*Documents of the American Revolution, 1770-1783,* K.G. Davies, ed. (21 vols., Dublin, Ireland, 1981), XXI: 165-166.

accept the blacks' freedom claim. If Abraham said he was "his own property," who would question that assertion? Twenty-seven year old Isaac Carrse, formerly the property of William Rolt of Great Neck, Long Island, said "a Quaker give him his Freedom" and went aboard without providing proof. But Joe, stating that he was "His property," showed his "Bill of Sale" before he went aboard the British transport.[527]

Why had Washington expected the liberated black to change his name when Harry Squash and Deborah his wife of Virginia admitted that they formerly belonged to General Washington? Some blacks admitted they were fugitives. Formerly a slave to Ben Churchwell of Rappahannock, Virginia, Harry Gray, age thirty, told how he "left him 6 years ago." Caught in the sting of battle between the tug of two competing armies trying to exterminate each other, caught up in the filth and the sickness of the war, the black, slave or free, made this choice: stand fast and endure all the calamities of the war or make a run for it while the opportunity existed. Mary Ann and her two children belonged to Governor Rutledge of South Carolina, but they "left him before the seizure of Charlestown and joined the British troops." Joseph, a sawyer, was formerly the property of Colonel DeVois whom he "left at the taking of Savannah."[528]

Eleanor Foster, "a thin woman" claimed she was free, but she might have been a borderline case. Commissioner Daniel Parks, a former army contractor, said that Eleanor, "Appears to be free to the satisfaction of Mr. Parks." One loyalist planter who journeyed to the New York ports to claim his slaves, saw the Commissioner. In July 1783, Doctor Teller claimed that Samuel Doran, who intended to go to Nova Scotia, was his slave, whereas a British commissioner noted Doran came within the "British lines under their sanction and claimed the Privilege of the Proclamation respecting Negroes heretofore issued for their security and protection." Since Teller declared himself a subject of Britain, the

---

[527]*Report on American Manuscripts in the Royal Institution of Great Britain* [Calender of Guy Carleton Papers] (4 vols., London, Dublin, Hereford, 1904-1909), II: 10428-19, 24.

[528]Ibid., II: 10427-24, 22, 58.

commissioners concluded they were not authorized "to determine the question between the claimant or the Negro;" they therefore referred the case to the commander. Weeks later Gerald Beeckman requested the commissioners to go on board and "bring to shore" Doran's two children, Peter and Elizabeth, whom he claimed as his property. According to Beeckman, Doran in April 1770 had taken "his two children from the House of Pierre Van Cortland, the former owner, and sent them to New York." The Commissioners returned the children to Beeckman.[529]

In May 1783, Bartram, a former slave, "complained that his daughter, Nancy, was detained by Henry Rodgers of Queen St. in order to send her to her former master in Connecticut." Bartram produced documentation showing he and his two daughters, Nancy and Flora, had come "in the British lines in July 1779." The commissioners freed Bartram's daughters. Planter Jonathan Gillech reported that a black woman, Judith Jackson, was on a British ship preparing to sail for Nova Scotia. The fugitive said General Birch issued her a certificate describing her as Jenny Jackson, property of John McLean of New York, and that "she came within the British lines under the sanction and claims the privilege of the Proclamation." After admitting that her name was Judith, that her owner had fled to England because of the war, and that she joined the army under General Alexander, a commissioner referred her case to the commander. Records exist for ten separate hearings during the time of embarkation in New York, which lasted from April 15 to November 30, 1783. Of the ten cases, four slaves received a favorable ruling, three an unfavorable ruling and two were referred to the commander.[530]

Peace treaty or not, Guy Carleton continued to load his ships with blacks and George Washington, save for firing off angry letters, could do little to stop it. He wrote Embarkation Superintendent, Daniel Parker, in New York on April 28, 1783, requesting that he prevent "their carrying off any Negroes or other property of the Inhabitants of the United States." The general also

---

[529]Ibid., II: 10427-24, 26, 27, 28, 29; Quarles, *American Revolution*, 169.

[530]Ibid., II: 10427-10, 11.

enclosed a "List and description of Negroes which has been sent to me by Governor Harrison of Virginia" with the hope that they could be recaptured. Washington asked that an eye be kept out for "Some of my own Slaves [and those of Mr. Lund Washington who lives at my Home] may probably be in N. York but I am unable to give you their descriptions their Names being so easily changed will be fruitless to give you."[531]

Aware that nothing could be done to retrieve the blacks, Washington told Harrison on April 30, 1783 that there was "little expectation that many will be recovered, several of my own are with the Enemy but I scarce ever bestowed a thought on them, they have so many doors through which they can escape from New York, that scarce anything but an inclination to return, or voluntarily surrender of themselves will restore them to their former Masters, even supposing every disposition on the part of the Enemy to deliver them."[532]

During the meeting with Carleton in May 1783, in which Governor Trumbull of Connecticut and Governor George Clinton of New York were present, Washington admitted the "Slaves which have absconded from their Masters will never be restored to them. Vast numbers of them are already gone to Nova Scotia, and the Construction which he (Sir Guy Carleton) puts on the 7th article of the provisional treaty differs widely from ours."[533]

Edmund Pendleton Sr., Virginia's legislative dean, had good reason to be skeptical of Carelton's "strange interpretation" of the Preliminary Treaty. He asked James Madison "to what purpose did he meet General Washington? Was it to deliver his private opinions whilst the treaty might be evaded, for amusement, whilst the Negroes were carrying away out of his and the owners power?"[534]

Madison could have talked to Carleton since he was in

---

[531]Fitzpatrick, *Wash. Writings*, XXVI: 364.

[532]Ibid., XXVI: 370.

[533]Ibid., XXVI: 401.

[534]Mays, *Pendleton Papers*, II: 449.

Philadelphia in 1783, but he too wrote letters instead, hoping this would stop the Negro embarkation. He wrote Thomas Jefferson on May 13, 1783, complaining about Carleton's "palpable & scandelous misconstruction of the Treaty, and by the necessity of adhering to the proclamations under faith of which the Negroes had eloped into their service." He also wrote Edmund Randolph about the "shameful evasion of the article for restoring the slaves."[535]

Even the old sage Benjamin Franklin wrote his friend Henry Laurens on July 6, 1783, stating that "General Carleton, in Violation of those Articles, has sent away a great number of Negroes, alleging, that, Freedom having been promised them by a Proclamation, the Honor of the Nation was concernd, &c. Probably another Reason may be, that, if they had been restored to their Masters, Britain could not have hoped any thing from such another Proclamation hereafter."[536]

Carleton expected to be deluged with complaints from aggrieved planters, demanding their liberated slaves. On April 28, 1783, Thomas Walke, a Princess Anne County justice of peace and House delegate, and Captain John Willoughby, a sheriff in Norfolk county, forwarded a memorial for the return of some 300 blacks, 90 of whom belonged to Willoughby. These two men, shortly after, journeyed to New York to see Carleton but the British general's aide, probably Major George Beckwith, told the two slaveowners that "no slaves were to be given up, who claimed the benefit of their former proclamations for liberating such slaves as threw themselves under the protection of the British government." Walke called this action a "glareing piece of injustice," that Carleton must be stopped, that he would take his case to the Congress and that "hundreds of the above mentioned slaves sailed during the last week to Nova Scotia." Captain Hugh Walker, a Middlesex County resident, visited New York at the behest of Governor Harrison and the British told him not to "take slaves without their own

---

[535]Hutchinson and Rachal, *The Papers of James Madison*, VII: 39, 40, 42.

[536]Smyth, *Benjamin Franklin Writings*, IX: 58.

concent."[537]

Should Carleton's and Leslie's liberation policy be viewed with suspicion given the fact they were white men fighting on behalf of a country which had traded in slaves for centuries? The offering of asylum to thousands of slaves should be looked upon as both an act of emancipation and part of the British overall policy of trying to break the colonists' will. During the war Major Frazier received instructions from his British superiors to "rescue the Negroes and bring them back" and to "collect all the slaves who belong to them [Americans] in arms against the British government." Frazier said, too, that "the Negroes of the enemy must be informed that it is the determination of the General never to return them to their masters, but to take care of them and their families and that they may depend upon the generosity of the English government should they behave with fidelity during the course of the war."[538] Governor John Rutledge, upset about the South Carolina devastation and the detention of General Christopher Gadsden, Colonel Charles Cotesworth Pinckney, and about ninety other South Carolina revolutionaries, wrote: "In short the Enemy seem determined if they can, to break every Man's Spirit, &, if they can't to ruin him."[539]

In South Carolina that certainly appears to be the case. The British laid siege to Charlestown, the capital and the site of the nation's leading seaport, in March of 1780. By May, the city had fallen. Lost were 6,000 American troops, seven of whom were generals and one lieutenant governor. One thousand seventy-seven were wounded. "Nothing but the evidence of my senses," wrote British General James Simpson to Sir Henry Clinton in the summer of 1780, "would have convinced me of that one half the distress I am witness to could have been produced in such a short

---

[537]Hutchinson and Rachal, *The Papers of James Madison*, V: 90, VII: 4-7.

[538]*Emery Papers*, New York Public Library, 15567; Hutchinson and Rachal, *The Papers of James Madison*, VII: 7.

[539]Joseph W. Barnwell, ed., "Letters of John Rutledge," *South Carolina Historical Magazine* (1916), XVIII: 44.

time in so rich and flourishing a country as Carolina when I left it."[540]

Rawlins Lowdnes, one-time deputy provost, Speaker of the House Assembly and President of the colony in 1778, remembered when he "annually made at least 1,000 barrels of Rice worth £15,000 Currency; I had as much Money at Interest or yielded, £8,000 Currency or more. My Houses in town brought in £3,000 so that my Annual income was £26,000 Currency, upwards of £3,799 Sterling which I was sure to have punctually paid." With his eighty slaves gone and his horses commandeered "for public Uses," his income barely reached "£250 Sterling a Year." Bankrupt, Lowndes blamed the British for "carrying off Negroes from the Province, for scarcely a vessel sails without some inhabitants who lost this kind of property. Many of my slaves are now in New York and in other parts beyond the Sea."[541]

Both sides were guilty of "plundering" and "carrying away Negroes" and both sides were trying to break each other's will. But it was the Americans who made a nationwide effort to wipe away the gains the liberated blacks had made while at large, who denied them asylum and who tried to reenslave them.

Did the planters try to recapture the indentured servants or did they allow or even goad them to make off. Did the British or French offer them solace? The *Pennsylvania Gazette* did publish fugitive advertisements describing 236 male servants and 24 women in 1775, 216 men and 23 women in 1776 and 43 men and 10 women in 1777. During 1778 the paper ceased publication and resumed in 1779. By 1779, either the *Gazette* decided to stop

---

[540]Alexander R. Stoesen, "The British Occupation of Charleston, 1780-1782," *South Carolina Historical Magazine*, 63 (1962), 71-72; "James Simpson to General S. Henry Catin, July 1," *Royal Institution of Great Britain* (London 1904), 149-150; George S. McMowen, Jr., *The British Occupation of Charleston, 1780-1782* (Columbia, 1972), 9-14.

[541]*Who Was Who in America Historical Volume, 1607-1896*, 394; *Report on American Manuscripts* [Calender of Guy Carleton Papers] 150; Vipperman, *The Rise of Rawlin Lowdnes, 1721-1800* (Columbia, South Carolina, 1978), 226-227.

publishing advertisements or the planters stopped taking our advertisements, for during 1779 and 1780 the planters published advertisements describing only 90 servants. During September 1774 and February 25, 1780, the *Maryland Gazette* published advertisements describing 133 male servants and 2 women. During the next four years the planters published advertisements describing 48 blacks, but no servants. The Virginia Gazette or American Advertiser published advertisements describing only 3 white servants during 1782-1784. Should it be concluded that as the war wore on the institution of servitude withered away and that therefore the need to track down servants and reinforce their indentured contracts was hardly an issue?

Indentured servitude may have declined in significance and the planters in Maryland and Pennsylvania may have muted any public outcry or public remonstration but Philadelphia alone had several hundred indentured servants working in that city. And shortly after the Paris Treaty the merchants in that city resume the importation of servants. On September 3, 1783, a Philadelphia paper, entitled *Freedman's Journal* published an advertisement describing "A number of healthy Young Men and Women Servants" who were recently imported and were for sale. And in 1784 this paper published advertisements describing 22 fugitive servants. The *Maryland Journal and Baltimore Advertiser* shows that the planter's desire to block servant escapes had not abated. This paper published 56 advertisements in 1785 describing 13 blacks and 22 servants. One planter wrote in his advertisement that the "practice of servants absconding is daily experienced by those masters who have paid every demand against them, and by the most tender and humane treatment render their situation much more comfortable than the honest laborer of the town or county."[542]

In 1786 Maryland planters published 74 advertisements describing 68 servants and 33 slaves and in 1787 they published 90 advertisements describing 52 servants and 34 blacks. Planter James Ramsey published an advertisement describing eight fugitives who escaped in 1786. One servant had his "eyebrows lately shaved in

---

[542]*Maryland Journal and Baltimore Advertiser,* April 15, 1785.

consequence of his running away and another had an iron collar and his back cut for running away some time ago."[543]

Save for the fugitive advertisements, source material is scarce concerning the servant experience during and after the war. George Washington, Thomas Jefferson, Alexander Hamilton and Benjamin Franklin, it appears, mention nothing about this class of laborers. Moreau de St. Mery's, a French traveler, maintains in 1794 that in "Philadelphia an indentured servant who runs away must, if retaken and convicted by justice of the peace, serve five days for each day of absence" and pay runaway fines. He discovered that a master could have his malingering servant placed in jail of have the servant whipped, that he could sell the servant, "just as any commodity," and that fugitive servants' "names are published as fugitives in the papers." The advertisements do show that the Revolutionary libertarian ideals had little to do with the servant on the run.[544]

---

[543]Ibid., June 13, 1786.

[544]Philadelphia *Freeman's Journal,* September 3, 1783; Sharon V. Salinger, "Colonial Labor in Transition: The Decline of Indentured Servitude in Late Eighteenth-Century Philadelphia Labor," *Labor History,* 22 (Spring 1981), 165-192; David Galenson, "The Rise and Fall of Indentured Servitude in the Americas: An Economic Analysis," *The Journal of Economic History,* 44 (March 1984), 1-26; Charlotte Erickson, "Why did Contract Labour not Work in the Nineteenth-Century United States?" in Shula Marks and Peter Richardson eds., *International Labour Migration: Historical Perspectives* (University of London, 1984), 37-38; Roberts, *Moreau de St. Mery's American Journey,* 300-310.

CHAPTER X
RUIN'D

President John Rutledge in 1776 told the South Carolina Provincial Assembly if that "there is no alternative but absolute unconditional submission, and the most abject slavery or a defense becoming men born to freedom" then Rutledge would not hesitate about the choice. Rutledge's keynote speech might have stirred his countrymen's hearts and excited their patriotic ardor, but it appears that during the war and its aftermath, the planters, mainly in South Carolina and Virginia, seemed to care less about the Revolutionary ideals and more about their plantation profits, less about the black's welfare and more about whether the slave tended crop or absconded. Consumed with their misfortunes, caught in the web of their self pity, the planters showed little concern about small pox epidemics, or about the food, clothing, and housing shortages, the abuse, the family breakups, the fear and terror that the war brought in its wake. Indeed, three years after the Revolution Senator Pierce Butler of South Carolina wrote Supreme Court Justice James Iredell of North Carolina saying that the "early pages of our history will be sullied by an uncommon greediness for property."[545]

Ambrose Serle, Secretary to Lord Howe, did show his concern. Serle visited the Eastern Shore of Maryland in September 1777, and noted that "Scarce a white person was to be seen; but Negroes appeared in great abundance. These live in Huts or Hovels near the Houses of their Owners, and are treated as a better kind of Cattle, being bought or sold, according to Fancy of Interest, having no Property not even in their Wives or Children. Such is the

---

[545]Moultrie, *American Memoirs*, I: 137; *Life and Correspondence of James Iredell: One of the Associate Justices of the Supreme Court of the United States* (2 vols., New York, 1857-1858).

Practice or Sentiment of Americans, while they are bawling about the Rights of *human Nature*, and oppose the freest Govt. and most Liberal System of Polity known upon the Face of the Earth!"[546]

After seventy days of a 1,243 mile journey from Providence, Rhode Island, traveler Elkanah Watson reached Charlestown, South Carolina on November 18, 1777. Near Savannah, Georgia, Watson met an old Irish woman who took him in and served him sweet potatoes. This woman owned a female slave. The "infuriated hag burst into our room," recalled Watson and "seizing one of our whips, rushed into an adjoining bed-room, with a pine torch in her hands, an impersonation of fury. Here she applied her heavy strokes to the poor, helpless wench, who could scarcely crawl, with the most diabolic purpose." After "knocking the Negroe down, she commenced pounding her head with the butt end of the whip. Fearing she might commit murder, we arrested her infernal arm, when she turned the full battery of her Billingsgate on us, swearing she had a right by J____ to kill her own nager if she plased." Still, he contended that the "relation between the native master and his slave, seems generally to be of the fondest and most affectionate character."[547]

Watson observed the plantations in Georgia in 1778, and wondered about the "vast expences of preparing the swamps for the cultivation of rice and stocking the plantations with the cheapness of the article, I have been astonished at the large fortunes which have been realized from the cultivation of this commodity." He saw "the large collection of Negroes" eating and "making a miserable meal upon boiled rice and pure water" and wondered "how the slave can sustain life with this wretched pittance, and even appear in good health and condition, compelled to labor from dawn to night, through the long summer days, under the scorching rays of the intense sun, with no shelter for his head, and in most instances his black and oily skin exposed to its full

---

[546]*The American Journal of Ambrose Serle, Secretary to Lord Howe, 1776-1778*, Edward H. Tatum, Jr., ed. (San Marino, Ca., 1940), 249.

[547]*Men and Times of the Revolution: In Memory of Elkanah Watson*, Winslow C. Watson, ed. (New York, 1856), 50.

beams; yet they seemed joyous and happy. In contemplating the wealth, and splendor, and magnificence of the Southern planter, I cannot divest my mind of the idea that they are all produced by the sweat and blood of the slave."[548]

Timothy Ford, soldier in the American Revolution and twice wounded, a Princeton graduate, lawyer, and later a member of the South Carolina Legislature, visited Charlestown, in 1785 when his sister married the noted judge Henry De Saussure. He discovered that the "most obvious division of the inhabitants of Charlestown is into *Black & White*, the former being to the latter as 5 to one. This sight occasions a reflection rather painful; that, in a land of Liberty & Christianity, that boasts & builds upon the irrefrayable rights of human nature; so many of the species should be torn from the enjoyment of them & devoted to perpetual slavery for no other cause but that God has formed them black. It begets a strange confusion of ideas and contradiction of principles − the general rule is Liberty, but the Exceptions form a majority of 5 to 1."[549]

Margaret Colleton of South Carolina, who showed little concern about human rights or liberty, owned 12,000 acres of land and one hundred blacks, lived in England and relied on her attorneys to manage her Wadboo estates. She wrote attorney Robert Muncrief of Charlestown in July 1778 complaining she had "not received the smallest remittance" from her estate and owing to "the calamity of the war," was in danger of losing the land to the Commissioners of Forfeited Estates. Colleton died on November 5, 1779 and an older brother, James Edward Colleton, who also lived in England, asked lawyer William Ancrum in July 1780 to oversee the estate. At Wadboo, the site of three major battles, Ancrum found "distraction and confusion" and discovered that "food is scarce, smallpox is rampant, and the blacks are leaving." Of the 169 blacks who belonged to Margaret Colleton, 109 had fled to Charlestown and hid on a British ship sailing for St. Augustine; but an American privateer blocked the transport from leaving the

---

[548]Ibid., 54-55.

[549]Joseph W. Barnwell, ed., "Diary of Timothy Ford," *The South Carolina and Genealogical Magazine*, 13 (1912), 142.

Charlestown bay, and carried sixty-two blacks back to Wadboo and sold forty-seven to the planters in North Carolina.[550]

Eliza Lucas kept watch on her South Carolina plantations, at Hilton Head, Auchland – 1,000, Marsh Lands – 500 acres, and her two homes in Charlestown. Her father, a wealthy planter, had been a lieutenant governor of Antigua and her husband Charles, representing St. Philip Parish, spent thirteen years in the Royal Assembly (1729-1742) and held various government posts, including the Chief Justice of South Carolina. Her oldest son Charles Cotesworth Pinckney, a lawyer, devoted the greater part of his life to the General Assemblies, 1769-1800 and held other posts including delegate to the federal Convention (1787) and Minister to France (1796). Her son Thomas Pinckney, a lawyer, was governor of South Carolina (1787-1789), Minister to Great Britain in 1792-1795, and House of Representatives member during 1797-1799. An adopted nephew, Charles Pinckney II had been a member of the Royal Assembly during 1754-1775, and the Provincial and General Assembly during 1776 and 1779. Eliza Pinckney herself gained attention when she helped introduce indigo to the colony and turned it into a major cash crop.[551]

---

[550]*Wadboo Baroney: Its Fate as Told in Colleton Family's papers, 1773-1793*, J.H. Easterby, ed. (Columbia, 1952), 3-5; Kathy Roe Coker, "The Case of James Nassau Colleton before the Commissioners of Forfeited Estates," *South Carolina Historical Magazine*, 87 (October 1986), 106-116; Henry A. M. Smith, comp., "The Colleton Family in South Carolina," *South Carolina Historical and Genealogical Magazine*, 1 (1900), 325-336.

[551]*The Letterbook of Eliza Lucas Pinckney, 1739-1762*, Eliza Pinckney, ed. (Chapel Hill, 1972), I-XXV; Francis Leigh Williams, *A Founding Family, The Pinckneys of South Carolina* (New York, 1978), 521, 523, 524; John E. Finding, *Dictionary of American Diplomatic History* (Westport, 1980), 387-389; *Appleton's Cyclopedia of American Biography*, James G. Wilson and John Fiske, eds. (7 vols., 1888), IV: 22-23; Reverend Charles Cotesworth Pinckney, *Life of General Thomas Pinckney* (Boston, 1895), 8-10; Edgar, *Biographical Directory of the South Carolina House of Representatives*, III: 521-529.

In 1778, under General Howe's command, Colonel Charles Cotesworth and Major Thomas Pinckney were busy trying to subdue the Spaniards in Florida. Meanwhile at her plantation the "distemper" had killed two blacks, George and Phebe; Abram and "Little Toby" were "extremely ill." In 1779, the threat to her wealth and children's lives became apparent. The British sacked Thomas Pinckney's Auchland plantation and Eliza wrote: "I have just received Yours with the account of my losses and your almost ruined fortunes by the Enemy, a severe blow!"[552] Thomas claimed that the British "took nineteen Negroes, among them were Betty, Prince, Chance and all the hand Boys. They left the sick women, and the young children, and about five fellows who are now perfectly free." His overseer had "concealed himself in the swamp and returned. I hope he will be able to keep the remaining property in some order" but Pinckney reported that the "Negroes pay no attention to his orders."[553]

In 1779, things were falling apart in the planter community. Eliza Pinckney, in her Charlestown home, harbored the elite: "Mrs. Middleton, Lady Mary, Mrs. E. Rutledge, Mrs. Charles Drayton, Mrs. Ralph Izard, Mrs. Matthews," and all their children. Before they left for Pedee, she harbored "Ms. D. Huger, Ms. William H. Drayton and children with Ms. Elliot and Ms. Haynes." At her plantation, Beach Hill and Belmont, the blacks had heard about the impending British invasion, and they probably made a decision about their destiny before Pinckney came for them: "I could hire a white man to go and fetch them away; or whether it would be best to remove them without if they chuse to come away for they all do now what they please every where, and several plantations of Negroes attached to their homes and the little they have there have refused to remove."[554]

---

[552]Elise Pinckney, "Letters of Eliza Lucas Pinckney, 1768-1782," *South Carolina Historical Magazine*, 76 (July 1975), 154-157.

[553]*Pinckney Letters* (Microfiche), Library of Congress Manuscript Division, May 17, 1779, 38.3.5.9.

[554]Eliza Pinckney, "Letters of Eliza Pinckney, 1768-1782," 154-158.

In 1782, the British captured Charles Cotesworth, shot Thomas in the leg, and finally Eliza's self pity surfaced. "It may seem strange," she wrote on May 14, 1782 to doctor Alexander Garden, that a "single woman, accused of no crime who had a fortune sufficiently to live Genteely in any part of the world, that fortune too in different kinds of property, and in four or five different parts of the Country should in so short a time be so intirely deprived of it as not to be able to pay a debt under sixty pounds Sterling." She moaned about the "fire and plunder both in Country and Town, as well as from the death and desertion of slaves," complained, too, that the "slaves I had working at my son Charles' Sequestered Estate, by Mr. Cruden's permission, has not produced one farthing since the fall of Charles town."[555]

The Pinckney's understood partly that the task of the day was not the preservation of their property or the capturing of fugitive slaves, but American independence. Though the British read her mail, Eliza did tell Thomas that "Independence is all I wish." Charles Cotesworth Pinckney told a Cornwallis aide Major Muney in June of 1780 that "I entered into this cause after much reflection, and through principle, my heart is altogether American and neither severity nor favour, nor poverty, nor affluence can induce me to sever from it." Two months later he learned that his slave Fortune had "runaway from his Mistress" and asked his brother to "tell the Negroes to let him know that if he will come over to me I will pardon him."[556]

The flight of blacks dispirited the planter and left its stamp on them after the war. Colonel Nathan Bryan told Governor Thomas Burke of North Carolina that the British, on their way to New Bern, "called on me and took off all my Negroes and horses and robbed my house of our clothing." Sixty blacks left Bryan for the British. "Your neighbors Colonel Taliaferro and Colonel Travis lost everything they had in the world, and Mr. Paradise has lost all

---

[555]Ibid., 159, 168-170.

[556]*Pinckney Family Papers*, Library of Congress Manuscript Division, Box III, June 30, September 7, October 22, 1780; *Pinckney Letters*, 1779, 36-38; Marvin R. Zahniser, *Charles Cotesworth Pinckney: Founding Father* (Chapel Hill, 1967), 64-65.

his but one slave," wrote Richard Henry Lee of Virginia to his brother William. "This has been the general case," wrote Lee, "of all those who were near the enemy." Lee told George Washington in 1781 that his brother "William has lost sixty-five, among whom are about 45 valuable grown slaves and useful Artisans." Perhaps the planter's disillusionment prevented him from understanding why the black wanted freedom, or perhaps he was just a product of his time, which may explain why Lee described the fugitives as "deluded" of "unhappy people," somehow misled by the British, but Washington admitted that twenty-six blacks escaped from him and that the fugitives had "scarcely anything but an inclination to return or voluntarily surrender of themselves willingly."[557]

In a letter to his brother-in-law in July 1781, Colonel John Banister of Petersburg, Virginia, claimed he lost eighty-two blacks. Joseph Martin, an American soldier, recalls in his narrative that when the local citizenry captured Banister's blacks in the woods, they refused to return them until Banister "promised not to punish them." Banister gave his promise and said the blame lay on Lord Cornwallis. Seven years after the war, Thomas Jefferson, writing from Paris told historian William Gordan that Cornwallis' army "took off also about 30 slaves. Had this been to give them freedom he would have done right but it was to consign them to inevitable death from the small pox and putrid fever then raging in his camp. This I knew afterwards to have been the fate of 27 of them."[558]

In his *Farm Book* Jefferson wrote "joined the enemy" and "Fled to the enemy," meaning that Cornwallis' troops did not force his slaves to defect. Hannibal, Patty, Sam, Sally, Nanny, Fanny, Prince

---

[557]Clark, ed., *North Carolina Records*, XIV: 634-635; *The Letters of Richard Henry Lee*, James C. Ballagh, ed., (2 vols., New York, 1912-1914), II: 242-256; Fitzgerald, *Washington's Writings*, XXII: 15; Duncan J. MacLeod, *Slavery, Race and the American Revolution* (New York, 1974), 62-108.

[558]Joseph Plumb Martin, *Private Yankee Doodle: Being a Narrative of Some of the Adventures, Dangers and Sufferings of a Revolutionary Soldier*, George F. Scheer, ed. (Boston, 1962), 241; *The Papers of Thomas Jefferson*, Julian P. Boyd, ed. (22 vols., Princeton, 1950-1958), XIII: 363-364.

and Nancy escaped from Jefferson's Cumberland plantation. These blacks had "Fled to the enemy and died." From the Elhill plantation: Flora (Black Sall's), Quomina (Black Sall's), Jame (Black Sall's) and Joe (Sue's) had "joined enemy & died." Sam and Jenny had "joined the enemy" and apparently survived. Barnaby of Monticello had "runaway returned & died." "Judy & Nat of Elhill with Wills Robin of Shadwell joined the enemy but came back again" and lived; so did Isabel and Hannibel's daughter, as well as York, Isabel, Jack, Hanah and her child.[559] Were the British responsible? A Monticello slave named Isaac, recalled that "The British treated them mighty well, gave them plenty of fresh meat and wheat bread. It was very sickly at York; great many colored people died there, but none of Mr. Jefferson's folks."[560]

Brigadier General William Moultrie recalled that upon his release, he returned to his plantation in South Carolina and listened to his slaves yell "Massa was come! Massa was come!" They shook his hand and sang songs and "tears stole from my eyes and ran down my cheeks." He claims that he possessed about two hundred slaves, and "not one of them left me during the war although they had great offers, nay, some were carried down to work on the British lines, yet they always continued to make their escapes and return home."[561]

On January 29, 1778, the South Carolina and American General Gazette published this ad:

---

[559]*Thomas Jefferson's Farm Book: with Commentary and Relevant Extracts From Other Writings*, Edwin Morris Betts, ed. (Princeton, N.J., 1953), 29.

[560]Isaac Jefferson, *Memoirs of a Monticello Slave: As Dictated to Charles Campbell in the 1840's by Isaac, one of Thomas Jefferson's Slaves*, Rayford W. Logan, ed. (Charlottesville, 1951), 23. For "Reminiscences of Israel Jefferson" see Fawn M. Brodie, *Thomas Jefferson, An Intimate History* (New York, 1974), 646-653; *Jefferson at Monticello*, James H. Bear, ed. (Charlottesville, Va., 1967), 9-11.

[561]Moultrie, *American Memoirs*, II: 326.

RUN away from the subscriber about 3 months ago, a Negro
Fellow named FRANK, about 5 feet 8 inches high, has a
remarkable cut on one of his hands, speaks good English,
and is 35 years of age; also a stout Negro Wench with her
Daughter, who is about 12 year[s] of age; she is a good
spinner, country born. They were seen lately at Mr.
Middleton's plantation. A reward of Twenty Pounds is
offered for each of the said Negroes, to any person who will
deliver them to the Warden of the Work-house.

WILLIAM MOULTRIE.[562]

Moultrie failed to mention that Jemmy, Clay, Bob, Prince, Cyrus,
John and Sharper had joined the British forces in 1780, and
worked with the Engineer Department, according to a list drawn
up by the Commissioners of Claims on March 14, 1781, and
published by the *Royal Gazette*.[563] Should the fact that General
Moultrie, at age seventy-two, published his *Memoirs* in 1802, two
decades after these events be cited as a reason for his hazy
memory?

Nowhere in Moultrie's *Memoirs*, which are rich in
documentation, did he mention the blacks' feelings about anything,
much less why his fugitive blacks escaped. This seems to also be
the case with Henry Laurens, James Madison, Thomas Jefferson
and George Washington, whose remarks about black liberation
combined illusion with truth. Yet these men understood that after
the Revolution certain contradictory preconceptions about blacks
had to be modified. "You know my Dear Sir" wrote Laurens in
1776 to his son John, "I abhor slavery." After blaming the "British
Kings & Parliaments and their laws for the establishment of
slavery in America," and claiming "I am not the Man who enslaved
them" the wealthy slavetrader declared "I am devising means for
manumitting many of them & for cutting off the entail of Slavery
— great powers oppose me. The Laws & Customs of my country,
my own & the avarice of my Country Men — What will my
Children say if I deprive them of so much Estate?" His son John

---

[562]*South Carolina American General Gazette*, January 29, 1778.

[563]*Royal Gazette* (Charlestown), March 14, 1781

Laurens, a lieutenant colonel during the Revolutionary War, noted in October 1776 that he had "scarcely ever met with a Native of the Southern provinces or the W. Indies, who did not obstinately recur to the most absurd Arguments in support of Slavery." One argument was that "Without Slaves how is it possible for us to be rich."[564]

In August 1776, Laurens senior had boasted to his son about how "My Negroes there all to a Man are strongly attached me, so are all of mine in this Country, hitherto not one of them has attempted to desert, on the contrary those who are more exposed hold themselves always ready to fly from the Enemy in case of a sudden descent."[565]

To understand Lauren's attitude toward self liberated blacks, it is necessary to understand that his hard line stance never changed: there was no evolution. He whipped, chained, and deliberately broke up black family unions throughout the war. It is important, too, to understand that by selling Africans, indentured servants, as well as rice, indigo, rum, beer, wine and deerskins, Laurens, the son of a wealthy Huguenot sadler, rose to become the wealthiest merchant in the American colonies. A member of the colony's Commons House of Assembly in 1757, a lieutenant colonel in the French and Indian War in 1761, and one of the presidents of the newly-formed Continental Congress in 1778, Laurens claims he punished his first fugitive in 1765; this was Sampson, an African who had been in America eighteen months, eight of which had been as a fugitive. Laurens, who promised he "would not keep a runaway," sold Sampson for over three hundred pounds. He indicated that "this is the first & only one that ever I had to be a bad example to the rest of my slaves who are in general very orderly & give me but little trouble." Henry Laurens' first documented fugitive escape actually occurred in 1753. He published an ad describing Footabea, "a tall well-made new Negro man (of the Mindingo country)." In 1765, Abraham, Jack and Nat

---

[564]Rodgers, *The Papers of Henry Laurens*, XI: 223-225.

[565]Ibid., XI: 223.

and "two or three" others escaped from his Mepkin plantation.[566] In 1773, three Africans made off named Somerset, Lymus and Mark. The following year another one made off and was captured with frostbitten feet. In 1777, plantation manager John Lewis Gervias told him that "4 Negroes ran away from Mepkin" and that "four Negroes run also away from Sante." The next month Laurens himself noted that "Since my Last another Negro came to me from Mepkin named Collonel. As I am afraid too many of them might take it in their heads to come to Town, I have kept my promise & ordered him a Gentle Whipping at the Work house with which he is gone back again well Satisfied, for the day he went to the Workhouse there was a Negro going to be Executed for endeavouring to go on board of the Men of War & carrying three Women & 2 Children belonging to Mr. Poaug with him."[567]

Why would Laurens tell his son John in August 1776 that blacks "are as well intitled to freedom as themselves" when he used his office as President of the Council of Safety to capture fugitive blacks? He asked General William Moultrie in 1775 to detach two hundred men "to land on Sullivan's Island" and "seize and apprehend a number of Negroes who are said to have deserted to the enemy, together with every person who may be found on that island." In January 1776 he ordered "Simon Tufts, a Charleston mariner, and captain of South Carolina armed vessels Defense and Prosper" to board a Spanish vessel, *The Snow*, to take five blacks harbored on this ship. In 1776, Laurens, responding to Colonel Steven Bull of Georgia's query concerning fugitive slaves on Tybee Island, acknowledged the "awful business notwithstanding it has the sanction of Law, to put even fugitive & Rebellious Slaves to death,

---

[566]Edgar, *Biographical Dir. of S.C.* II: 390-393; Philip Hamer and George C. Rodgers, eds., *The Papers of Henry Laurens*, IV: 537, 567, 573, 645, 656, XI: 414; *South Carolina Gazette*, September 3, 1753, July 4, 1761, October 11, 1773; *South Carolina American General Gazette*, January 15, 1768, September 9, 1769; *South Carolina Historical Magazine*, 4 (1903), 205-206; David D. Wallace, *The Life of Henry Laurens: With a Sketch of the Life of Lieutenant Colonel John Laurens* (New York, 1918), 405, 456.

[567]Rodgers, *The Papers of Henry Laurens*, VII: 411, XI: 414.

the prospect is horrible."[568]

In 1777, fearful of a slave named Sam "who expects to absond," Laurens told his plantation manager that "After due Correction cause Irons to be put upon him which he cannot disengage." Laurens said "it will be the first instance of any Negro of mine put in Irons, but his Ingratitude will deserve the punishment. Spare no expence to take him if he attempts to run away." Why would an overseer care about the first "Negro " in irons especially when it seems that Laurens' policy was to chain fugitive slaves? The year before Laurens asked a planter to find Jack, a black who intended to "get on board Some of the Enemy's Vessels, which I would not have him Suceed in for twice his value." He sent a letter about Jack to his overseer asking him to "Secure him in Irons if he can be taken & watch him with the utmost attention until he can Send him Safely to me."[569]

In 1777, Laurens did admit that United States Senator Ralph Izard, owner of 8,000 oxen and 808 blacks, who was in England during the revolution, needed help. Laurens asked Izard to return to South Carolina and take charge of his estates. He claimed that Izard's "Negroes are continually deserting the plantations and going there where I have no doubt many of them would have embark'd in Men of War and other Vessels, and have been totally lost to you if I had not been upon the Spot sometimes to shield them against the Tyranny and Villainy of Overseers and Sometimes to restrain their own vicious Designs – nothing more troublesome than that Branch of plantation Business and I have had more of it fall to my Lot from your Negroes within two last Years than I had experienced in twenty years with my own." Laurens never manumitted a single slave nor sdid he support the gradual abolition of slavery legislatively in spite of his anti-slavery utterances and credited himself for having inserted "Article 7 of the Paris Treat prohibiting the carrying away of Negroes or other

---

[568]Ibid., X: 40, 546, XI: 172, 410, 414.

[569]Rodgers, *The Papers of Henry Laurens*, XI: 264-265, 350, 386, 387.

property."[570]

Madison's, Washington's, and Jefferson's writings called for the gradual abolition of slavery, but they continued to track down fugitives, whip them, sell them and break up their families. In the summer of 1783, Madison's slave Billey escaped from Virginia to Philadelphia. Madison barred Billey's return because the fugitive's mind was "too thoroughly tainted to be a fit companion for fellow slaves in Virginia" and because he could not "expect to get the near worth of him." But the fourth president could not punish Billey "by transportation merely for coveting that liberty for which we have paid the price of so much blood, and have proclaimed so often to be the right, and worthy pursuit of every human being." Were Madison's days of tracking down blacks over? No. In November 22, 1786, he published an ad describing a "Mulatto Slave named Anthony, about 17 years old who probably procured a Pass or a Certificate of his Freedom and has changed his name and cloathes." A year later Madison, writing from Philadelphia, informed his father that Anthony had escaped again and that "the enquiries which I have at different times made of Billey concerning Anthony satisfied me that he either knows, or will tell nothing of the matter."[571]

George Washington's attitude toward the fugitive showed itself in 1786. In a letter to Pennsylvania governor Robert Morris, Washington complained about a fugitive and an impending Quaker lawsuit designed to free that black. Washington asserted: "None of those whose *misfortune* it is to have slaves as attendants, will visit City if they can possibly avoid it; because in doing so they hazard their property or they must be at the expense (and this will not always succeed) of providing servants of another description for the trip." Washington did not "wish to hold the unhappy people, who are the subject of this letter in slavery. I can only say there is not a man living who wished more sincerely that I do, to see a plan

[570]Rodgers, *The Papers of Henry Laurens*, XI: 349-350; Wallace, *The Life of Henry Laurens*, 456.

[571]Hutchinson, *Papers of James Madison*, VII: 304, IX: 108, 155, XI: 208; *Virginia Gazette or American Advertiser* (Hayes) November 22, 1786.

adopted for the abolition of it, but there is only one purpose and effectual mode by which it can be accomplished, and that is by Legislative authority."[572]

"Happy and contented" slaves should not be "tampered with and seduced" to leave "their masters" said Washington. Oney Judge was apparently an unhappy woman; this black woman, treated "more like a child than a Servant," who had waited on Martha Washington for over a decade, had escaped to Portsmouth, New Hampshire, in the late summer of 1796. Joseph Whipple, the United States Collector of Customs found her, and he told Washington that Oney demanded immediate emancipation before she would return to Mount Vernon, a compromise Washington found "inadmissible." "For however well," he added, "disposed I might be to gradual abolition, or even to an entire emancipation of that description of People (if the latter was in itself practicable at this moment) it would neither be politic or just to reward *unfaithfulness* with a premature preference; and thereby discontent before hand had all the minds of all her fellow servants who by their steady attachments are far more deserving than herself of favor."[573]

A year later the President told his nephew Lawrence Lewis that he was "sorry to hear of the loss of your servant; but it is my opinion these elopements will be Much More, before they are Less frequent and the persons making them should never be retained, if they are recovered, as they are sure to contaminate and discontent others." And the President continued: "I wish from my soul that the Legislature of this State could see the policy of a gradual Abolition of Slavery; it would prevent much future mischief."[574]

Washington died on December 14, 1799, leaving behind 317 slaves, all of whom he willed free after his wife's death. Martha died twenty-nine months later. Abraham (1794), French Will (1795), French Paul (1795), Caesar (1796), Oney Judge (1796), and

---

[572]Fitzpatrick, *Writings of Washington*, XXVIII: 407-408.

[573]Ibid., XXXV: 201-202, 297.

[574]Ibid., XXXVI: 2-3.

Hercules (1797) made off before the executor read the last will and testament. The President claimed he could not free his slaves during his or his wife's lifetime because of their intermixture by marriages with the Dower blacks who belonged to Martha through a former marriage. But these Dower blacks numbered fifty-three, leaving 124, not including the forty he leased from a neighbor. The aged, the sick and the young might not be able to fend for themselves, still it is difficult to believe that he could not free Oney Judge. He gave his "Mulatto-man William" immediate freedom "for his faithful services during the Revolutionary War."[575] Oney Judge displayed "unfaithfulness" and Washington felt that to free her would cause blacks such as William who did not abscond to be up in arms. Certain fugitives if freed "prematurely" could cause havoc. When Oney left, who did the sewing — Martha? Who did the cooking at Mount Vernon while Hercules laid low in Philadelphia — George? "The running of my cook, has been a most inconvenient thing to this family," wrote the President on November 13, 1797 to his household steward Frederick Kitt in Philadelphia. Three months later he asked Kitt to keep searching "as I neither have nor can get a good cook to hire, and am disinclined to hold another by purchase."

Washington's slaves left little evidence of what they felt about the abolition of slavery other than the act of running away. Oney Judge's escape did provoke Washington to ponder the issue of gradual abolition for certain loyal blacks, but should the President's statement be blindly accepted without inquiry? Fortunately a Benjamin Chase tracked down Oney Judge in Greenland, New Hampshire and interviewed her in 1846 for the *Liberator*. Judge recalled that she was a "chambermaid for Mrs. Washington, that she was a large girl at the time of the revolutionary war; that when Washington was elected President, she was taken to Philadelphia, and that, although well enough used as to work and living, she did not want to be a slave always, and she supposed if she went back to Virginia, she would never have a chance to escape." Once in New Hampshire Judge married a man named Staines, and had three children. Washington sent a man named Basset to persuade Judge to return but she refused to go

---

[575]Ibid., XXVI: 70-71, XXXIV: 104, 154, 301, XXXVII: 277.

with him. Basset left and returned *"with orders to take her by force."*
Bassett even visited New Hampshire's governor who asked Oney
Judge to leave the state or be arrested. Judge who had to go into
hiding criticized America's first President. The "nearly white, very
much freckled" black said she never received the least mental
instruction of any kind while she remained in Washington's family."
She maintained that the "stories told of Washington's piety and
prayers so far as she ever saw or heard while she was his *slave,
have no foundation.*"[576]

What about America's third president, Thomas Jefferson, the
author of the Declaration of Independence? In his acclaimed *Notes
on the State of Virginia*, which he labored on from 1780 to 1781,
Thomas Jefferson used such terms as "unremitting despotism,"
"degrading submissions," and "miserable conditions" to describe the
plight of blacks under chattel slavery.[577] Aware that the black had
been denied the benefits of liberty, Jefferson appeared to
empathize with their plight, but could he sympathize with the
black who had fled to Florida to escape this "unremitting
despotism"?

After the war Washington asked Jefferson to quit his post as
Minister to France and in 1790 to become Secretary of State in
America's first Cabinet; Washington needed both him and James
Seagrove, the superintendent of Creek Indians, to help recapture
the blacks who escaped to Florida during the Revolutionary War.
The President ordered Seagrove to stop the "further reception of
fugitive slaves" and "to seek the restitution of those who have fled
to Florida," an action requiring diplomatic skill, for Governor Juan
Nepomuceno de Quesada of Florida might have viewed this as an
intrusion. Washington, therefore ordered Jefferson to pave the way
for Seagrove and by October 1790, Jefferson had notified Edward
Telfair of Georgia about the King of Spain's orders "not to permit
that Persons held in Slavery within the United States to introduce

---

[576]Blassingame, *Slave Testimony*, 245; Mechal Sobel, *The World
They Made Together: Black and White Values in Eighteenth-Century
Virginia* (Princeton, New Jersey, 1987), 139.

[577]Thomas Jefferson, *Notes on the State of Virginia*, William
Peden, ed. (Chapel Hill, N.C., 1755), 162.

themselves as free persons into the Province of Florida."[578]

Seagrove pressured Quesada on August 2, 1791 to issue a proclamation "ordering all Officers, civil and military, within this colony, but particularly, those on the River St. Mary's, to stop all such fugitive Slaves, and without delay convey them to the Spanish Post on Amelia Island." The Commissioner asked that harboring penalties be enacted and that "all fugitive Slaves belonging to the United States, who have taken shelter in Florida since the date of his Catholic Majesty's order on that head, be immediately restored on the preceding terms." Four days later Quesada claimed that "There is no account of even a single Slave being in the Province, who fled from the United States," and if there were such "fugitives it is the opinion of Government that they ought not to be restored, nor can it be agreed to without an express order from the King."[579]

What was Jefferson's attitude toward blacks who escaped from his home at Monticello after the war? Before the war, he published one ad, which called for the capture of Sandy, a shoemaker and carpenter. This is his only recorded advertisement:

[7 September 1769]

RUN away from the subscriber in *Albermarle*, a Mulatto slave called *Sandy*, about 35 years of age, corpulent, and his complexion light; he is a shoemaker by trade, in which he uses his left hand principally, can do coarse carpenters work, and is something of a horse jockey; he is greatly addicted to drink, and when drunk is insolent and disorderly, in his conversation he swears much, and his behavior is artful and knavish. He took with him a white horse, much scarred with traces, of which it is expected he will endeavour to dispose; he also carried his shoemakers tools, and will probably endeavour to get employment that way. Whoever conveys the said slave to me in *Albermarle* shall have 40 s. reward, if taken up within the county, £4. if elsewhere within the

---

[578]Fitzpatrick, *Writings of Washington*, XXXI: 288-290; Boyd, *Papers of Thomas Jefferson*, XVIII: 491.

[579]Boyd, *Papers of Thomas Jefferson*, XXII: 407-408.

colony, and £10 if in any other colony, from[580]

THOMAS JEFFERSON

According to Jefferson's son, Madison Hemings, when Jefferson became minister to France "during our revolutionary troubles," he invited his two daughters Maria and Martha, who took along James and Sally Hemings (Madison's mother), to accompany him. They stayed twenty-six months. Madison revealed that his mother, Sally, aged sixteen or seventeen, was Jefferson's concubine. Hemings wrote that Jefferson "desired to bring my mother back to Virginia with him but she demurred. She was just beginning to understand the French language well, and in France she was free, while if she returned to Virginia she would be re-enslaved. So she refused to return with him." After Jefferson promised Sally "extraordinary privileges and made a solemn pledge that her children should be freed at the age of twenty-one years," she returned to Virginia and gave birth to five children. "The first died" and four – Beverly, Harriet, Madison, and Easton – survived. All became free because of the "treaty entered into by our parents before we were born."[581]

Had Madison Hemings interview occurred during Jefferson's presidency an argument could be made that the Federalists were using this slave's memoir to unseat the third president of the United States, but the Ohio newspaper, *Pike County Republican*, interviewed Hemings in 1873, long after Jefferson's death. And still the interview might be at worst a hoax and at best marred by a few inaccuracies. Whatever the case, Madison's memoir and Jefferson's relationship with his mother might have never received the public's attention if Jefferson had remained out of politics and had he steered clear of James Thompson Callender. Callender was

---

[580]*Virginia Gazette*, September 7, 1769.

[581]Blassingame, *Slave Testimony: Two Centuries of Letters, Speeches, Interviews and Autobiographies*, 474-480; Brodie, *Thomas Jefferson, An Intimate History*, 471-476. For skeptics of Hemings' claim that Jefferson was his father, see Merrill D. Peterson, *The Jefferson Image in the American Mind* (New York, 1960), 185-186, 482-483; Jordan, *White Over Black*, 468-489.

a man that the British chased out of their country for his seditious writings, a man who pressured Alexander Hamilton to admit that he had committed adultery and a man who even compelled Jefferson to admit the "incorrectness" of his behavior when he tried to seduce his neighbor's wife. Jefferson employed Callender to keep his Federalist detractors at bay. These detractors included President John Adams whom Callender attacked at Jefferson's behest and received a consequent jail sentence under the 1798 Sedition Act for libeling a government official. When Jefferson assumed the presidency he pardoned Callender who then asked his erstwhile employer for the position of postmaster at Richmond, only to be turned down. Dejected, discouraged and disheartened, Callender sought to get even.[582]

When W.A. Rind had attacked Jefferson's sexual indiscretions in his *Virginia Federalist* in 1800. Callender "believed the surmise an absolute calumny." By 1802, Callender was writing in the *Richmond Recorder* that "it is well known that the man *whom it delighteth the people to honor*, keeps, and for many years has kept, as his concubine, one of his own slaves. Her name is *Sally*. The name of her oldest son is Tom. His features are said to bear a striking though sable resemblance to those of the president himself."[583] Callender did not survive to corroborate his charges for six months later he supposedly drowned himself in three feet of water in the James River. Still, Jefferson scholar Merrill Peterson claims that "it is difficult to imagine Jefferson caught up in a miscegenous relationship. Such a mixture of the races, such a ruthless exploitation of the master-slave relationship, revolted his whole being." Another scholar Dumas Malone found it "inconceivable" that Jefferson would engage in this "vulgar liaison." Besides, Martha Jefferson Randolph, Jefferson's daughter, considered him to be a devoted husband and father. When the

---

[582]Jordan, *White Over Black*, 468-489; Brodie, *Thomas Jefferson*, 416-428; Betts, ed., *Thomas Jefferson's Farm Book*, 130; Blassingame, *Slave Testimony*, 477; *Pike County Republican*, March 13, 1783; Charles A. Jellisow, "The Scoundrel Callender," *Virginia Magazine of History and Biography*, 57 (1959), 295-306.

[583]*The Richmond Recorder*, September 1, 1802.

third president's wife had passed away in September of 1782, she remembered that Jefferson had fainted, that he "kept his room for three weeks" that he "walked almost incessantly night and day" and that he had "many violent bursts of grief."[584]

Jefferson in his *Notes on Virginia* had showed in 1785 his concern about the black's intellectual capabilities and sexual proclivities. Why would he mount a black woman when he claimed they have a "strong and disagreeable odor," when they have "inferior reason," when they had hardly "uttered a thought above the level of plain narration; never seen even an elementary trait of painting or sculpture." Strangely enough this never stopped other white men from desiring black women.[585]

James Johnston's book on Virginia's "Race Relations" show that the Virginia legislature had preserved the written testimonies of numerous white women who demanded divorces because of their husbands' relationship with female slaves. In 1814, a woman from Augusta charged her husband with being 'carnally intimate' with

---

[584]Dumas Malone, *Jefferson The President, First Term 1801-1805* (Boston, 1970), 212-214; Sidney P. Moss and Carhin Moss, "The Jefferson Miscegenation in British Travel Books," *Journal of the Early Republic*, 7 (Fall 1987), 254; Merrill D. Peterson, *Thomas Jefferson and the New Nation: A Biography*; William Cohen, "Thomas Jefferson and the Problem of Slavery," *Journal of American History*, 56 (1969), 503-526; Fawn Brodie, "The Great American Taboo," *American Heritage*, 23 (1972), 48-57; Bar Sera, Chase-Riboud, *Sally Hemmings* (New York, 1979); Malone and Steven H. Hochman, "A Note On Evidence: The Personal History of Madison Hemings," *Journal of Southern History*, 41 (1975), 523-528; Virginius Dabney, *The Jefferson Scandals: A Rebuttal* (New York, 1981), 40-50; James A. Bear Jr., "The Hemings Family at Monticello," *Virginia Calvalcade*, 35 (1979), 78-87; William Bottorff, *Thomas Jefferson* (Boston 1979), 51-53; Jack McLaughlin, *Jefferson and Monticello: The Biography of a Builder* (New York, 1988) 121; Elizabeth Langhorne, *Monticello: A Family Story* (Chapel Hill, 1987), 109.

[585]*Notes on the State of Virginia*, William Peden, ed. (Chapel Hill, 1955), 137-143.

a black woman named Milly, in his "own wife's bed" and the "said Negro woman Milly has since been delivered of a mulatto child." Another woman in 1817, said in her petition that a witness had "heard the said husband boast to his wife in her absence he had taken of his own Negro woman into her bed and that he would do it again whenever it suited him." One woman complained in 1820 that her husband took up with a female slave cook and that for three months 'night after night' "he would before her eyes and in the very room in which your petitioner slept go to bed with the said slave or cause the said slave to come in and go to bed with him." How widespread was this practice is hard to tell because only the determined white woman would openly defy her husband by testifying in front of the legislators.[586]

These cases may well have been the tip of the iceberg. Jefferson's father-in-law, John Wayles had three wives who gave birth to four daughters. After the death of his third wife, Wayles took an African woman named Betty Hemings, from his plantation and she bore him six children, one of whom was named Sally Hemings. Upon marrying Martha Wayles, Thomas Jefferson inherited these slaves.[587]

The Virginia legislature kept records describing white women giving in to their sexual fantasies, and having sexual relations with black men and as a result white men too, asked for divorces. In 1801 a Fluvanna county citizen said his wife Elizabeth was "delivered of a mulatto child, and is now so bold as to say it was begotten by a Negro man slave in the neighborhood." The following year a Norfolk citizen told the legislators that his wife Lydia was "delivered of a child, which on your petitioner's return and to his inexpressible grief and astonishment proved to be a mulatto, and which she shortly afterwards confessed was the child of a Negro slave."[588]

Madison Hemings' claim that he had a white father would not

---

[586]James Hugo Johnston, *Race Relations in Virginia & Miscegenation in the South, 1776-1860* (Amherst, 1970), 239-242.

[587]Blassingame, *Slave Testimony*, 477.

[588]Johnston, *Race Relations*, 250-253.

have roused such a stir had he not named Thomas Jefferson. Had it not been for Callender, the citizens in Charlottesville, Jefferson's hometown, would have probably shrugged it off. But since the country probably heard about or read the charges, it would be difficult for the third President to free the Hemings. Yet if Jefferson reneged in freeing Sally Hemings' children, it might have caused discontent or an escape attempt, but perhaps that was what Jefferson hoped his detractors would believe when he listed Beverly and Harriet as having "ranaway" in his *Farm Book*. Madison Hemings reported: "Beverly left Monticello and went to Washington as a white man. He married a white woman in Maryland, and their only child, a daughter was not known by the white folks to have any colored blood coursing in her veins." Harriet married a white man in Washington city and "assumed the role of a white woman." Jefferson's Monticello overseer, Edmund Bacon, recalled that "she was nearly as white as anybody and very beautiful. People said he freed her because she was his own daughter. She was not his daughter: she was – 's daughter." Bacon also said Jefferson "paid her stage fare to Philadelphia and gave her fifty dollars." Jefferson freed Easton and Madison, as well as three others; he did not free Sally Hemings.[589]

Did Jefferson allow others to "run away"? Joe, aged twenty-six, twelve years a blacksmith, escaped in the summer of 1806. "Joe left," claimed Jefferson, "without the least word of difference with any body & indeed having never in his life recieved a blow from anyone." Two other blacks, hired out to Jefferson on a yearly basis, escaped to Fredericksburg where their master lived. In 1807, Jefferson ordered Bacon to find them because "they will make out a sad story to her, which it would be well for you to set to rights by letting her know how little they have to complain of as to severity, food or clothing, being always treated as my own, & better whenever any difference is made." James Hubbard, a black, escaped from Monticello in 1805 and managed to live free in Lexington for at least a year. Jefferson ordered overseer Isham Chisolm to capture him. Chisolm brought Hubbard back in irons, and Jefferson had him "severely flogged in the presence of his old

---

[589]Blassingame, *Slave Testimony*, 477; Bear, *Jefferson at Monticello*, 102.

companions and committed to jail." Jefferson felt: "All circumstances convinced me he will never again serve any man as a slave. The moment he is out of jail and his irons off he will be off himself."[590]

Thomas Jefferson suffered in 1816 from poor hearing and needed glasses to see at night. He depended on overseer Jeremiah Goodman to whom he paid 200 pounds a year to manage the Tomahawk plantation in Poplar Forest where sixteen blacks worked 209 acres of land. Harvesting tobacco, hemp, wheat, pumpkins, clover and peas, the blacks had families and they frequently lived far from Poplar Forest. Phil Hubbard yearned to see his wife named Hanah at Bearcreek; Goodman refused his wish and Hubbard escaped. He made it to Monticello on December 27, 1814, and told Jefferson why he escaped. After considerable thought, Jefferson informed his overseer that certainly "there is nothing I desire so much as that all the young people in the estate should intermarry with one another and stay at home. They are worth a great deal more in that case then when they have husbands aboard. Phil has long been petitioning me to let him go to Bearcreek to live with his family and Nanny has been long at me to let her come to the Poplar Forest." Hubbard's escape finally moved Jefferson to send Hubbard to Bearcreek, and Nanny to Poplar Forest. Should Hubbard be punished? "I would by no means have Phil punished for what he has done; for all others I had let them all know that their running away should be punished, yet Phil's character is not that of a runaway."[591] Despite his threat to whip fugitive blacks, Jefferson seemed to understand that work productivity would decrease and discontent increase if he blocked family reunification at his plantation.

Words about the need to abolish slavery and the need to manumit blacks flowed from the Founding Father's mouths, but what comes to mind is Samuel Johnson's 1774 essay entitled "Taxation No Tyranny" where he wrote: "We are told, that the subjection of Americans may tend to the diminution of our own

---

[590]Betts, *Jefferson's Farm Book*, 22, 24, 26-27, 34-37.

[591]Thomas Jefferson, *Garden Book: 1766-1824*, (Philadelphia, 1944), 540.

liberties: an event, which none but very perspicacious politicians are able to foresee. If slavery be thus fatally contagious, how is it that we hear the loudest yelps, for liberty among the drivers of Negroes."[592] None of the Founding Fathers, including Jefferson, could claim that they had not heard the black's freedom yelps for the noted Benjamin Banneker wrote Jefferson in 1791, complaining about his "narrow prejudices." Banneker complimented Jefferson's *Notes:* "This Sir, was a time when you clearly saw into the injustices of a State of Slavery, and in which you had Just apprehensions of the horror of its condition." But "Sir, how pitiable is it to reflect, that although you were so fully convinced of the benevolence of the Father of Mankind, and of his equal and impartial distribution of these rights, and privileges which he hath conferred upon them, that you should at the Same time counteract his mercies, in detaining by fraud and violence so numerous a part of my brethen, under groaning captivity, and cruel oppression, that you should at the Same time be found guilty of that most criminal act, which you professedly detested in others, with respect of yourselves."[593]

Archibald McCalester, a "Carolina Rice Planter" also wrote Thomas Jefferson in 1791. A former officer in the "Maryland Line," McCalester expressed concern about the "British Troops that ravaged the Carolinas, carried off Twenty-eight Negroes from my Plantation, and a number more from an Estate to which I am an Executor. Several of my Negroes were after the Peace at Birch Town in Nova Scotia; but I never could reclaim them, as the British would not give them up. – Query, are not the British bound to pay for them, and is there any possibility of obtaining Payment"?[594]

---

[592]*Samuel Johnson: Political Writings*, Donald J. Greene, ed. (10 vols., New Haven, 1977), 452.

[593]Aptheker, *A Documentary History of the United States*, I: 22-23; Silvio A. Bedini, *The Life of Benjamin Banneker* (New York, 1971), 154-155.

[594]Charles T. Cullen, *The Papers of Thomas Jefferson*, XXII: 253-254.

Ten years after the war the planter still remembered the self-liberated blacks and apparently Jefferson was the man with whom he felt comfortable enough to talk about slave compensation. Compensation was an old argument first advanced by the Quakers in 1740 and 1756 and sometimes it worked, given the proper political clout. McCalester had heard that the "British Court are sending out a Mr. Hammond with a view to negotiate a Treaty of Offensive and Defensive Alliance with the United States" and rather than give them a "commercial advantage," the South Carolina planter had hoped that the United States "will reject such a connection with disdain."[595]

This appears to be what Jefferson had in mind when he wrote George Hammond, the English ambassador, on December 15, 1791, regarding the "large embarkation of Negroes, of the property of the inhabitants of the U. S." in which some three thousand blacks had been carried away. Unprepared for Jefferson's query, Hammond wrote the British foreign affairs secretary and stated: "the treaty of peace cannot be supposed to apply to any other description of Negroes than such as were the actual property of the inhabitants of the United States, at the period of the cessation of hostilities — that, of the Negroes, carried away from New York, under the permission and protection of Lord Dorchester, part may be presumed to have been captured during the war, and were consequently booty acquired by the rights of war: But that the principal part of them had fled to the British lines, in consequence of proclamations issued by the British Commanders in Chief (who were at the time in the exercise of legal authority in the country) which promised to them freedom upon their joining the British army — and that this description of Negroes, thus emancipated, had acquired indefeasible rights of personal liberty, of which the British government was not competent to deprive them, by reducing them again to a state of slavery, and to the domination of their ancient masters."[596]

Because of the founding fathers' attitudes, it is not surprising to find attention devoted to Article Seven of the Paris Peace Treaty

[595]Ibid.

[596]Ibid, XXII: 410-411.

calling for the return of black evacuees. How many blacks were missing? The British transported at least 17,000 blacks out of the country as the war wound down in 1781-1782. Thomas Jefferson estimated that Virginia in 1778 lost 30,000 blacks. Dr. David Ramsay, a Continental Congressman (1782-1785) and an historian, an eye witness, claimed a loss of 25,000 slaves for South Carolina. Authorities said that 6,000 blacks belonging to loyalists left Georgia for Florida. Again, Dunmore's incursion brought in its wake 700-800 blacks. Extant gazettes between 1776-1781 in North and South Carolina, Georgia, Virginia, Maryland, Delaware, Washington, New Jersey, Pennsylvania and New York described 300 blacks and 60 white servants going off. At least 100,000 blacks were missing out of a total of 600,000 after the war.[597]

Jefferson might have sought compensation from Britain because the same planter who cried "Ruin'd" in the 1780s remained so in the 1790s. Virginia still owed the British merchants over 20,000 pounds and with a depleted treasury, the colonist had no way to pay it. Even Jefferson himself was in debt. In fact, he owed his creditors over $100,000 when he died. Compensation for the 30,000 slaves could go a long way towards paying creditors.[598]

Mindful that the British compensation issue might be revised by the planter, Jay wrote in 1787 that "there is no doubt but that Britain has violated the 7th Article" by its evacuation of New York. "Negroes belonging to American Inhabitants were carried away" but distinctions must be made, Jay claims, between the blacks who were captured as "bounty," and those who stayed within the British lines, responding to the British proclamations and promises of freedom or protection." The Secretary of Foreign Affairs maintained that " By the Laws by War all goods and

---

[597]Quarles, *The Negro in the American Revolution.*

[598]Myrr C. Rich, "Speculations on the Significance of Debt," *Virginia Magazine History and Biography* (June 1968),??76; Charles F. Hobson, "The Recovery of British Debts in the Federal Circuit Court of Virginia, 1790-1797, *Virginia Magazine History and Biography*, 92 (April 1985), 176-200; Emory G. Evans, "Private Indebtedness and the Revolution in Virginia, 1776-1796," *William and Mary Quarterly*, 3rd Ser., 28 (July 1971), 349-374.

Chattels captured and made booty flagrante Bello" became British property and that this Article applied to those "Negroes kept as slaves" who remained within the British lines. Moreover, blacks could not by "merely flying or eloping extinguish the right or title of their masters, nor was that title destroyed by their coming into the enemy's possession, for they *were received not taken* by the enemy; they were received not as Slaves but as friends and freeman." Jay concluded that the British violated the 7th Article and that they should do "substantial justice to the Masters by paying them the value of those Slaves."[599]

In the long run the Federalists, led by Alexander Hamilton, won the battle; Jay drafted the treaty and handed it Washington in April of 1795. In the dead of night the Senate ratified the treaty. Virginia Senator George Mason leaked the details of the Jay Treaty to the press causing Jay's life to be put in danger. Southern demonstrators burned Jay in effigy and torched British ships, but Washington held fast and signed the treaty, a treaty that left out any reference to the 7th Article or to the blacks who left America. An angry James Madison stood up in Congress in April 1796 and said that "Apologies had been attempted also for the very extraordinary abandonment of the compensation due for the Negroes." A cautious Hamilton told Washington that Britain's "proceedings in seducing away our Negroes during the War were to the last degree infamous – and form an indelible stain in her annals. But having done it, it would have been still more infamous to have surrendered them to their Masters." And James Hillhouse of Connecticut, a Jay supporter, felt that it did not matter whether the citizen was captured and enslaved in Barbary nations in Africa or in the United States: "The first principle that is laid down in the rights of man, is that all men are born free and equal, it does

---

[599]Frederick Austin Ogg, "Jay's Treaty and the Slavery Interests of the United States," *American Historical Association Annual Report for 1901*, I: 275; Samuel E. Bemis, *Jay's Treaty: A Study in Commerce and Diplomacy* (Westport, 1962), 448; Richard B. Mollis, *John Jay, Winning of the Peace, Unpublished Papers, 1780-1784* (New York, 1980), 523; *The Negro in the Continental Congress*, Peter Bergman and Jean McCarroll, comp. (New York, 1969), 130-133.

not say all *white* men." He ended by stating that slavery was an
"evil which existed at the commencement of our Revolution," and
he trusted every part of the Union would "get rid of the evil as
soon as it should be practical and safe." Indeed, that is exactly
what began to occur in some states and the fugitive played a role
in this process.[600]

---

[600]Peter M. Bergman and Jean McCarroll, *The Negro in the
Congressional Record* (10 vols., New York, 1969), I: 82, 92-96;
Donald Robinson, *Slavery in the Structure of American Politics,
1765-1820* (New York, 1971), 352-354; *Alexander Hamilton Papers*,
Syrett, ed., XVIII: 415.

CHAPTER XI
HOPPER VERSUS BUTLER

The Revolutionary War led the local citizenry in eleven states to draft constitutions and in some cases caused them to abolish slavery and slave trading as well. Vermont banned slavery in 1777; three years later Pennsylvania followed suit with a gradual abolition provision. Judicial decisions nudged Massachusetts down that path. Rhode Island (1784), Connecticut (1784), New York (1799) and New Jersey (1784) passed gradual abolition laws. New Hampshire had no slaves by 1810. In Delaware, Maryland and Virginia, lawmakers, various committees and anti-slavery societies denounced slavery, but to no avail. Private manumission laws and not the gradual abolition of slavery arose in Virginia (1782), Delaware (1787) and Maryland (1782). North Carolina required County court approval, Georgia, legislative approval. South Carolina rejected gradual abolition, privately and legislatively.[602]

Massachusetts' constitution created restlessness among blacks. In 1795 a sixty-nine year old Boston merchant, Samuel Dexter, responding to the query of the secretary of the Massachusetts Historical Society, Reverend Jeremy Belknap, about slavery's end in Massachusetts, claimed slavery "never was" formally and "expressly abolished." But the first article in the Massachusetts Constitution declared: "All men are born free and equal, and have

---

[602]*The Federal and State Constitutions Colonial Charters, and other Organic Laws...*, Francis N. Thorpe, comp. and ed. (7 vols., Washington, D.C., 1909), VI: 3739; Willi Adams, *The First American Constitutions: Republican Ideology and the Making of the State Constitutions in the Revolutionary Era* (Chapel Hill, North Carolina, 1980), 180-183; Arthur Zilversmit, *The First Emancipation: The Abolition of Slavery in the North* (Chicago, 1967), 112-116; Jordan, *White Over Black*, 345-346.

certain natural, essential and unalienable rights, among which may
be reckoned the right of enjoying and defending their lives and
liberty." Dexter also recalled that "soon after the establishment of
the Constitution of Massachusetts, one Negro after another
deserted from the service of those who had been their owners till
a considerable number had revolted." Some of them were seized
and remanded to their former servitude. Some blacks brought suits
against their owners which "operated to the liberation of all who
did voluntarily remain with their former owners." And "Thus ended
slavery in Massachusetts," claimed Dexter.[603]

Black fugitive Quock Walker played a role in the judicial
decision to free blacks in Massachusetts. James Caldwell of
Worcester, who purchased Walker on May 4, 1754, died in 1763.
Caldwell bequeathed "one third of the property" including Walker,
to his wife, Isabell, who married Nathaniel Jennison. In 1766,
Isabell died, whereby Jennison, and Isabell's two sons, laid claim
to Walker. Quock Walker, who claimed his former master had
promised him freedom at age twenty-eight, worked briefly for
Jennison, but absconded ten days later and found a job with Seth
and John Caldwell, probably the children of James Caldwell. In
June 1781, according to the clerk of Worcester's Common Pleas
Court, Jennison "seized the said Quock, & threw him down &
struck him several violent blows upon his back & arm with the
handle of a whip" and had the slave jailed. The jury found that
Quock was a "freeman, and not the proper Negro slave of the said
Nathaniel Jennison" and ordered Jennison to pay a fifty dollar fine.
In June 1781, Jennison sued the Caldwells for harboring Quock
Walker. The court found the Caldwells guilty and fined them
twenty-five pounds. The Caldwells appealed to the Supreme
Judicial Court in Worcester for redress and the court reversed the
decision five months later.[604]

---

[603]"Belknap Papers," *Collections of the Massachusetts Historical
Society*, 5th Ser., IV: 306; Zilversmit, *The First Emancipation*, 112-
116.

[604]"Brief of Levi Lincoln in the Slave Case Tried 1781," *Coll.
of Mass.*, 1st Ser., IV: 440-442; William O'Brien, S.J., "Did the
Jennison Case Outlaw Slavery in Massachusetts?," *William & Mary*

On June 10, 1782 the House of Representatives in that colony examined Jennison's petition claiming he was "deprived of ten Negros" because of a clause in the Declaration of Rights stating that "all men are free and equal." Between 1781 and 1783 the judiciary discussed the legality of slavery in one of the Jennison court cases. Chief Justice William Cushing, a Supreme Judicial Court clerk during that time wrote:

> And upon this ground our Constitution of Government, by which the people of this Commonwealth have solemnly bound themselves, sets out with declaring that all men are born free and equal – and that every subject is entitled to liberty, and to have it guarded by the laws, as well as life and property – and in short is totally repugnant to the idea of being born slaves. This being the case, I think the idea of slavery is inconsistent with our own conduct and Constitution; and there can be no such thing as perpetual servitude of a rational creature, unless his liberty is forfeited by some criminal conduct or given up by personal consent of contract... Verdict Guilty.[605]

Massachusetts appears to have responded to the blacks' plea for liberate them, for by 1790, slavery had withered away.[606]

The Pennsylvania council drafted America's first gradual abolition bill in February 1777 and these issues came under discussion. Should a black who descended from a slave mother after March 1, 1780 be forced to serve until age twenty-one or

---

Quarterly, 3rd Ser., 17 (1960), 219; Robert M. Spector, "The Quock Walker Cases: The Abolition of Slavery and Negro Citizenship in Massachusetts, 1781-1783," *Journal of Negro History*, 8 (1968), 12-32.

[605]Quoted in John D. Cushing, "The Cushing Court and the Abolition of Slavery in Massachusetts: More Notes on the Quock Walker Case," *American Journal of Legal History*, 5 (1961), 118-144.

[606]Green, *American Population Before* 1790, 12-19.

twenty-eight? Should the colony continue to prohibit racial intermarriage? Should the colony indenture the unemployed free blacks? And should the black be allowed to vote or hold office? The Council decreed that slavery be gradually abolished in March 1780 and ordered the planters to register their slaves between March and November 1, of 1780 or lose them.[607]

Hoping to make it easier to sell his slaves outside Pennsylvania's borders, the planter requested a registration extension, but Quaker lobbyists and a black outcry waylaid the request. One black, Cato, published this plea in the *Freeman's Journal* on September 21, 1781:

> MR. PRINTER
> I am a poor Negro, who with myself and children have had the good fortune to get my freedom, by means of an act of assembly passed on the first of March 1780, and should now with my family be as happy a set of people as any on the face of the earth; but I am told the assembly are going to pass a law to send us all back to our masters. Why dear Mr. Printer, this would be the cruelest act that ever a set of worthy good gentlemen, could be guilty of. To make a law to hang us all, would be *merciful*, when compared with this law; for many of our masters would treat us with unheard of barbarity, for daring to take advantage (as we have done) of the law made in our favor. Our lots in *slavery* were hard enough to bear: but having tasted the sweets of *freedom* we should now be miserable indeed – surely no Christian gentleman can be so cruel! I cannot believe they will past such a law – I have read the act which made me free, and I always read it with joy – and I always dwell with particular pleasure on the following words spoken by the assembly in

---

[607]Edward Turner, *The Negro in Pennsylvania* (New York, 1911), 78-80; *Pennsylvania Packet*, March 3, 1780; Zilversmit, *The First Emancipation*, 112-114.

top of the said law.[608]

Cato's plea did not deter the planter from selling blacks. During the period between 1780 and 1784 the *Pennsylvania Packet* published sixty-eight ads describing eighty blacks up for sale. In 1788, the Pennsylvania lawmakers ordered planters to register the birth of children born to slave women, prevented them from separating a slave couple for more than a distance of eleven miles, and made it illegal for them to send pregnant women out of the state. Blacks fortunate enough to be born after March 1, 1780, still had to serve their mother's master until age twenty-eight; the act bounded blacks during the best years of their lives. Blacks entitled to indentured contract, court redress, and freedom dues, still faced punishment for contractual breaches. In the long run, it was not the black indentured servants who benefitted, but their offspring.[609]

Twenty-three members of the assembly who represented the Scotch-Irish Presbyterians of the back country called the bill "premature," claiming that it might lead the "Negroes of these states to demand their immediate and entire freedom," that blacks would want to vote and to be "voted into office" and that they would want to marry "with white persons."[610] To insure the bill's passage, Anthony Benezet, the noted anti-slavery crusader, solicited the assembly's votes. If Benezet and some Quakers had their way, they would have abolished slavery before the Revolutionary War, especially those Quakers who belonged to America's first anti-slavery organization, set up in 1775 and called The Society for the Relief of Free Negroes, Unlawfully Held in Bondage.[611]

Old-fashioned, wearing broad-trimmed hats, straight collars, drab colored jackets and unmetallic shoes, the Quakers refused to smoke, sing, dance or play cards, or pick up arms or swear

---

[608]*Freeman's Journal,* postscript, September 21, 1781; Zilversmit, *The First Emancipation,* 136.

[609]*Pennsylvania Packet,* March 3, 1780.

[610]*The Pennsylvania Society for Promoting the Abolition of Slavery,* Edward Needles, comp. (New York, 1848, 1969), 1-10.

[611]Jordan, *White Over Black,* 357-359.

allegiance to the American government during the American Revolution. The government enacted the Test Act demanding the Quakers to pay a double tax, to desist from working if they were merchants, traders, lawyers, physicians, druggists or school teachers and to discontinue using the courts, making out wills, or acting as guardians. The authorities in the summer of 1777 arrested Quaker leaders James, John, and Israel Pemberton, Henry Drinker, Thomas Wharton, Samuel Pleasants, and banished them to Winchester, Virginia until early 1778, where some fell sick or died.[612]

After the war the authorities expected the Quakers to remain silent, stop politicking, cease their attacks on the slave trade, stop their support of the black freemen and their harboring of fugitive slaves. In 1785, the *New York Packet* wrote: "Blacks, in combination with their friends, the Quakers, would give assistance to our enemies and fight against us by whole regiments. It was these pretended supporters of liberty who now preach up, let us emancipate the slaves, conceiving it more for the benefit of their souls to have the Negroes now set at liberty, than they thought it just that white people should have it in the years 1776 and 1777."[613]

The early southern congressmen tried to discredit the Quakers. Aedanus Burke of South Carolina "denied that they [Quakers] were the friends of freedom," but felt they were "spies," that "they supplied the enemy with provisions;" that "they were guides and conductors to their armies; and whenever the American army came into their neighborhood, they found themselves in an enemy's country." In March 1790, Representative William Loughton Smith of South Carolina said of the Quakers: "in time of war they would not defend their country from the enemy, and in time of peace they were interfering in the concerns of others, and doing everything in their power to excite the slaves in the Southern States to insurrection." The Northerners as a rule defended the

---

[612]Sydney V. James, "The Impact of the American Revolution on Quakers' Ideas About Their Sect," *William & Mary Quarterly*, 3rd Ser., 19 (1962), 360-382.

[613]*New York Packet*, April 4, 1785.

Quakers and their antislavery activities. He "believed them to be good friends of order," said Albert Gallatin of Pennsylvania. New York's Edward Livingston said the Quakers did not deserve "the character given them."[614]

To increase their influence, the Quakers began to organize abolitionist societies in a number of states, and exerted considerable influence throughout the country. A year after the Pennsylvania Abolitionist Society reopened, the New York Manumission Society opened its offices in Manhattan. Similar societies opened in Wilmington, Delaware (1788); Washington County, Pennsylvania (1789); Rhode Island (1789); Virginia (1791); Maryland (1790); and Connecticut (1790). By 1791, twelve abolitionist societies had sprung up from Massachusetts to Virginia, signaling a new stage in the fight against chattel slavery.[615]

Why did the pro-slavery congressmen single out the Quakers when the Methodist and Baptist denominations also freed blacks, when the Baptist General Committee in Virginia in 1785 found 'hereditary slavery to be contrary to the work of God,' and when during the late eighteenth century the Methodist Church contended "Slavery is contrary to the laws of God, man, and nature" and proceeded to prevent slaveholders from attending their

---

[614]Owen S. Ireland, "The Ethnic-Religious Dimensions of Pennsylvania Politics, 1755-1786," *William & Mary Quarterly*, 3rd Ser., 30 (July 1973), 423-448; *The Negro in the Congressional Record, 1789-1801*, Peter M. Bergman and Jean McCarroll, comp. (10 vols., New York, 1969-1971), II: 29, 32, 167-169.

[615]Jordan, *White Over Black*, 345. For a definitive list see *Minutes of the Proceedings of a Convention of Delegates from the Abolition Societies Established in Different Parts of the United States, Assembled at Philadelphia* (Phila., 1794), 37-43; Mary S. Locke, *Anti-Slavery in America: From the Introduction of African Slaves to the Prohibition of the Slave Trade, 1619-1808* (Boston, 1901, 1968), 97-99; Leon F. Litwack, *North of Slavery: The Negro in the Free States, 1790-1860* (Chicago, 1961), 7.

services?[616] Planters even accused Methodists of harboring their slaves:

> A Young Negro man slave, the property of the subscriber, named Sam, left the service of Charles Gosnell near Soldiers Delight, in Baltimore County, on Sunday last, to whom he was hired; he was seen the same day traveling towards Baltimore, where he has several relations (manumitted blacks) who will conceal and assist him to make his escape. HE WAS RAISED IN A FAMILY OF RELIGIOUS PERSONS, COMMONLY CALLED METHODISTS, AND HAS LIVED WITH SOME OF THEM FOR YEARS PAST, ON TERMS OF PERFECT EQUALITY; the refusal to continue him on these terms, the subscriber is instructed, has given him offence, and is the sole cause of his absconding. Sam is about twenty-three years old, 5 feet 8 or 9 inches high, pretty square made, has a down look, very talkative among persons whom he can make free with, but slow of speech; HE HAS BEEN IN THE USE OF INSTRUCTING AND EXHORTING HIS FELLOW CREATURES OF ALL COLORS IN MATTERS OF RELIGIOUS DUTY...[617]

Unlike the Baptists or the Methodists, the Quakers did not

---

[616]James David Essig, "A Very Wintry Season: Virginia Baptists and Slavery, 1785-1797," *The Virginia Magazine of History and Biography*, 88 (1980), 170-185; W. Harrison Daniel, "Virginia Baptists and the Negro in the Early Republic," *The Virginia Magazine of History and Biography*, 80 (1971), 61; Carlos R. Allen, Jr., ed., David Barrow's, "Circular Letter of 1798," *William & Mary Quarterly*, 3rd Ser., 20 (1963), 440-451; Donald G. Mathews, *Slavery and Methodism: A Chapter in America's Morality, 1780-1845* (Princeton, 1965). Presbyterians were reluctant to emancipate slaves," see W. Harrison, "Presbyterian and the Negro in the Early National Period," *Journal of Negro History*, 38 (1973), 291-295.

[617]Quoted in "Eighteenth Century Slave Ads As Advertised by Their Masters," *Journal of Negro History, 1*, (1916), 202-203.

restrict their antislavery activities to manumissions or harboring alone; they pressured the government as well. During 1789 and 1790, the capital of the Federal government was Philadelphia, where the Quakers held sway and therefore Quakers could walk to the Federal building and attack the slave trade, the kidnapping of free blacks, the Fugitive Act, and slavery itself. On February 11, 1790, Quakers, representing societies from New York to Virginia, presented a petition in America's first Congress condemning "the licentious wickedness of the African trade for slaves" and calling for its abolition. The following day another memorial signed by Benjamin Franklin of the Pennsylvania Abolitionist Society promised to use all "justifiable endeavors to loosen the bands of slavery, and promote a general enjoyment of the blessings of freedom."[618]

The Southern congressmen denounced the memorials. "Do these men expect a general emancipation of slaves by law? This would never be submitted to by the Southern States without a civil war" roared Thomas Tucker of South Carolina. William Loughton Smith of South Carolina felt any discussion of the slave trade or emancipation was "an attack upon the paladium of the property of our country is therefore our duty to oppose it by every means in our power." He asked a month later in March 17, 1790 about the plan to manumit blacks: "Would not such a step be injurious even to the slaves themselves? It was well known that they were indolent people, improvident, averse to labor: when emancipated, they would either starve or plunder." Using Jefferson's *Notes on Virginia* as a source, Smith concluded that "Negroes were by nature an inferior race of beings." The Quakers, too, were a special object of scorn for Smith. He criticized the Quaker memorial, calling it an "indecent attack on the character of those States which possess slaves." He wondered if any had "ever married a Negro, or would any of them suffer their children to mix their blood with that of

---

[618]Bergman and McCarroll, *The Negro in the Congressional Record*, 1789-1801, II: 14-15, 120. By 1780 the Pennsylvania Society called itself "The Pennsylvania Society for Promoting the Abolition of Slavery for the Relief of Free Negroes Unlawfully Held in Bondage, and for Improving the Condition of the African Race." Jordan, *White Over Black*, 343.

a black? They would view with abhorrence such an alliance."[619]

The Quakers refused to be ignored. "The gallies were thronged with the Quakers who had presented the Petitions" Congressman Smith wrote to Governor Edward Rutledge in February, 1790. "Their appearance had a manifest influence on those members who apprehended the loss of their Election if they displeased the Quakers who vote by System. They therefore voted for the Commitment without wishing to take the step in the business," Smith claimed. During that same period Senator William Maclay of Pennsylvania recorded in his journal that "our Vice-President [John Adams] produced the petitions and memorials of the Abolition Society. He did it rather with a sneer, saying he had been honored with a visit from a society, a self constituted one, he supposed." He remembered that South Carolina's Senator Ralph Izard "in particular, railed at the society; called them fanatics, etc." but Maclay alluded to the "benevolent intentions of the society."[620]

The Pennsylvania Congressmen supported the Quakers. Thomas Scott of Pennsylvania described the slave trade as being one of the "most abominable things on earth." He promised "to support every Constitutional measure likely to bring about its total abolition." If he was "one of the Judges of the United States, and those people were to come before me and claim their emancipation; but I am sure I would go as far as I could." James Jackson of Georgia predicted that the "existence of such a Judge might be in danger" in Georgia and that if Quakers continued to push the slave-trade issue it would "light up the flame of civil discord."[621]

Quakers pressed another congressional issue in December, 1796,

---

[619]Ibid., II: 30, 31.

[620]George C. Rodgers, Jr., ed., "The Letters of William Loughton Smith to Edward Rutledge, June 6, 1789 to April 8, 1794," *South Carolina Historical Magazine* (1968-1969), 69-70, 107-108; *Journal of William Maclay: United States Senator From Pennsylvania, 1789-1791*, William S. Maclay, ed. (New York, 1890), 196.

[621]Bergman and McCarroll, *The Negro in The Congressional Record*, II: 21.

criticizing ship captains who kidnapped free blacks and sold them into slavery. William Murray of Maryland "wished to know what was fully meant by the idea of preventing kidnapping. He confessed he did not rightly understand the idea of preventing kidnapping. He confessed he did not rightly understand the meaning of the word. Was the intention of the committee to have reference to the taking of free Negroes and selling them as slaves, or the taking of slaves to make them free."[622]

Pennsylvania representative John Swanwick claimed that "it was intended to prevent both evils. It was intended to prevent their being stolen from their masters; and also, to prevent the power of the Master taking them to other States to sell them." Murray was hoping that the word kidnapping would not justify the "harboring of Negroes" for "at present Negroes through the influence of their own mind, through the insinuation of others, or both, frequently leave their masters and are harbored by other persons." Murray argued that the harborer and the ship captain who sold free blacks were both kidnappers, and the real aim was to weaken the "Fugitive Slave Clause" in the Constitution, which "orders the return of any person held to Service or Labour in one State, under the laws thereof, escaping into another to the Party to whom such Service or Labour may be due."[623]

Murray invoked the spectre of the fugitive slave law because it awarded the planter the right of recaption, a right that had Federal backing since 1787. Fearful that slaves would seek solace in the Northwest Territory where slavery was prohibited, the planter managed to extract from a congressional committee packed with northerners, a declaration that "any person escaping into the same, from whom labor or service is lawfully claimed in any one of the original States, such fugitive may be lawfully reclaimed and conveyed to the person claiming his or the labor or service as aforesaid." Because the Continental Congress possessed no coercive powers under the Articles of Confederation, this clause could not be enforced. Yet it shows how some northern representatives

---

[622]Ibid., II: 113-115.

[623]Ibid.

compromised and bargained away the black's right to be free.[624]

On August 28, 1787 Pierce Butler and General Charles Cotesworth Pinckney of South Carolina prodded the Federal convention to adopt a fugitive slave law without congressional opposition. Madison recorded in his "Federal convention notes" that "Mr. Butler and Mr. Pinckney moved to require fugitive slaves and servants to be delivered up like criminals." James Wilson of Pennsylvania worried about "public expense" and Roger Sherman of Connecticut "saw no more propriety in the public seizing and surrendering a slave or servant, then a house." The next day, Butler inserted after Article XV "If any person bound to service or labor in any of the United States shall escape into another State, he or she shall not be discharged from such service or labor, in consequence of any regulations subsisting in the State to which they escape, but shall be delivered up to the person justly claiming their service or labor."[625]

The kidnapping issue did not peter out. In North Carolina, manumitted blacks feared being kidnapped and forced into slavery, especially if they were former fugitives. In 1741 and 1777, North Carolina's lawmakers said "that no person within this Government shall make any contract with his Negroes for his freedom or Liberty that are Runaway or Refractory Negroes. This act shall not hinder any man from setting his Negro free as a reward for his or their honesty and faithful service." In 1778, the North Carolina legislature clamped down on illegal manumissions in order to "prevent Domestic Insurrections and for other purposes." The

---

[624]Robinson, *Slavery in the Structure of American Politics*, 228-230; Thomas D. Morris, *Free Men All: The Personal Liberty Laws of the North, 1780-1861* (Baltimore, 1974), 16-22; Staughton Lynd, *Class Conflict, Slavery, and the United States Constitution* (Indianapolis, New York, 1967) 154, 159, 189, 205, 208, 213; Don E. Fehrenbacher, *Slavery, Law, and Politics: The Dred Scott Case in Historical Perspective*, (New York, 1981), 17-25; Max Farrand, *The Records of the Federal Convention* (4 vols., New Haven, 1911, 1937, 1960), II: 453-454; Jay A. Barrett, *Evolution of the Ordinance of 1787* (New York, 1891), 89.

[625]Farrand, *Federal Convention Records*, II: 473.

lawmakers declared that "no person shall liberate his or her slave except for meritorious service, to be judged and allowed by the County Court," and that "liberated slaves shall be apprehended and sold." They put to rest the fear and "doubts" of "purchasers" who had brought liberated slaves by stating that "all such sales made bona fide."[626]

Ebenezer Hazard, a Princeton graduate, New York postmaster and surveyor, traveled to North Carolina to regulate the postal route between Philadelphia and Savannah. En route he stopped in Edenton, North Carolina and discovered that "Some Quakers in North Carolina have lately emancipated their Negroes, & the Assembly have passed a Law for apprehending the Negroes, and selling them as Slaves; the Money to be put in the public treasury." He called it "repugnant to every principle upon which we contend for Liberty."[627]

In 1791 the North Carolina paper published a fugitive ad describing a black man named Luke who had "once been set free, but the manumission being illegal he was sold anew." Another planter from that colony claimed that a "Negro fellow Job 5 foot 6 inches, rather black, 20 or 30 years old was one of the Negroes emancipated by the Quakers, and taken up and sold by the order of the court; it is more than probable they wish to Secret him."[628]

---

[626]Ibid., II: 453; Ernest M. Lander, "The South Carolinians at the Philadelphia Convention," *South Carolina Historical Magazine*, 57 (1956), 134-155; Clark, *State Records., N.C.*, XXIII: 65, XXIV: 14, 203-204, 221.

[627]Hugh Buckner Johnston, ed., "The Journal of Ebenezer Hazard in North Carolina, 1777 and 1778," *The North Carolina Historical Review*, 36 (1959), 362-363.

[628]*State Gazette of North Carolina*, June 2, December 12, 1796; Don Higginbothan and William S. Price, Jr., "Was it Murder for a White Man to Kill a Slave? Chief Justice Martin Howard Condemns the Peculiar Institution in North Carolina," *William and Mary Quarterly*, 3rd Ser., 36 (October 1979), 573-601; Duncan J. MacLeod, *Slavery, Race and the American Revolution* (Cambridge, 1978), 42.

Neither the fugitive ad nor the North Carolina statutes could match the power of the black freeman's testimony to Congress in 1797. In that year four black freemen made their way out of North Carolina and into Philadelphia. In their petition, these men: Jacob Nicholson, Jupiter Nicholson, Job Albert and Thomas Pritchet told the House of Representatives, the Senate and President Washington a harrowing tale about being "hunted day and night, like beasts of the forests by armed men with dogs and made a prey of as free and lawful plunder." Jupiter Nicholson said he was "pursued by men with dogs and arms; but was favored to escape to Virginia, with my wife who was manumitted by Gabriel Cosan, where I resided about four years in the town of Portsmouth, chiefly employed in sawing boards and scantling; from thence I removed with my wife to Philadelphia where I have been employed, at times by water, working along the shore or sawing wood."[629]

Jacob Nicholson, despite being freed, "continued to live" with his owner, Joseph Nicholson, but he said "being pursued day and night, I was obliged to leave my abode, sleep in the woods, and stacks in the fields and to escape, leaving a mother, one child, and two brothers, to see whom I dare not return." Job Albert had been captured and placed in a jail in North Carolina, but he escaped and made it to Portsmouth, Virginia with his wife where he continued "unmolested about four years, being chiefly engaged in sawing boards and plank." Albert and his wife moved to Philadelphia. He maintained that both his mother and sister were "set free," but both were "taken up and sold in slavery, myself deprived of the consolation of seeing them, without being exposed to the like grievous oppression."[630]

And lastly, there was Thomas Pritchard, a hard working man. He reported: "My master furnished me with land to raise provisions for my use, where I built myself a house, cleared a sufficient spot of woodland to produce ten bushels of corn; the second year about fifteen, and the third, had as much planted as I supposed would

---

[629]Bergman and McCarroll, *The Negro in the Congressional Record*, II: 130-131.

[630]Ibid.

have produced thirty bushels." When Pritchard's master died, a Holland Lockwood married the master's widow and demanded that Thomas serve him or be banished to the West Indies. Another man named Enoch Ralph threatened to send "me to jail, and sell me for the good of the country" recalled Thomas Pritchard "and being thus in jeopardy, I left my little farm with my small stock and utensils and my corn standing and escape by night into Virginia where shipping myself for Boston, I was through stress of weather landed in New York, where I served as a waiter for seventeen months."[631]

Despite his successful escape, the black fugitive was unhappy because "my mind being distressed on account of the situation of my wife and children, I returned to Norfolk, Virginia with a hope of at least seeing them, if I could not obtain their freedom; but finding I was advertised in the newspaper, twenty dollars the reward for apprehending me, my dangerous situation obliged me to leave Virginia, disappointed of seeing my wife and children, coming to Philadelphia, where I resided in the employment of a waiter upward of two years."[632]

The planters or their agents slipped into Philadelphia, prowled the city, hoping to abduct these blacks. The black petitioners told of "a fellow black now confined in the jail of this city, under the sanction of the Act of General Government, called the Fugitive Law." This black had been manumitted in North Carolina, sold back into slavery for a period of six years, "made his escape to Philadelphia, where he has resided eleven years, having a wife and four children; and by an agent of the Carolina claimant, had been lately apprehended and committed to prison."[633]

Thomas Blount of North Carolina brought the halls alive by claiming that "Agreeably to a law of the State of North Carolina, he said they were slaves, and could, of course, be seized as such." Massachusetts' representative, George Thatcher, derided Blount's claim and concluded that the petitioners had been manumitted and

---

[631]Ibid.

[632]Ibid., 131-133.

[633]Ibid.

that "their manumissions were sanctioned by a law of that State, but that a subsequent law of the same State, subjected them to slavery." Accept the petition and revise the fugitive act, argued Thatcher. In the same vein, Swanwick attacked the law and criticized the "atrocity of that reward of ten dollars offered for one of them if taken alive, but that fifty should be given if found dead and no questions asked."[634]

James Madison of Virginia, unmoved by Thatcher or Sitgreaves or the petitioners, felt the petition should be given to "a Court of Appeal in that State." If the fugitives were slaves "the Constitution gives them no hopes of being heard here," claimed Madison. Smith felt the petitioners would "spread an alarm throughout the Southern states."[635]

Eleven months later, the Quakers urged Congress to prevent planters in North Carolina from re-enslaving blacks freed by Quakers under the pretext that the blacks were fugitive slaves. Congressman Nathaniel Macon of North Carolina, after berating the Quakers for trying "to stir up insurrection among the blacks," denied knowing anything about 132 kidnapped blacks. In 1800, Quaker Robert Waln presented a petition on behalf of noted pastor Absalom Jones, and other free blacks of Philadelphia calling on Congress to halt the slave trade, rescind the fugitive act and consider a general emancipation of blacks.[636]

The Quakers' impact in Philadelphia cannot be underestimated. Their petitions alone kept the issue of slavetrading, kidnapping and fugitives in the public eye. Even the *North Carolina Gazette* acknowledged the Quakers were "a peril" and "danger" and claimed that they had "corrupted" the slave's mind and that they had "protected and harbored fugitives."[637]

The real peril was the planter himself for during the

---

[634]Ibid., II: 131-132.

[635]Ibid., II: 131-133.

[636]Ibid., II: 241-242; Hiram H. Hilty, *Toward Freedom for All: North Carolina Quakers and Slavery* (Richmond, Ind., 1984, 27-29).

[637]*State Gazette of North Carolina*, June 2, 1796.

Revolutionary War and well after the independence of America had become a reality the planter continued to beat and maim blacks. The North Carolina fugitive ads tell it all. One planter noted that his slave's ears had been "slit about an inch at the top." Yellow Hannah, aged 35, "had her right ear cut off, and a scar on the underpart of her right cheek." Another owner claimed that Tom was "branded on each cheek, the brand very large, both ears cropt, his back very much marked with the whip."[638]

Dead-or-alive notices received space in the gazette both during and after the war. In 1778, James Davis, owner of the *North Carolina Gazette*, placed an ad describing Smart but received no response. About a year later he traveled to New Bern County and had two justices draw up a proclamation that gave the sheriff the right to apprehend the slave. If the fugitive refused to surrender, Davis said, "any person may kill or destroy him." Davis offered fifty dollars for the delivery of Smart or twenty dollars for his head.[639]

A fugitive black in North Carolina or in any other state, including Pennsylvania, could not expect the Quaker to openly assist him. Save for the local North Carolina Gazette, not a single newspaper mentioned the Quakers in their fugitive notices or their editorials as harborers of blacks. It appears, then, that either the Quakers proved ineffective once they filed their petitions and left the Federal building in Philadelphia or that they were reluctant to lift a hand to assist a black escapee in the heart of Philadelphia where there were 15,000 Quaker families.[640]

In early America a few Quakers did assist fugitive blacks; George Keith was one. In 1693, in *An Exhortation and Caution to Friends Concerning Buying and Keeping of Negroes*, he noted that the Bible said: "Thou shall not deliver unto his Master the Servant that is escaped from his Master unto thee, he shall dwell with thee, even amongst you in that place which he shall chuse in one

---

[638]*State Gazette of North Carolina*, October 2, 1792; Halfax, *North Carolina Journal*, February 12, 1794.

[639]*North Carolina Gazette*, June 27, 1777, November 30, 1778.

[640]Thomas G. Drake, *Quakers and Slavery in America* (New Haven, 1950), 5.

of thy Gates, where it liketh him best; thou shall not oppress him, Deut.23.15.16. By which appeareth, that those which are at Liberty and freed from their Bondage, shall not by us be delivered into Bondage again."[641]

Noted Quaker Assemblyman Isaac Norris sold blacks long after Keith's entreaties. In 1712, Norris wrote a friend about a "Negro woman being bigg with child is not of ready Sale." He noted, however, that he was willing to sell her for 40 pounds because he thought she was "worth it."[642]

The Quaker anti-slavery faction consisted of a few dedicated members who openly assisted fugitives. Anthony Benezet, the noted Quaker anti-slavery critic, began to assist the fugitives when one anxious black came to his school and appealed for assistance. In 1783, Benezet wrote Thomas Pemberton, a Quaker activist, that "the case of the oppressed Black people becomes rather more weighty with us, my situation in the Negro school lays me very open to frequent solicitation. Indeed, 'the matter' has been so close with some of the black people that redress being refused, or delayed, the poor disconsolate creatures have made away with themselves." Benezet recalled the "case of a French Negro who from the most clear evidence was a freeman, and on whose behalf I had in vain requested a habeas corpus; redress being thus delayed and uncertain the poor fellow hung himself."[643]

Without a writ of *habeas corpus*, and the security bond, Benezet could not assist these "special people" who had "special suffering," therefore he recruited activists willing to assist fugitive slaves or kidnapped black freeman. Benezet needed the American Quakers, but he claimed they were "averse to engage in it" and that it would

[641]George Keith, "The First Printed Protest Against Slavery in America, "*Pennsylvania Magazine of History and Biography*, 13 (1889), 268.

[642]Quoted in Darold D. Wax, "Quaker Merchants and the Slave Trade in Colonial Pennsylvania," *Pennsylvania Magazine History and Biography*, 76 (1962), 149.

[643]George S. Brookes, *Friend Anthony Benezet* (London, 1937), 378-395.

be preferable to obtain the monies from the Quakers in England.[644]
Had the Quakers lost every cent during the American
Revolutionary War and lacked donation monies? A decade after
the war, the Quakers, riding the wave of prosperity, at least in
Philadelphia, owned five churches, one hospital, one bank worth
three millions dollars, and scores of other businesses, enough
money to build and staff scores of anti-slavery societies and to
contribute to a special fund for fugitive blacks.[645] Was it racism?
French publicist Moreau de St. Mery believed that the "color
prejudice is more deeply rooted in Philadelphia and in
Pennsylvania than in any other state of the union and among the
Quakers more than in any other sect." Moreau's sharp eye
discovered that "colored and whites do not eat together" in the
Philadelphia prisons; that there was a cemetery exclusively for
blacks in Philadelphia, that the churches were segregated and that
the Quaker form of protection was nothing more that an
"ostentatious display of humility," which was "a form of
condescension which many businessmen use to their own
advantage."[646]
Joseph Drinker, a Quaker of Philadelphia, declared in 1796 that
the Quakers "are the only People I know who make any objections
to Blacks or People of Color joining them in church Fellowship."
In that year, Cynthia Miers, a black, stirred the members in the
Rayway Monthly meeting because one member noted that this was
"a case of singular nature amongst us" and that they should
"proceed very cautiously." In the next meeting John Wigham, a
journalist who was present, wrote that she was well "received."[647]

---

[644]Ibid.

[645]Duc De La Rochefoucault, *Travels Through The United States of North America* (London, 1799), II: 375.

[646]Roberts, *Moreau de St. Méry's American Journey*, 302, 303, 309.

[647]Henry J. Cadbury, "Negro Membership in the Society of Friends," *Journal of Negro History*, 21 (1936), 173-174; "Another Early Quaker Anti-Slavery Document," *Journal of Negro History*, 27,

One Quaker beat a slave to death. In 1780, the Rhode Island Friends called on the Society to expel one Quaker woman planter for "encouraging the unmerciful whipping or beating of her Negro man servant." The black died and the "Friend utterly disowned all such actions."[648]

Why the furor in Congress about the Quakers when they posed little threat to chattel slavery? Their refusal to carry arms, or to employ violence should have swept away the planter's worry. The Quakers did pose an ideological threat; they understood the black condition after the war and the tactics needed to solve the problem. Aware that slavery could not be uprooted in one feel swoop, barring a civil war, they sought to inform everybody about the need to support the gradual abolition of slavery. Warner Mifflin, "a great fellow near seven feet high," paid a visit to President Washington. "I was visited (having given Permission), by Mr. Warner Mifflin, one of the People called Quakers, active in the pursuit of the Measures laid before Congress for emancipating the Slaves," wrote Washington in his diary in March 1790. The Quaker told the President about "the immorality – injustice – and impolicy of keeping these people in a state of Slavery, with declarations, however, that he did not wish for more than a gradual abolition or to see any infraction of the Constitution to effect it."[649]

Another Quaker tactic was to set up anti-slavery institutions. Under the administration of the Pennsylvania Abolition Society the Quakers set up several committees to aid both the free black and the slave: the Committee of Employment, the Committee to Visit

210-215. Quoted in Lorenzo J. Greene, *The Negro in Colonial New England* (New York, 1969), 232-233.

[648]Quoted in Greene's, *The Negro in Colonial New England*, 233; Thomas E. Drake, "Joseph Drinker's Plea for Admission of Colored People in the Society of Friends," *Journal of Negro History*, 32 (1947), 111-112; David Brion Davis, *The Problems of Slavery in the Age of Revolution, 1770-1823* (Ithaca, New York, 1975).

[649]George Washington, *The Diaries of George Washington*, Donald Jackson, ed. (6 vols., Charlottesville), VI: 46-47.

the Colored People, the Committee of Guardians, and the Committee of Education. Probably the most prestigious committee and the most active was the Acting Committee (A.C.) which began operating in 1784. The A.C., consisting of five members, met every two weeks in a Negro school house operated by Quakers to discuss how to protect the kidnapped and the fugitive black. With ten lawyers on hand, the A.C. could subpoena planters for violating the Pennsylvania Gradual Abolition Act.[650]

George Washington alluded to the A.C. in his complaint to Governor Robert Morris in 1785 about an impending lawsuit concerning a fugitive seeking to be free. Washington warned that slaveholders would not visit Philadelphia because they "hazard their property." The A.C. led Smith the South Carolina Congressman to say in 1790 that "A gentleman can hardly come from that country with a servant or two either to this place or Philadelphia, but there are persons trying to seduce his servants to leave him." The same group stirred Edward Rutledge, another representative from that state, to call for the "censure" of those who "attempt to seduce the servants of gentlemen traveling to the seat of Government."[651]

George Washington's Hercules, James Madison's Billy, and the slaves of two South Carolina congressmen, Jacob Read and Pierce Butler had found refuge in Philadelphia, though the 1780 Gradual Abolition Act stated that "this Act nor anything in it contained shall not give any relief or shelter to any absconding runaway Negro or Mulatto slave or servant who absented himself from his or her owner, master or mistress residing in any other state or country." Possibly these officials had failed to register their slaves and possibly these fugitive blacks were free. But the Gradual

---

[650]Margaret Hope Bacon, *Lamb's Warrior: The Life of Isaac T. Hopper*, 41-43; Ira V. Brown, "Pennsylvania, Immediate Emancipation and the Birth of the American Anti-Slavery Society," *Pennsylvania History*, 54 (July 1987), 163-178.

[651]Fitzpatrick, *Washington's Writings*, loc. cit.; Bergman and McCarroll, *The Negro in the Congressional Record*, I: 22-23, II; 668. See Ira V. Brown, "Pennsylvania's Anti-Slavery Pioneers, 1688-1776," *Pennsylvania History*, 55 (1988), 60-77.

Abolition Act exempted from registration those "Delegates in Congress from the American states, foreign Ministers, lawsuits or persons passing through, or sojourning in this State."[652]

How the Acting Committee circumvented The Gradual Abolition Act can be understood by examining the exploits of Thomas Harrison and Isaac Hopper. Thomas Harrison was born in Cumberland, England in 1738 where he served as a tailor's apprentice, before working as a journeyman in London for a few years. He migrated to America, set up a tailoring business in Philadelphia, embraced the Quakers and married a Quaker elder. Isaac Hopper, born in Woodbury, New Jersey in 1771, also served as a tailor's apprentice and eventually set up a tailoring business in Philadelphia and also turned to Quakerism and married a Quaker woman.[653]

Because of his pacifistic beliefs, Harrison, recalled Hopper, was strongly opposed to the American Revolution, believing it would be "attended with the effusion of much blood" and "waste of property." Harrison criticized the war, despite the danger of being expelled from Pennsylvania and banished to Virginia, "merely on a vague suspicion of being inimical to the American cause, without being allowed a hearing or permitted to defend themselves." Harrison was a marked man, said Hopper, for he was one of the "number of those selected for this persecution; and one of the Committee of safety, as they were called, gave Thomas this information privately." Forced into hiding, Harrison continued to operate his tailor business in strict secrecy. Hopper was a pacifist as well. He maintained: "I myself have suffered because I could not conscientiously comply with military requisitions, and the Friends have suffered much in England on account of ecclesiastical demands. I therefore have cause to know in some degree, how hateful are persecutions in the Divine right of man."[654]

---

[652]*Pennsylvania Packet and General Advertiser*, March 30, 1780; Catterall, *Judicial Cases Concerning American Slavery*, IV: 267.

[653]*National Anti-Slavery Standard*, February 8, 1844, hereafter referred to as *Standard*; Bacon, *Lamb's Warrior*, 7-18.

[654]*Standard*, loc. cit.

Harrison's anti-slavery activity began formally and purposely in 1774, when he was elected to the office of Secretary in the P.A.S., but the war forced the organization to suspend their operations until 1784. Two years later Thomas was again elected Secretary of the P.A.S. and appointed to the Standing Committee, later to be called the Acting Committee. The Quaker's Philadelphia monthly meeting admitted Hopper in 1792; from there he joined the South District monthly meetings in Philadelphia, where he counseled youths, raised money, printed Quaker books, taught in black schools and assisted kidnapped blacks. All of these activities paved the way for his admission to the P.A.S. in 1795 at age twenty-five. During this period he formally took over the reins of the A.C. because he claimed "he was an old man, and nearly worn out, and he felt glad that I had entered with so much feeling into the cause in which he had so many years engaged. He said that he already felt the burden in great measure taken from off his shoulders, and hoped when he was removed from the stage of action that I would fill his place."[655]

Before Harrison handed the reins of leadership to Hopper, the A.C. minutes showed that Thomas Harrison spent a great deal of his time in court defending the black who had not been properly registered, or indentured and who was consequently eligible for manumission. Friend Hopper recalled that some planters "neglected to furnish the clerk with necessary documents to make the registry until it was too late to make the entry; others again made informal returns." Harrison kept one book for recording admissions and another for recording indentures. Whether he be free, servant or slave, the black could take his grievance to the P.A.S. where Thomas Harrison or any A.C. member would assist him. In sparse sentences the A.C. minutes noted in 1787 that "Adam isn't registered and not indentured to a person" and that "T. Harrison believed Adam shouldn't be held beyond age of 21." The committee wrote that "J. Thomas and T. Harrison removed Kate but Cooke gave Bond and Kate was returned, a writ of habeas corpus was given."[656]

---

[655]Ibid., Bacon, *Lamb's Warrior*, 42-43.

[656]Ibid.; *Standard*, loc. cit.

Hundreds of cases came to the attention of the A.C. but Hopper was the first committee member who saw the need to publish the black's testimony in a daily newspaper. Hopper penned stories in the 1840's in the *New York National Anti-Slavery Standard* about seventeen black women and sixty-seven black men of whom 25% were fugitives because he thought that the "readers of the *Standard* would be interested in facts, from authentic sources, relating to the sufferings of the slaves and their efforts to escape from their fetters, and having a great abundance of such facts in my possession I have concluded to offer them for publication in your columns."[657]

Graphic, action packed, adventurous in tone and spirit, Hopper's *Tales* revealed what it meant to be a slave in the late eighteenth century. The *Tales* gave the fugitive the opportunity to speak about his fears, his dreams and his disappointments. The fugitive ad, though it mirrored the planters' views, remains the primary source of testimony for the study of the eighteenth century fugitive, but while the fugitive notices helped capture the fugitive, Hopper's *Tales* helped liberate the black.[658]

Hopper's *Tales* showed that George Washington, Jacob Read, William Loughton Smith, Edward Rutledge, Pierce Butler and other representatives had good reason to suspect the Quakers of harboring their slaves. In Tale XLIV, Friend Hopper wrote that "Jacob Read, of Charleston, South Carolina, was a member of the Senate of the United States; and as Congress then sat in Philadelphia, he went there in the latter part of the year 1797, to discharge the duties of his station and took his family with him and several slaves to wait upon them." One of those slaves, Red Betsey, "a bright mulatto," was "determined to make an effort to be free." Betsey left Read, found work as a domestic, but feared "going into the street for water and again reduced to slavery: though she was not advertised, and it did not appear that her

---

[657]*Minutes of the Pennsylvania Abolition Society: The Executive Committee, Acting Committee,* See Vol. 7, 1787; *Standard,* October 22, 1840.

[658]Blassingame, *The Slave Community,* see his "Critical Essay on Sources," 367-382.

master took any measures to recover her." She worked for a few months, but her depression, her discomfort, her inability to sleep never left her so she visited Isaac Hopper. "I referred her to my wife who agreed to employ her; and accordingly, she came to reside with us." Betsey, "an excellent cook," had "always lived amidst great affluence." Hopper maintained that "she was rather too extravagant to suit my circumstance" and he managed to find her a new employer who paid higher wages.[659]

Betsey visited Hopper, therefore, Read could not accuse Hopper of luring his cook away. Hopper could hardly afford to hire or offer every needy fugitive a room; he, like any harborer, had his limitations. What Hopper possessed that other harborers might have lacked was an understanding of the law. To prevent the planter from reclaiming Betsey, Hopper recalled: "The plan I had devised to secure her freedom in case of her arrest, was this, I would have obtained a Homine replegiando, and in this way she must have a trial in the Supreme Court." By the time the case was over Betsey "would have been safely out of the way, and I would have paid her master what a court and jury decided to be her value."[660]

The blacks did not need Hopper to understand slavery's unjustness. Tale VII describes Benjamin Jackson of Virginia who told Hopper "that when he was about sixteen years old, he became awakened to a sense of his situation as a slave, he could not reconcile it with the justice and goodness of his Creator, that one man should be born to serve another, without compensation; to be driven about, and treated as the beast of the field." In 1792 Jackson made it to Philadelphia, got a job as a seaman and headed for sea, far from the Virginia fields, hoping his master would never find him. At age thirty, Jackson returned to Philadelphia, married and chauffeured Benjamin Rush, the fifty-four year old pioneer in medicine and mental health and a noted abolitionist. After completing his indentured time as a coachman for Rush, Jackson

---

[659]*Standard*, November 25, 1841.

[660]Ibid., *Standard*, loc. cit.

received a freeman's certificate.[661]

"Some time after, about 1797, his master came to that city, and had him arrested as his fugitive slave," wrote Hopper. The black freeman was taken to Justice Joseph Bird where Jackson's owner "demanded the usual certificate to authorize him to take the man to Virginia." Jackson "neither denied nor admitted that he was a slave" but showed Bird his freedom's certificate and asked for Hopper to track down Rush. Friend Hopper found Rush that night, but the doctor hardly remembered Jackson.[662]

Unable to verify the black's claim to freedom, Hopper went to see the fugitive. "The poor fellow was in great distress," said Isaac Hopper and "I endeavor to impress upon him the necessity of telling me the real state of his case; and he open his situation fully. He acknowledged he was a slave, and belonged to the person who claimed him. I told him not to be discouraged, and I would see what could be done for him."[663]

Hopper could not stage a jailbreak and rescue Benjamin Jackson from his captors. Nor could Jackson's owner take him to Virginia without receiving a hearing in Bird's office because both actions amounted to a violation of the Fugitive Law of 1793. Because Hopper knew both the magistrate and Judge Bird, both of whom were in sympathy with Jackson, Hopper was able to ask the magistrate to have Jackson in Bird's office at 8:45 in the morning, fifteen minutes before the scheduled hearing time. When everybody arrived as scheduled, Hopper "demanded the discharge of the prisoner claiming Jackson's owner had no legal proof" that Benjamin Jackson was his slave and that "Dr. Rush would not have given such a certificate as he had done, without some reason for doing so." He also "urged that the claimant was appraised of the time to which the case was adjourned." Joseph Bird told "Jackson he was at liberty."[664]

---

[661]Ibid., November 12, 1840.

[662]Ibid.

[663]Ibid.

[664]Ibid.

A few minutes after nine Jackson's owner came to Bird's door and "Benjamin saw his master and ran for his life." Jackson lived with Hopper for a week and returned home, but Isaac Hopper told him "to go to New York, and go to sea but his wife was unwilling that he should leave her." Hopper told Jackson "the great danger he would be in, as long as he remained in Philadelphia."[665]

Jackson and his wife remained in Philadelphia. Ever watchful for any surprise seizures, Benjamin placed a rope ladder outside their second floor apartment in order to insure a quick escape, and as long as they had each other what other worries could they have? Two weeks after his arrest, Jackson's "door was suddenly burst open, and his master, with a constable rushed in," reported Hopper. Down the ladder and straight to Hopper's house Jackson went. Hopper urged Jackson to leave Philadelphia. Jackson went to sea, returned to Philadelphia again, and discovered that Hopper had recovered his freedom for $150.00. But it was too late for the "mental suffering his wife had endured, was too much to bear; she had sunk into a state of melancholy, from which she never fully recovered."[666]

No matter what his standing in the community, no matter how august his name, no matter how industrious, how religious, the black freeman was at all times a step away from slavery and two steps away from being forced to assume the role of fugitive. No man in Philadelphia personified the backbone and the spirit of the black community as did Richard Allen. It was Allen and his colleague Absalom Jones who in 1787 could no longer tolerate sitting in the rear gallery of the St. George Methodist Church, a place reserved solely for blacks who wished to attend Sunday services. Allen eventually headed the Bethel African Methodist Episcopal Church; Jones set up the St. Thomas Protestant Episcopal Church, both of which were independent denominations designed to serve the needs of blacks.[667]

Hopper remembered well this unvanquished man named Allen,

---

[665]Ibid.

[666]Ibid.

[667]Ibid., December 30, 1840.

who was "born in Maryland, a slave to Benjamin Chew of Philadelphia. After some years of servitude, Allen purchased his manumission, and went to that city, where he married and settled." Hopper also remembered that Allen "swept chimney sweeps, and had a considerable business in that line," that he had a shoemaking business and "several apprentices" working for him, that he "became possessed of considerable property," and that he owned a three story apartment. If a Philadelphian wanted a well fitted shoe, or his chimney swept clean, or to hear a good sermon, Bishop Allen was the man to see.[668]

With the planter on the move, combing the city for the fugitive black, even Richard Allen could not be safe in his brick house. "A man who lived in Maryland, brought a slave *running*," recalled Hopper in Tale IX, "that is, one who had runaway" and sent one of his sons to Philadelphia to ferret him out. "In passing along one of the streets of that city, this man saw the name of Richard Allen on a window, and a colored man standing in the door. He stepped up to him, asked if his name was Richard Allen, and was answered in the affirmative."[669]

The man sped back to Maryland, returned to Philadelphia with his brother and father, took out a warrant for a "runaway slave by the name of Dick," and then "secured a peace officer, walked into Allen's front room where the shoe apprentices were busy at work, and called Allen who came toward strangers. 'Well Dick, do you know me?' Richard replied, 'No, I do not know you.' 'Well, I will make you know me. Seize him Constable.'" Both parties eventually ended up in front of a magistrate who said that "there must be some mistake about this business for that he had known Richard Allen for more than twenty years, and knew he was a freeman." The magistrate dismissed the case against the planter's wishes and Allen "inquired whether redress was not to be had for this outrage upon him," for had it not been for the "kindness of the officer, he might have been dragged through the streets like a felon."[670]

---

[668]*Standard*, December 12, 1840.

[669]Ibid.

[670]Ibid.

Isaac Hopper said the magistrate "proposed that I be sent for; and as I lived but a short distance from the officer, I was soon on the spot." Friend Hopper recommended that the "father and the two sons should be committed to prison" and they were. He recommended that a "civil suit be filed and a two thousand dollar bail set" and it was. The planter's children made bail at $800.00 and were released; the father remained in jail for three months.[671]

Had it not been for the Fugitive Law of 1793, Richard Allen could have been whisked away without any questions asked. In 1793, three white men abducted a black man in Pennsylvania and took him to Virginia. The Pennsylvania authorities charged the white men with kidnapping and asked the Virginia governor to return the black freeman. The governor refused, claiming the absence of a fugitive rendition statute. The case was given to President Washington who gave it to Congress and that body ordered the planter to apply to a circuit judge for a certificate to take a black out of a state. This gave Isaac Hopper and other Acting Committee members more time to uncover the circumstances surrounding a kidnapping.[672]

Whereas the 1793 Fugitive Slave Law offered no protection to the fugitive slave, it did legitimize the planter's right to take the black into custody. Again, neither the Federal Constitution nor the local northern state constitutions offered protection to the fugitive. But Hopper, the Quakers and the free black community made it their business to understand the laws pertaining to the slave. Once when confronting a planter on a ferry boat heading to New Castle, Delaware with a ten year old kidnapped slave, Hopper recalled "I pulled a small volume out of my pocket containing the laws of Pennsylvania, and of some of the other States, as well as those of the United States, on the subject of slavery, the slave trade, & c. I read to him the clause in relation to removing colored people out of the State, circumstanced as this lad was."[673]

---

[671]Ibid.

[672]Stanley W. Campbell, *The Slave Catchers: Enforcement of the Fugitive Slave Law: 1850-1860* (Chapel Hill, 1970), 7-9.

[673]*Standard*, April 29, 1841.

The key provision in the Pennsylvania Constitution requiring the planter entering Pennsylvania to set free his slave if he remained in that state over a period of six months, forced the A.C., the planter, and the slave, to keep a close eye on the calendar. Senator Pierce Butler of South Carolina, owner of 441 slaves in 1793 and over 9,000 acres of land, served as a South Carolina representative between 1779 and 1789 and as a senator from 1789 to 1796. In 1803 he was an influential force on behalf of his constituents as well as a scathing critic of the Quaker abolitionist. Butler owned a mansion in Philadelphia and a retreat close to German Town during that period. He owned, too, a thirty-six year old slave named Ben who waited on him wherever he went. In August 1804, Ben left Butler and applied to the A.C. because Butler "proposes taking him to Georgia, whereby he will be separated from his wife who needs his support, she being in delicate health."[674]

Believing that Ben could obtain his freedom, the A.C. instructed Hopper to serve Major Butler with a writ of habeas corpus. On August 3, 1804 the A.C. provided Ben with an attorney. Judge John Inskeep, a friend of Hopper, presided over the case. According to Hopper, "Butler contended he was only a sojourner in Pennsylvania, and that Ben had not resided six months at any one time in that state, except while he was a member of Congress, and that he had a right, agreeably to the laws of Pennsylvania to keep him as long as he pleased." Inskeep adjourned the case until September 3rd and ordered Ben to return to Butler's residence. The A.C. called in William Lewis, a leading trial lawyer in Pennsylvania and the author of the Gradual Abolition Act of Pennsylvania.[675]

In December 1804, Butler stepped down as Congressman and by then Philadelphia had ceased being the "seat of the Government." Lewis therefore claimed "there can be no such thing here as the domestic slave attending Delegates in Congress from the other American States." Butler had no special privileges and Ben walked away free only to see Inskeep's decision "reversed" and to be jailed months later by a Federal marshall "by writ of Homine

---

[674]Ibid., July 9, 1840.

[675]Ibid.

Replegiando at the suit of Pierce Butler and two thousand dollar bail was demanded." In October 1806, the Circuit Court of the United States received Ben's case, and again Ben was set free. According to Hopper, the "court discharged Ben, and he enjoyed his liberty thence forth without interruption."[676]

According to Lydia Maria Child in *Isaac T. Hopper: A true Life* Butler told Hopper that he was a benevolent man. "'Thou benevolent! Why thou are not even just, retorted Hopper, 'Thou hast already sent back into bondage two men who were legally entitled to freedom by staying in Philadelphia during the term prescribed by law. If thou hadst a proper sense of justice thou wouldst bring those men back and let them take liberty that rightfully belongs to them.'"[677]

Was Butler a benevolent man? He did fight for the debtors and the back country parishes in his home state, yet on the other hand, he told his colleagues at the Federal Convention in May 1787, that "an election by the people was an impracticable mode." By June 6 of that year he was for an "election by the people as to the 1st branch and by the States as to the 2d."[678]

Butler claimed to be benevolent toward blacks, despite being an absentee planter. While his overseer Roswell King complained that "the management of the estate is a heavy burthen very heavy on me," Butler said that "if I reside constantly on the estate, I would have everything go on with the regularity of clock work." Despite King's burden, Pierce Butler said: "I shall never give to any person on whom I employ the power to act [?] or rely as he may think right. When I expressely desire a measure to be done I expect

---

[676]Ibid.

[677]See in Malcolm Bell, Jr., *Major Butler's Legacy: Five Generations of a Slaveholding Family* (Athens, 1987), 141; Paul Finkelman, *The Law of Freedom and Bondage: A Casebook* (New York, 1986), 61-62; Lydia Maria Child, *Isaac Hopper: A True Life* (New York, 1881), 98-103.

[678]Francis Coghlan, "Pierre Butler, 1744-1822, First Senator from South Carolina," 78 (1977), *South Carolina Historical Magazine*, 118; Farrand, *Federal Convention*, I: 50, 137.

strict compliance by the person entrusted with my property – he is responsible to me only."[679]

Butler showed great concern about the treatment of his slaves. In 1796, in a letter to overseer William Page, he maintains that black ditch diggers "should do a reasonable days work & no more than that," and he would "rather the Island was sunk in the sea than I should cause the death of one Negro – they are slaves but they are human beings – give them a moderate reasonable days work, what that shall be I leave to your own judgment, and approved humanity." Yet he warned Page some "blacks will take advantage of indulgence and wish to do no work, but where you meet with such characters they must be made to work."[680]

Whether it was in 1787, or in 1821, a year before his death, Butler expected a black to perform his duty. In 1819, 1820, and 1821 he had a poor crop because the "people do not do their duty and that those who are set over to see them working do not oblige them to do so." Although Butler wanted "a reasonable day's work" from his slaves "he abhors putting them in work to the utmost of their strength, but there is a medium, which medium I wish to be observed. I am gratified very much so in having them contented. I have not been unfeeling in Clothing or Diet. There is a reciprocity which I expect and required for the last 3 or 4 years."[681]

The work medium and the reciprocity he expected did not come readily because the blacks continued to escape. They made it to Nova Scotia. "A Negro man of Mine" wrote the South Carolina planter, "ran from me and is now in Nova Scotia." He gave merchant John Coffin the Power of Attorney to "recover him" and "not to let him escape."[682]

Another fugitive made it to St. Croix. "I yesterday received

---

[679]*Pierce Butler's Letterbooks (1787-1822 and 1794-1822),* Historical Society of Pennsylvania, PB to RK, January 3, April 14, 1821.

[680]*Butler's Letterbooks,* PB to WP, November 9, 1797.

[681]Ibid., PB to RK, October 21, 1821.

[682]Ibid., PB to JC, June 25, 1790.

certain assurance that a Servant of mine, a slave, who fled from hence last March is at Saint Croix professing as free," reported Butler to Henry Cooper, the United States Consul to St. Croix. Butler admitted that the eighteen year old hair dresser named Sommerset was a "good Lady's hair dresser," who could make "£40 sterling a year for him," but he left it up to Cooper about where he should be sold.[683]

The fiery senator swore in 1798 that he had seen the last of his "runaways," yet during that year he had heard from Page about "six men running away from the rice Island – I was hopeful that every disposition of that kind had long ceased, and that I was never again to experience the mortification of owning a runaway." He ordered the overseer to "punish the ringleaders."[684]

How did Butler try to restore his notion of reciprocity? In May 1804 King wrote: "In my absence three of the New Negroes Ranaway for Two days and was taken near Doby, in a Cannoe, bound to Africa as they Say the leader was well whipped & the other Two forgiven. This is the 2nd time that fellow [named] Morris has Ranaway."[685]

Butler pleaded with the blacks, threatened them, called them names, sold them, and even blamed the Quakers. The Senator said Molly and Hannah could no longer work in the house, they must be "put in the field." "She [Hannah] is a Monster of ingraditude." Butler had "raised her from the Brink of the grave, after being many days speechless and apparently without a pulse – would you believe it she has attempted to run off – my boy Sam absconded thro the baseness of some Quakers I shall lose him," said Butler on June 26, 1798.[686]

A month later he wrote Page again: "On the subject of the runaways, punish Titus and Morris when you get them." He told

---

[683]Ibid., PB to HC, August 27, 1793.

[684]Ibid., PB to WP, June 4, 1798.

[685]*Butler Family Papers*, Historical Society of Pennsylvania, RK to PB, May 12, 1804.

[686]*PB Letterbook*, PB to WP, June 26, 1798.

Page "do not ill treat them. I am mortified that any of them should run off. Call all the runaways before you and tell them how much it hurts me and how much displease[d] I am with their behavior, believing as I do that they had no just cause for going away."[687]

Butler could not admit that his "runaways" cared nothing about his "paternal kindness," or "reciprocity." Hopper had told him that slavery was unjust, the anti-slavery senators had complained of the unjustness of the peculiar institution at the Federal Convention and during the congressional session in the late eighteenth century, his slaves had made clear they wanted to be free. But still Butler, like Jefferson, would not let them go. Was it the overseer's fault? King worked the blacks hard. "After considerable Labour, good talk, some severe, and a little Whipping. I have got the Negroes to Thresh in a tolerable manner. In two days this week 40 hands (say 12 women & 18 men) thresh over 1,500 [sic] barrels of rice say an average of 19 barrels a day."[688]

King disliked the slaves, but was not above having sex with them. He told Butler that "Nine Tenths of your Negroes are rascals," but he considered himself "poor and proud." The overseer distrusted the driver Sambo: though he got this black's wife pregnant, and though King himself had a wife and child.[689]

Both King and Butler showed confusion and disillusionment during the War of 1812. In January 1815, 2,500 British soldiers landed in Georgia and headed towards Hampton where hundreds of slaves waited for the opportunity to escape. Roswell King intended to "keep myself Cool Determined and resolute." He told Butler to depend on him or *"You are a Ruined Man."* He calmed the senator by saying that "Your Negroes truely behave well, I have ordered them all to be in there houses to take care of them, and their poultry, which they can sell if it is not Stolen from them, but for the men to keep out of the way for they will take them to

---

[687]Ibid., PB to WP, July 24, 1798.

[688]*Butler Family Papers*, RK to PB, July 19, 1806.

[689]Ibid., July 26, 1806; Bell, *Major Butler*, 165.

drag their Guns instead of horses."[690]

A month later the British captured King. He complained about his bad "health" and he could "hardly hold a pen in hand. I am in Constant pain from head to foot." He told the senator the "Negroes are all declared free that will go off with them and the most of yours as well as the Others on this Island appear to have a wish to try their New Master, but few have yet to come from the Main or other Islands." Trying to console Butler, the overseer noted that "it is not you, and myself, but the Inhabitants generally have all been deceived in the Ethiopian race. Your Sons observation is now verified, that Negros have neither honor or gratitude." He praised the house servants, "Bram and Gabriel as they behaved well but have no influence." Angry King went on: "God cursed the Negroes by making them Black — I cursed the Man that brot the first from africa and the curse of God is still on them to send them away to a yet the black appeared to be infactuated miserable death. I have no doubt but the Negroes will be got back in time of peace but who can look at Negroes that have been so humanly treated as yours a degree of madness."[691] And King claimed, too they were "stupid Negroes, half intoxicated with liquor and nothing to do but to think their happy days had come."[692]

The mass escapes had weakened King's spirit: "It appears that I shall never be fit for much active business, I cannot get the use of my limb and as for my mind I can never get over the business of your ungrateful Negroes." The plantations seemed deserted: "We have only eight field workers left on St. Simons. Not a shoemaker or Tanner left. The blacksmiths left. Jack Sawney and Boy Billy (they was at Island at work) 2 Bricklayers left." And Sancho

---

[690]Ibid., RK to PB, January 20, 1815; Bell, *Major Butler*, 170-171.

[691]Ibid., RK to PB, February 26, 1815, February 12, 1818; Bell, *Major Butler*, 182.

[692]Ibid., RK to PB, February 14, 1815.

"wouldn't go with his family."[693]

So King's twelve years of Negro management had been for naught. He had tried to make these "ungrateful wretches comfortable but it is all nonsense and folly to treat Negroes with humanity is like giving pearls to swine, it is throwing away Vallue and geting insult and ingratitude in return."[694] For the blacks who missed the opportunity to escape they could expect the worst. "I call myself a humane man, but if I live I will teach them good behavior before the year is out" reported King. Claiming he could not "bear the sight of a Negro without a melancholy sensation" the overseer said, "Those animals must be ruled with a rod of Iron which might be painful to yourself as well as me."[695]

Hopper hit the mark when he questioned Butler's notion of benevolence and paternal kindness. The mere fact that blacks kept leaving his plantation is in itself proof that something had gone wrong under his rule. Blaming King might be the easy way out, but that overseer and others faithfully carried out his orders or faced immediate dismissal. Butler owned the plantation, owned the slaves, and virtually owned the overseers and consequently had the responsibility of the management of the plantation. It was his greed that forced him to keep blacks in their state, greed that even he seemed to be concerned about.

---

[693]Ibid., RK to PB, February 24, 1815.

[694]Ibid., RK to PB, February 26, 1815.

[695]Ibid., RK to PB, February 28, 1815.

BIBLIOGRAPHICAL ESSAY

This dissertation has drawn upon several categories of evidence; data needed to understand the fugitive's world before 1800.

Primary Sources – Newspapers

The most important category of evidence has been the colonial newspapers. There the planter published his fugitive notices, described his slave or servant, offered his reward, poured forth his tale of woe, and issued his ultimatum to kill or forgive the fugitives. Nonspecialists interested in capturing the planter's belligerent attitude should begin with the South Carolina newspapers: *South Carolina Gazette, South Carolina Gazette and General Advertiser, South Carolina Country Journal, South Carolina American General Gazette, Royal Gazette, Gazette of the State of South Carolina, Charleston Gazette,* the *South Carolina Royal Gazette,* and *Charleston Morning Post and Advertiser.*

Less belligerent are the fugitive ads in the North Carolina newspapers: New Bern *North Carolina Gazette, Wilmington Chronicle, North Carolina* and *Weekly Advertiser,* Halifax *North Carolina Journal, North Carolina Minerva* and *Fayetteville Advertiser,* Edenton *State Gazette of North Carolina,* New Bern *North Carolina Gazette* or *Impartial Intelligencer,* and *Weekly Advertiser,* New Bern *North Carolina Magazine*; or *Universal Intelligencer,* Fayetteville *North Carolina Chronicle* and *Fayetteville Gazette, Wilmington Centinel* and *General Advertiser, Edenton Intelligencer,* and Wilmington *Cape Fear Mercury.*

For fugitive ads that show a large number of group escapes see the Georgia newspapers: Savannah *Georgia Gazette,* Savannah

Royal Gazette, Savannah *Gazette of the State of Georgia,* Augusta *Georgia State Gazette* or *Independent Register.* Virginia's newspaper fugitive ads have one noted characteristic – they used the term "outlaw." The slave outlaw could be shot on sight. Virginia newspapers include *Virginia Gazette* (Williamsburg) *Virginia Gazette* or *American Advertiser, Virginia Gazette* and *Weekly Advertiser, Virginia Independent Chronicle* and *General Advertiser* (Richmond).

Northern fugitive ads lacked the mordacity and passion of the southern newspapers. This does not mean the planters were any more merciful but that they rarely openly called for the slave or servant to be whipped or mutilated. Maryland fugitive ads describing slaves and servants found space in the *Maryland Gazette* which has a long uninterrupted run (1745-1801). The *Maryland Journal* and the *Baltimore Daily Intelligencer* should be drawn on as well.

I relied on the *Pennsylvania Gazette* to study the indentured servant in that colony. After 1780, the black fugitive received fugitive ad coverage in this colony. For New York I mostly utilized the *New York Gazette.*

The South Carolina, Virginia, Maryland and Pennsylvania newspapers are on microfilm. The Delaware Historical Society had the Delaware newspapers; the New York Historical Society, the North Carolina and New York newspapers, and the Library of Congress, the Georgia newspapers.

Fugitive Statutes

Another important category of evidence has been the fugitive slave and servant statutes. Do not expect the statutes to be orderly because the legislators enacted them to deal with problems as they arose. The author drew heavily on Thomas Cooper and David J.

McCord, eds., *The Statutes at Large of South Carolina* (10 vols., 1836-1841); William L. Saunders, Walter S. Clark, and Stephen B. Weeks, eds., *Colonial and State Records of North Carolina* (10 vols., Raleigh, Winston, Goldsboro, and Charlotte, 1886-1914); William W. Henig, ed., *The Statutes at Large, Being a Collection of All the Laws of Virginia...* (13 vols., Richmond, 1809-1823); and William H. Browne, ed., *Archives of Maryland* (69 vols., Baltimore, 1883).

Slave Narratives

Slave and servant autobiographies greatly help one to understand the fugitive's world. The following can be found in the Schomberg Library (New York City): Silvia DuBois, *Silvia DuBois (now 116 years old a biography of the slave who whipt her mistress and gained her freedom* (Ringos, New Jersey); Olaudah Equiano, *The Interesting Narrative of the life of Olaudah Equiano; or Gustavus Vassa, the African* (London, 1789); Moses Grandy, *Narrative of the Life of Moses Grandy; Late a Slave in the United States of America* (Boston, 1867); James Roberts, *The Narrative of James Roberts, soldier in the Revolutionary war and at the battle of New Orleans* (Hattiesburg, 1945), Julius Melbourn, *Life and Opinions of Julius Melbourn...* (Syracuse, 1847). See also "Notes and Documents: James Carter's Account of His Suffurings in Slavery" ed., Linda Stanley *The Pennsylvania Magazine* CV (July, 1981), 335-341; "Notes and Documents: Chattel with a Soul: the Autobiography of a Moravian Slave" ed., Daniel B. Thorpe, *The Pennsylvania Magazine*, CXII (July, 1988), 433-453; David George, "An Account of the Life of Mr. David George, From Sierra Leone in Africa, given by himself in a Conversation with Brother Rippon of London, and Brother Pearce of Birmingham" *Baptist Annual Register for 1790-1793*, 413-422.

For an indentured servant narrative, see T.H. Breen, James H. Lewis and Keith Schlesinger, "A Motive For Murder: A

Servant's Life in Virginia, in 1768" *The William and Mary Quarterly* XL (January, 1983), 107-111; John Harrower, *The Journal of John Harrower*.

Planter Sources

Unpublished and published planter collections were used in this study. The unpublished manuscript collections were: Robert "Councillor" Carter Papers (Duke University Manuscript Division); Pinckney Family Papers (Library of Congress); Butler Papers (The Historical Society of Pennsylvania); and John Hanson Collection (Maryland Historical Society).

Published planter sources were: *Henry Callister Papers* (5 vols., Yale University); John C. Fitzpatrick, ed., *The Writings of George Washington From the Original Manuscript Sources, 1754-1797* (39 vols., Wash., 1931-1944); William T. Hutchinson and William M.E. Rachel, eds., *James Madison Papers* (15 vols., Chicago, 1962-1972); William Moultrie, *Memoirs of the American Revolution* (2 vols., New York, 1802); "Letters of Joseph Clay Merchant Savannah 1776-1793," *Collections of the Georgia Historical Society* VIII (1913); "The Correspondence of Arthur Middleton, Signer of the Declaration of Independence," ed., Joseph Barnwell, *The South Carolina Historical and Genealogical Magazine*, XXVI (1925); "John Rutledge Letters," ed., Joseph Barnwell, *The South Carolina Historical and Genealogical Magazine XVII* (1916); J.H. Easterby, ed., *Wadboo Barony: Its Face as Told in a Collection Family Papers 1773-1793* (Columbia, 1952); *The Papers of Thomas Jefferson*, Julian P. Boyd, ed. (22 vols., Princetown, New Jersey 1950-1988); Edwin M. Betts, ed., *Thomas Jefferson's Farm Book* (Princeton, New Jersey, 1953).

Planter Diaries

The *Diary of Colonel Landon Carter*, Jack P. Greene, ed., (Charlottesville, 1965) is rich with detail about the fugitive blacks' efforts to get beyond the reach of Landon Carter. And *The Secret Diary of William Byrd of Westover, 1709-1712* (Richmond, 1941), eds., Louis B. Wright and Marion Tinling, while less revealing than Carter's diary, contains enough data to show that blacks did not stand idly while Byrd and his wife pummeled them. For a sympathetic account of the slaves' plight, see the "Diary of Timothy Ford, 1785-1876, "*The South Carolina Historical and Genealogical Magazine* XIII (1912).

Traveler's Accounts

The traveler's recorded impression helped unlock some of the mysteries of chattel slavery. John Martin Bolzius, an Austrian Lutheran minister who eventually settled in Georgia, tried to attract more Salzburg settlers from his country to emigrate while trying to allay their fears about the blacks and indentured servants. See Klaus G. Loewalk, Beverly Starika, and Paul S. Taylor, trans., and eds., "Johann Martin Bolzius Answers a Questionnaire on Carolina and Georgia" *William and Mary Quarterly* XIIV (1957) and XV (1958); John Martin Bolzius' "Trip to Charleston, October, 1742," ed., George Fenwick Jones. For a view of miscegenation in the South as well as the treatment of a fugitive, Ebenezer Hazard's account should be consulted: "A View of Coastal South Carolina in 1778; The Journal of Ebenezer Hazard," ed., Roy Merrens, *William and Mary Quarterly*, LXXIII (October, 1972); Winslow Watson, ed., *Men and Times of the Revolution* (New York, 1856).

Parish Transcripts

This trove contains hundreds of documents bearing on the activities of slaves in South Carolina as well as their attempts to reach St. Augustine and their masters' efforts to deter them. This collection of documents, miscellaneous papers, and official letters have yet to be fully exploited (New York Historical Society).

British Headquarters Papers

During the American Revolution, over five thousand blacks made it to New York, with the hope of leaving America for Nova Scotia. The British embarkation officer kept a list of the slaves and their owners (New York Public Library).

Tales of Oppression

Issac Hopper's "Tales of Oppression" published in the *National Anti-Slavery Standard* is one man's effort to provide an account of the fugitive slaves' experience in their own words. The Tales reveal a great deal about the anxieties of fugitives trying to stay one step ahead of the planter while trying to build a life of their own.

Secondary Works

The first extensive treatment of fugitive slaves is Gerald Mullin's *Flight and Rebellion: Slave Resistance in Eighteen-Century Virginia* (New York, 1972). Mullin makes some perceptive comments about the acculturation process, but continues to subscribe to the Phillips' notion of paternalism.

Unlike Mullin, Lathan Windley focuses strictly on resistance. "A Profile of Runaway Slaves in Virginia and South Carolina from

1730 through 1787" is an unpublished Ph.d dissertation, University of Iowa, 1974. Other background works include the following: John Blassingame, *The Slave Community: Plantation Life in Antebellum South*, Revised and Enlarged Edition (New York, 1979); Peter Wood, *Black Majority: Negroes in Colonial South Carolina From 1670 through the Stono Rebellion* (New York, 1974); Daniel C. Littlefield, *Rice and Slaves: Ethnicity and the Slave Trade in Colonial South Carolina* (Baton Rouge: Louisiana State University Press, 1981); Eugene D. Genovese, *Roll, Jordan, Roll* (New York, 1974); Betty Wood, *Slavery in Colonial Georgia, 1730-1775* (Athens, 1984).

Articles include: "Eighteenth Century Slaves as Advertised by their Masters, "*Journal of Negro History*, 1 (April, 1916); Lorenzo J. Greene, "The New England Negro as seen in Advertisements for Runaway Slaves," *Journal of Negro History*, 29 (April, 1944); Marvin L. Michael Kay and Lorin Lee Kay, "Slave Runaways in Colonial North Carolina, 1748-1775," *The North Carolina Historical Review*, 63 (January, 1986); Daniel E. Meaders, "South Carolina Fugitives as Viewed through Local Colonial Newspapers with Emphasis on Runaway Notices, 1732-1801," *Journal of Negro History*, 60 (April, 1975).

Published Manuscript Sources

Adams, John, *Diary and Autobiography*, 4 vols., ed. L. H. Butterfield, Cambridge, Mass.: Belknap Press of Harvard University Press, 1962.

American Archives, 4th Series, ed. Peter Force, 6 vols., Washington: M. St. Clair and Peter Force, 1837-1846. 5th Series. 3 vols. Washington: M. St. Clair and Peter Force, 1848-1853.

Ames, Susie M., ed. *County Court Records of Accomack-*

Northampton, Virginia 1632-1640, Virginia, 1973.

Barbour, Philip L., *The Jamestown Voyages Under The First Charter, 1601-1609,* Cambridge, England: Hakluyt Society of the University Press, 1969.

Brown, Alexander, *The Genesis of the United States,* Boston, New York: Houghton, Mifflin and Company, 1890.

Brown, William H., et al. eds., *Archives of Maryland,* 66 vols., Baltimore, 1883.

Byrd, William, *The Secret Diary of William Byrd of Westover, 1709-1712,* eds. Louis B. Wright and Marion Tinling, Richmond, Virginia: Dietz Press, 1941.

_____, *Another Secret Diary of William Byrd of Westover, 1739-1741, With Letters & Literary Exercises, 1696-1726,* edited by Maude H. Woodfin, transcribed by Marion Tinling, Richmond, Va.: Dietz Press, 1942.

_____, *The Correspondence of the Three William Byrds of Westover, Virginia, 1684-1776,* 3 vols., ed. Marion Tinling, Charlottesville, Va.: University Press of Virginia, 1977.

Cadbury, H. J., "Another Early Quaker Anti-Slavery Document," *Journal of Negro History,* 27 (April 1942), 210-214.

Carter, Landon, *The Diary of Colonel Landon Carter of Sabine Hall, 1752-1778,* 2 vols., ed. Jack P. Greene, Charlottesville: University Press of Virginia, 1965.

Catterell, Helen T., ed., *Judicial Cases Concerning American Slavery and the Negro,* 5 vols., Washington, D.C.: Carnegie Institution of

Washington, 1926-1937.

De La Warr, W., *The Relation of the Right Honorable The Lord De La Warr*, London: W. Hall, 1611.

Farrand, Max, *The Records of the Federal Convention of 1787*, 3 vols., New Haven: Yale University Press, 1911.

Fitzpatrick, John C., ed., *The Writings of George Washington*, 37 vols., Washington: Government Printing Office, 1931-1940.

Franklin, Benjamin, *The Papers of Benjamin Franklin*, ed. Leonard W. Labaree, et al., New Haven: Yale University Press, 1970.

Georgia Historical Society, *Collections*. Published by the Society. "... Letters from Governor Sir James Wright to the ... Secretaries of State for America, August 24, 1774 to February 16, 1782," Savannah, 1873.

_____, "Letters of Joseph Clay, Merchant of Savannah, 1776-1793," Savannah, 1913.

Hamer, Philip M. and George C. Rogers, et al., eds., *The Papers of Henry Laurens*, 9 vols., Columbia: University of South Carolina Press, 1968.

Hamilton, Alexander, *The Papers of Alexander Hamilton*, 27 vols., ed. Harold C. Syrett et al., New York: Columbia University Press, 1987.

Hazard, Samuel, ed., *Pennsylvania Archives...*, Philadelphia: Printed by Joseph Severas & Co., 1853.

Hening, William W., *Statutes at Large: A Collection of the Laws of Virginia*, 13 vols., Richmond & Philadelphia: various publishers, 1819-1823.

Izard-Laurens Correspondence, *The South Carolina Historical and Genealogical Magazine*, 22 vols., January, 1921, 1-11, 39-52, 73-88.

Jefferson at Monticello, edited with an introduction by James A. Bear, Jr., Charlottesville, Virginia: University Press of Virginia, 1967.

Jefferson, Thomas, *The Papers of Thomas Jefferson*, ed. Julian P. Boyd, et al., 22 vols., Princeton: Princeton University Press, 1956-1972.

_____, *The Family Letters of Thomas Jefferson*, eds. Edwin M. Betts and James A. Bear, Columbia, Mo.: University of Missouri Press, 1966.

Journals of the Council of the State of Virginia 1776-1781, 5 vols., ed. H.R. McIlwaine, 1931-1939.

Madison, James, *The Papers of James Madison*, eds. Thomas Mason, Robert Rutland, and Jeane K. Sisson, 15 vols., Charlottesville: University Press of Virginia, 1985.

Mason, George, *The Papers of George Mason*, ed. Robert A. Rutland, 3 vols., Chapel Hill: University of North Carolina Press, 1969.

McIlwaine, H.R., ed. *Official Letters of the Governors of the State of Virginia.* 3 vols., Richmond: Virginia State Library, 1926-1929.

Morgan, William J., ed. *Naval Documents of the American Revolution*, 9 vols., Washington, D.C., 1980.

Pendleton, Edward, *The Letters and Papers of Edward Pendleton 1734-1803*, ed. David J. Mays, Charlottesville: University of Virginia Press, 1967.

Pinckney, Elise, *Letters of Eliza Lucas Pinckney, 1768-1782*, South Carolina Historical Magazine, 143-

_____, *The Letterbook of Eliza Lucas Pinckney, 1739-1782*, Chapel Hill: University of North Carolina Press, 1972.

Pringle, Walter, *The Letterbook of Robert Pringle*, ed. Walter B. Edgar, 2 vols., Columbia: University of South Carolina Press, 1972.

Rutledge, John, *Letters of John Rutledge, South Carolina Historical and Genealogical Magazine*, 18 (1917), 42-49, 59-64, 131-142.

The Colonial Records of North Carolina, 10 vols., Raleigh: State of North Carolina, 1886-1890.

The Colonial Records of South Carolina, edited by J.H. Easterby, et al., 9 vols., Columbia, 1950-1961.

The Colonial Records of the State of Georgia, 1732-1782, edited by Allen D. Candler, et al., 26 vols., Atlanta, Ga.: The Franklin Company, 1904-1916.

The Statutes at Large of South Carolina, Thomas J. Cooper and David J. McCord, 10 vols., Columbia, 1836-1841.

Journals (Primary Sources)

Brown, Marvin L., ed., *Baroness von Riedesel and the American Revolution: Journal and Correspondence of a Tour of Duty, 1776-*

1783. Chapel Hill: University of North Carolina Press, 1965.

Campbell, Colin, ed., *Journal of An Expedition Against the Rebels of Georgia in North America Under the Orders of Archibald Campbell Esquire Lieut. Colol. of His Majesty's 71st Regimt., 1778,*

Darien, Georgia: Ashantilly Press, 1981.

Ford, Timothy, "Diary of Timothy Ford," *The South Carolina Historical and Genealogical Magazine*, 13 (1912), 133-203.

Herdon, Melvin, "A Young Scotsman's Visit to South Carolina, 1770-1772," *South Carolina Historical and Genealogical Magazine*, 85 (1984), 187-194.

Howe, Mark DeWolf A., "Journal of Josiah Quincy, Junior, 1773," *Massachusetts Historical Society Proceedings*, 49 (1916), 424-481.

Johnston, Buckner H., "The Journal of Ebenezer Hazard in North Carolina, 1777 and 1778," *North Carolina Historical Review*, 36 (1959), 358-377.

"Journal of A French Traveler," *American Historical Review*, 26 (July 1921), 726-747.

MacMaster, Richard K., "News of the Yorktown Campaign: The Journal of Dr. Robert Honyman, April 17-November 25, 1781," *The Virginia Magazine of History and Biography*, 79 (October 1971), 393-399.

Parkinson, Richard, "Tour in America in 1798, 1799, and 1800," London: Printed for J. Harding, 1805.

Pringle, Robert, "Journal of Robert Pringle, 1746-1747," *South*

Carolina Historical and Genealogical Magazine, 26 (1925), 21-30.

Robbins, Walter L., "John Tobler's Description of South Carolina (1753)," *South Carolina Historical and Genealogical Magazine*, 71 (1970), 141-161.

Salley, S. A., "Diary of William Dillwyn During a Visit to Charles Town in 1772," *South Carolina Historical and Genealogical Magazine*, 36 (1935), 1-7, 24-35, 73-78, 107-110.

Shelley, Fred, "The Journal of Ebenezer Hazard in Virginia, 1777," *The Virginia Magazine of History and Biography*, 62 (1954), 400-423.

Smith, Josiah, "Josiah Smith's Diary, 1780-1781," *South Carolina Historical and Genealogical Magazine*, 33 (1933-34), 1-28, 79-116, 197-207.

Smith, William Loughton, "Journal of William Loughton Smith, 1790-1791," *Massachusetts Historical Proceedings*, October, 1917-June, 1918, 200-213.

Taitt, David, "Journal of David Taitt's Travels From Pensacola, West Florida, To and Through the Country of the Upper and the Lower Creeks, 1772," ed. Newton D. Mereness, New York: MacMillan, 1916.

Von Closen, Baron Ludwig, "The Revolutionary Journal of Baron Ludwig von Closen, 1780-1783," Chapel Hill: University of North Carolina Press,

Watson, Winslow C., *Men and Times of the Revolution; or Memoirs of Elkanah Watson, including Journals of Travels in Europe and America, 1777 to 1842...*, New York: Dana and Company, 1856.

Newspapers

Connecticut:

Connecticut Gazette (New Haven) (New London), 1763-1800

Delaware:

Delaware Gazette (Wilmington), 1785-1799
Delaware Gazette or The Faithful Centinel (Wilmington), 1788

Georgia:

Georgia Gazette (Savannah), 1763-1775
Royal Georgia Gazette (Savannah), 1779-1782
Savannah Gazette at the State of Georgia (Savannah), 1783-1788
Augusta Georgia State Gazette or Independent Register (Augusta), 1786
Savannah Georgia Gazette (Savannah), 1788-1790
Augusta Georgia, The Augusta Chronicle and Gazette & The State (Augusta), 1789-1790

Maryland:

Maryland Gazette (Annapolis), 1727-1734: 1745-1800
Maryland Journal and Baltimore Advertiser (Baltimore), 1773-1797

Massachusetts:

Boston Gazette, 1719-1798
Boston Evening Post, 1725-1744

New York:

New York Gazette, 1747-1773

North Carolina:

North Carolina Gazette (New Bern), 1751-1775
State Gazette of North Carolina (New Bern), 1785-1790
State Gazette of North Carolina (Edenton), 1788-1790

Pennsylvania:

Pennsylvania Gazette (Philadelphia), 1728-1780

South Carolina:

Gazette of the State of South Carolina (Charleston), 1777-1780; 1783-1785
Royal Gazette (Charleston), 1781-1782
South Carolina and American General Gazette (Charleston), 1764-1781
South Carolina Gazette and Country Journal (Charleston), 1766-1775
South Carolina Gazette and General Advertiser (Charleston), 1783-1785
South Carolina Weekly Gazette (Charleston), 1783-1786
State Gazette of South Carolina (Charleston), 1785-1793
City Gazette and Daily Advertiser (Charleston), 1783-1800
Royal South Carolina Gazette (Charleston), 1780-1782

Virginia:

Virginia Gazette (Williamsburg–Rind, Pinkney), 1766-1776
Virginia Gazette (Williamsburg–Purdie, Clarkson & Davis), 1775-

1780
Virginia Gazette and Independent Chronicle (Richmond–Dixon & Hope), 1783-1797
Virginia Gazette and Weekly Advertiser (Richmond–Nicolson & Prentis), 1781-1789
Virginia Gazette, or American Advertiser (Richmond–Hayes), 1781-1786 (Richmond Davis), 1786-1790
Virginia Independent Chronicle and General Advertiser, 1786-1790
Virginia Gazette and General Advertiser (Richmond–Davis), 1790-1799

Secondary Works

Alden, Richard, *The American Revolution, 1775-1783.* New York: Harper & Row, 1954.

Aptheker, Herbert, *The American Revolution.* New York: International Publishers, 1970.

_____, *American Negro Slave Revolts.* 5th ed. New York: International Publishers, 1976.

_____, *Early Years of the Republic.* New York: International Publishers, 1976.

_____, *A Documentary History of the Negro People in the United States from the Colonial Period to the Establishment of the NAACP.* New York: International Publishers, 1951.

Austin, Allan D, *Muslims in Antebellum America: A Source Book.* New York: Garland, 1984.

Bacon, Margaret, *Lamb's Warrior: The Life of Isaac T. Hopper.* New York: Thomas W. Crowell, 1970.

Bassett, John S, *Slavery in the State of North Carolina*. Baltimore: John Hopkins University Press, 1899.

Beard, Charles A, *An Economic Interpretation of the Constitution of the United States*. New York: MacMillan Company, 1935.

Bell, Malcolm, *Major Butler's Legacy: Five Generations of a Slaveholding Family*. Athens: University of Georgia Press, 1987.

Berlin, Ira, *Slaves Without Masters: The Free Negro in the Antebellum South*. New York: Oxford University Press, 1981.

Blassingame, John, *The Slave Community: Plantation Life in the Antebellum South*. Revised and enlarged edition, New York, Oxford: Oxford University Press, 1979.

_____, *Slave Testimony: Two Centuries of Letters, Speeches, Interviews, and Autobiographies*. Baton Rouge: Louisiana University Press, 1976.

Brackett, Jeffrey R., *The Negro in Maryland: A Study of the Institution of Slavery*. Baltimore: John Hopkins University, 1889.

Brodie, Fawn, *Thomas Jefferson: An Intimate History*. Toronto, New York, London: Bantam, 1975.

Brookes, George S., *Friend Anthony Benezet*. Philadelphia: The University of Pennsylvania Press, 1937.

Campbell, Stanley W., *The Slave Catchers: Enforcement of the Fugitive Slave Law, 1850-1860*. Chapel Hill: University of North Carolina Press,

Chapin, Bradley, *Criminal Justice in Colonial America, 1606-1660*.

Athens: The University of Georgia Press, 1983.
Clark, Ronald W., *Benjamin Franklin: A Biography.* New York: Random House, 1983.

Cohen, Hennig, *The South Carolina Gazette, 1732-1775.* Columbia: University of South Carolina Press, 1953.

Coleman, Kenneth, *Colonial Georgia: A History.* New York: Charles Scribner's Sons, 1976.

_____, *The American Revolution in Georgia, 1763-1789.* Athens: The University of Georgia Press, 1958.

Collier, Christopher and James L. Collier, *The Constitutional Convention of 1787.* New York: Random House, 1986.

Craton, Michael, *Searching for the Invisible Man: Slaves, Plantation Life in Jamaica.* Cambridge, Mass.: Harvard University Press, 1978.

Craven, Wesley Frank, *White and Black: The Seventeenth Century Virginian.* Charlottesville: Virginia Press, 1971.

Crowe, Jeffrey J., *The Black Experience in Revolutionary North Carolina.* Raleigh: North Carolina Dept. of Cultural Resources, Division of Archives and History, 1977.

_____, *Black Americans in North Carolina and the South.* Chapel Hill: The University of North Carolina Press, 1984.

_____, *The Southern Experience in the American Revolution.* Chapel Hill: The University of North Carolina Press, 1978.

Cunningham, Noble E., *In Pursuit of Reason: The Life of Thomas*

Jefferson. Baton Rouge: Louisiana State University Press, 1987.
Curtin, Philip D., *Africa Remembered; Narratives by West Africans from the Era of the Slave Trade.* Madison: University of Wisconsin Press, 1967.

_____, *The Atlantic Slave Trade: A Census.* Madison: The University of Wisconsin Press, 1969.

Donnan, Elizabeth, *Documents Illustrative of the History of the Slave Trade in America.* 4 vols. Washington, D.C.: Carnegie Corp., 1930-1935.

Elkins, Stanley M., *Slavery: A Problem in America Institutional and Intellectual Life.* Chicago: University of Chicago Press, 1959.

Evitts, William J., *Captive Bodies, Free Spirits: The Story of Southern Slavery.* New York: J. Messner, 1985.

Finkelman, Paul, *The Law of Freedom and Bondage: A Casebook.* New York: Oceana Limitations, 1985.

Flanders, Ralph B., *Plantation Slavery in Georgia.* Chapel Hill: The University of North Carolina Press, 1933.

Flemin, Thomas, *The Man Who Dared The Lightning: A New Look at Benjamin Franklin.* New York: WIlliam Morrow, 1971.

Flexner, James T. George Washington and the New Nation, 1783-1793. Boston: Little Brown, 1965-1972.

Fogel, Robert W. and Stanley L. Engerman, *Time On The Cross, The Economics of American Negro Slavery.* Boston: Little Brown and Company, 1974.

Franklin, John Hope, *From Slavery to Freedom: A History of American Negroes.* New York: Knopf, 1974.

Galenson, David W., *Traders, Planters, and Slaves: Market Behavior In Early English America.* Cambridge, New York: Cambridge University Press, 1985.

_____, *White Servitude in Colonial America: An Economic Analysis.* Cambridge, New York: Cambridge University Press, 1981.

Genovese, Eugene D., *Roll, Jordon, Roll; The World the Slaves Made.* New York: Pantheon Books, 1974.

_____, *From Rebellion to Revolution: Afro-American Slave Revolts in the Making of the Modern World.* Baton rouge: Louisiana State University Press, 1979.

Goveia, Elsa V., *The West Indian Slave Laws of the 18th Century.* Bridgetown BWI: Caribbean Universities Press, 1970.

Grant, Douglas, *The Fortunate Slave: An Illustration of African Slavery in the Early Eighteenth Century.* New York: Oxford University Press, 1968.

Gray, Lewis C., *History of Agriculture in the Southern United States to 1860.* 2 vols. Washington, D.C.: The Carnegie Institution of Washington, 1933.

Greene, Lorenzo J., *The Negro in Colonial New England, 1620-1776.* New York: Columbia University Press, 1942.

Harding, Vincent, *There is a River: The Black Struggle for Freedom in America.* New York: Harcourt Brace Jovanovich,

1981.

Hawke, David Freeman, *Franklin.* New York: Harper & Row, 1976.

Herrick, Cheesman A., *White Servitude in Pennsylvania: Indentured and Redemption Labor in Colony and Commonwealth.* New York: Negro Universities Press, 1969.

Higginbotham, Leon A., *In the Matter of Color: Race and the American Legal Process.* New York: Oxford University Press, 1978.

Hill, Hiram H., *Toward Freedom for All: North Carolina Quakers and Slavery.* Richmond: Indiana University Press, 1984.

In Resistance: Studies in African - American and Afro-American History. ed. Gary Y. Okihiro. Amherst: University of Massachusetts Press, 1986.

Jordan, Winthrop D., *White Over Black: American Attitudes Toward the Negro 1550-1812.* Chapel Hill: University of North Carolina Press, 1968.

Katz, Stanley N. and John M. Mullin, *Colonial America, Essays in Politics and Social Development.* 3rd edition. New York: 1983.

Lambert, Robert Stansbury, *South Carolina Loyalists in the American Revolution.* Columbia: University of South Carolina Press, 1987.

Lefler, High T. and William I. Powell, *Colonial North Carolina: A History.* New York: Charles Scribner & Sons, 1973.

Littlefield, Daniel C., *Rice and Slaves*. Baton Rouge: Louisiana State University Press, 1981.

Lopez, Claude-Ann and Eugenia W. Herbert, *The Private Franklin: The Man and His Family*. New York: W.W. Norton, 1975.

MacLeod, Duncan J., *Slavery, Race, and the American Revolution*. New York: Cambridge University Press, 1974.

Mannix, Daniel P., *Black Cargoes: A History of the Atlantic Slave Trade, 1518-1865*. New York: Viking Press, 1962.

Morgan, Edmund S., *American Slavery, American Freedom: The Ordeal of Colonial Virginia*. New York: Norton, 1975.

Mullin, Gerald, *Flight and Rebellion; Slave Resistance in Eighteenth Century Virginia*. New York: Oxford University Press, 1972.

Munro, John A., *Colonial Delaware: A History*. New York: KTO Press, 1978.

Newton, James E. and Ronald L. Lewis, *The Other Slaves: Mechanics, Artisans and Craftsmen*. Boston, Mass.: G.K. Hall Company, 1978.

New Perspectives on Race and Slavery in America: Essays in Honor of Kenneth M. Stampp. Robert H. and Stephen E. Maizlish, editors. Lexington, Kentucky: University Press of Kentucky, 1986.

Patterson, Orlando, *Slavery and Social Death: A Comparative Study*. Cambridge: Harvard University Press, 1982.

Phillips, Ulrich B., *American Negro Slavery*. Baton Rouge: Louisiana State University Press, 1966.

Proctor, Samuel, ed. *Eighteenth-Century Florida: The Impact of the American Revolution.* Gainesville, Florida: University of Florida, 1978.

_____, *Life and Labor in the Old South.* Boston: Little Brown, 1963.

Quarles, Benjamin, *The Negro in the American Revolution.* Chapel Hill: North Carolina Press, 1961.

Race and Slavery in the Western Hemisphere; Quantitative Studies. Stanley L. Engerman and Eugene D. Genovese, editors. Princeton University Press,

Ramsey, David, *The History of the American Revolution.* 2 vols. London, 1793.

Robinson, Donald L., *Slavery in the Structure of American Politics, 1765-1820.* New York: Norton, 1979.

Rose, Willie Lee and William W. Freshling, *Slavery and Freedom.* New York: Oxford University Press, 1982.

Saunders, Gail, *Bahamian Loyalists and Their Slaves.* London: Macmillan, 1983.

Sellers, James B., *Slavery in Alabama.* Alabama: University of Alabama Press, 1950.

Smith, Abbot E., *Colonists in Bondage: White Servitude and Convict Labor in America, 1607-1776.* Chapel Hill: University of North Carolina Press, 1947.

Smith, James Morton, ed. *Seventeenth Century America, Essays in*

Colonial History. Chapel Hill: University of North Carolina Press, 1959.

Smith, Julia Floyd, *Slavery and Rice Culture in Lower Country Georgia, 1750-1860.* Knoxville: University of Tennessee Press, 1985.

Smith, Warren Thomas, *Wesley and Slavery.* Knoxville: Abington Press, 1986.

Stampp, Kenneth M., *The Peculiar Institution: Slavery in the Antebellum South.* New York: Vintage Books, 1956.

Sydnor, Charles, *Slavery in Mississippi.* New York: 1956.

Tate, Thad W., *The Negro in Eighteenth-Century Williamsburg.* Williamsburg, Va.: Colonial Williamsburg; Charlottesville: The University Press, Virginia, 1965.

Tise, Larry E., *Proslavery: A History of the Defense of Slavery in America, 1701-1840.* Athens: University of Georgia Press, 1987.

Robert Higgins, ed. *The Revolutionary War in the South: Power and Conflicts and Leadership.* Durham: Duke University Press, 1979.

Van Doren, Carl, *Benjamin Franklin.* New York: Viking Press, 1938.

Windley, Lathan A., *Runaway Advertisements, A Documentary History From the 1730's to the 1790's.* Westport, Connecticut: Greenwood Press, 1983. "A Profile of Runaway Slaves in Virginia and South Carolina from 1730 through the 1787." Unpublished Ph.D. dissertation, University of Iowa, Iowa, 1974.

Wood, Betty, *Slavery in Colonial Georgia, 1730-1775.* Athens: University of Georgia Press, 1984.

Wood, Peter H., *The Black Majority: Negroes in Colonial South Carolina from 1670 through Stono Rebellion.* New York: Alfred A. Knopf, 1974.

Zilversmit, Arthur, *The First Emancipation: The Abolition of Slavery in the North.* Chicago and London: The University of Chicago Press, 1957.

INDEX